DEEP

STATE

DEFECTOR

RAHUL

MANCHANDA

508 West 26th Street KEARNEY, NE 68848
402-819-3224
info@medialiteraryexcellence.com

CONTENTS

The subversion of the judiciary in America was one of the slowest but greatest tragedies in the fall of the American Republic. Now if one has the gumption or fortitude to challenge an unjust statute or law, you are immediately given a judge who will "tow the political line" in tune with his masters ideals and proceed to subjugate and suppress your ability to air your grievances or concerns or to seek justice against your tormentors or oppressors.

CHAPTER 1

Why the Courts of America Don't Work Anymore
(Especially in the Major Cities)

The American courts used to be a public forum and place where grievances could be brought as claims and publicly aired in order to enforce the rights vested in the people by the US Constitution, and all of their subsidiary rules and regulations thereto.

B ut now the courts are political arms of power- and they are used and staffed strategically by the money powers, global elites, and banking cartels to further suppress, humiliate, target, and enslave the people they were enacted to serve.

The subversion of the judiciary in America was one of the slowest but greatest tragedies in the fall of the American republic-now if one has the gumption or fortitude to challenge an unjust statute or law, you are immediately given a judge who will "tow the political line" in tune with his masters ideals, and proceed to subjugate and suppress your ability to air your grievances or concerns, or to seek justice against your tormentors or oppressors.

You will be unilaterally shunted into "mediation programs" against your will, where your case will be hushed up and heard only by "arbitrators" who also know what side their bread is buttered on and will further see to it that your case or cause is relegated to the dustbin of history-and justice. This is especially true if you try to take on unlawful police, governmental action, legislation, or unconstitutional enactments, which destroy your freedoms.

If, however, your case can serve the interests of the powers that be, even if you are publicly humiliated and flogged, your case will be vaunted and uplifted, with a million dazzling lights shone upon you, with the "presstitute" media quickly following in the lurch, transcribing and photographing you relentlessly in your time of shame.

Since the public court reporters are nowadays privately owned by a handful of websites and whose leadership are invariably linked and bought out or beholden to those money-masters who control the races, whether or not your case gets mentioned on the internet again depends entirely on whether or not it helps, or hurts, the money power and global elite.

This again is instrumental in your ultimate case success or failure, and your legal destiny becomes pre-ordained.

The American courts (especially growing on the federal level) are completely and totally dead and controlled.

CHAPTER 2

Institutional Corruption of the Federal Judiciary through Rule 83.10: Stifling of Public Hearings, Pleadings, and Court Proceedings

The federal courts are the final arbiters of the US Constitution, and to silence them, after buying off nearly every single member of the federal judiciary through the big banks with their subgroups of special interests, is yet another indication of the death knell of the US judiciary and court system.

A few years ago, some hitherto unnamed and unknown "enlightened beings" presumably in the thoroughly corrupted and now infamous New York City government decided that Rule 83.10 would be a good idea that is, "certain" civil rights cases being brought under 42 § 1983 would now be shunted and shifted from the public hearing, public pleading, and public informing process of a federal lawsuit, where all people in the United States could observe the case and its process, into the hinterland dead zone of the private, hushed up, gag-ordered, muffled Rule 83.10 Civil Mediation process.

Enacted in only 2010, almost twenty years after the enactment of the Violent Crime Control and Law Enforcement Act (VCCLEA) and VAWA, which resulted in 1/3 of all blacks, 1/6 of all Latinos, and 1/13 of all whites in America getting incarcerated without evidence or probable cause, the 42 § 1983 civil rights federal lawsuit has historically been one of the only methods that poor, indigent, or wrongfully arrested/prosecuted litigants have been able to "fight back" and embarrass those scoundrels in the US federal and state government who have unlawfully deprived them of their rights pursuant to the First, Second, Fourth, Fifth, Sixth, Thirteenth and Fourteenth Amendments of the US Constitution.

But of course, the powers that be, the elite that actually wrote and passed such draconian laws, which effectively reduced the US government and its corrupt law enforcement into kings rather than public servants got wind of this impending flurry of civil rights litigation, and put their heads together to hurriedly draft and enact this 83.10 mediation rule, whereby these types of cases, if they are meritorious, are then silenced and thrown into the hole of nonpublic disclosure, secrecy, while protecting those human rights transgressors by not embarrassing them in public.

It is bad enough that bad police officers and federal agents have the US attorney general or state's attorney generals defending them at the taxpayers' expense, but to now also shield them from public scrutiny with having to answer for their criminal conduct is another slap in the face of the entire purpose of this third branch of government, the judiciary, which is now also corrupted by the global elite, international banking cartels, and money power in this country.

Without meaningful public discourse and disclosure in the federal courts, we would not have had the watershed case decisions, which freed the slaves, gave women the right to vote, banned Japanese concentration/internment camps, protected minorities from institutional discrimination, and other progressive developments in American history, now taken for granted.

The federal courts are the final arbiters of the US Constitution, and to silence them, after buying off nearly every single member of the federal judiciary through the big banks with their subgroups of special interests, is yet another indication of the death knell of the US judiciary and court system.

It's bad enough that the entire congress/senate (legislative) and the president (executive) have been co-opted by the elite international banking cartel/money power, but now that the courts (judiciary) is almost nearly under the thumb of these insidious global powers, there is little to no hope for the people to escape their inevitable enslavement and servitude to the whims of the plutocracy.

People need to wake up, and wake up fast, as freedom and their civil liberties, human rights, and constitutional rights are literally in the last gasping throes before permanent death.

CHAPTER 3

America Must Reclaim Moral Authority

America needs to once again ask itself in order to recalibrate itself-just what do we stand for? What are our values? What will we tolerate, and what will we fight to defend?

The United States of America is at a crossroads yet again. The balkanization of this great country and the constant internecine warfare between the citizenry may be the end goal of some of the international elitists and plutocrats who want this nation to fracture and break up, relegated to the dustbin of history, but it would be a very sad development if the great experiment that is the charter of this great nation should be forgotten.

Our nation has been battered and whipped by malevolent forces, both external and internal, by those with money and power who have sought to sow the seeds of discord, disunity, and distrust among members of the American family, often through legislation or elected (or non-elected) members of government who have come together to drive us all in different directions, with no common purpose, no common denominator, no common destiny, and no common future.

America needs to once again ask itself, in order to recalibrate itself-just what do we stand for? What are our values? What will we tolerate, and what will we fight to defend? Many in the US argue that our nation is exceptional-that is, we have a God-given mandate to exist and to bring everyone in the world under our umbrella of enlightenment, freedom, solid values, equality, and progress.

Our nation, in order to reclaim our place as a "shining city on a hill," a place where people want to come to, must immediately begin to do the following:

1   We must stop attacking other nations overseas for the sake of the military- industrial complex, special interest groups, and other nations who buy and sell our elected leaders, judges, and legislators like baseball cards-we must treat other nations as they would want to be treated, with respect, trade, and comity of nations, as Thomas Jefferson spoke about.

2   We must stop creating terrorists as proxies to accomplish foreign policy goals, as is caused when the above elements are allowed to dominate our political discourse through think-tanks and cold, hard cash bribes paid to the elected (and non-elected) officials of the US government.

3   We must encourage peaceful solutions and negotiations as well as diplomacy among nations to resolve conflict, and we must be consistent throughout, as a reflection of our own values, all across the world —rather than bombing nations into submission (which never works), we should be using diplomatic chambers and boardrooms to settle our differences, with war only as a last resort, and only to be declared by congress after full disclosure (to the extent possible) to the American people.

4   We must recreate the middle class, not by force through Socialist measures as espoused by some candidates running for office but through the American way -free trade, laissez-faire economics, production of solid and well—crafted goods and services, the mobilization of industry and technology, and the encouraging of Americans of all stripes to become business owners, patent holders, tradesmen, innovators, and producers once again.

5   We must abolish all social engineering laws and programs in the United States that tend to always have a blow-back effect and that are unconstitutional in their application and effect. Criminal justice and family court reform are essential aspects to forge and reclaim our once-great nation. We are imprisoning far too many innocents in this country, leaving tens of millions of families, children, and individuals   broken,   shattered,   ruined   bankrupted,   and psychologically, emotionally, financially, physically, and spiritually.

6   We must encourage charitable giving and love in our popular entertainment and media rather than the glorification of gratuitous violence, sex, and substance abuse. Such exposures often desensitize the viewing population after generational years and decades of enduring such type of experiences, and skew our inherent man-made urges to create, strengthen, and fortify our families and societies rather than tearing them down.

7   We must return to the rule of law in this country, and that means cleaning up the corrosive and corrupting forces of money on our judges and their courts. Too many federal and state judges cut their teeth working for huge law firms where their clients were banks and mega-corporations whose sole motives were higher profits at the

expense of the people they were supposed to serve. Activist judges or those who are far too close to special interest and lobbying groups must be driven out and not allowed to serve on the bench.

8   We must balance our budget and escape the yoke of central banking somehow to a nameless, faceless elite who are not elected by the people and who often force our government officials into foreign and domestic policies that actually hurt our nation and exhaust our people and resources, leaving the people and their hard work and labor spent and used up, like the ashes of a smoked cigar.

9   We must teach common moral values in our schools, media, television, movies, and families from birth until death. Freedom and the first amendment are paramount, but common decency should prevail, and abuse of those freedoms are not beneficial to a healthy nation.

10 We must constantly police our elected and non-elected government officials and oligarchs, ensuring that they are not selling or blotting out our collective freedoms or direction of this great nation. With great power comes great responsibility, but the people are the ultimate guardians of their own freedoms, not their elected or non-elected government officials or the oligarchs/plutocrats who think they are demigods.

To recap, we must once again become a nation that people want to flock to, not a nation that people cower away from in revulsion, disgust, and fright, which unfortunately our nation is fast becoming. We must once again become a beacon of hope, light, and inspiration to the world rather than a darkened gaggle of balkanized mouth-breathers with no common purpose, decency, morality, direction, value system, or destiny.

CHAPTER 4

Obama's Plutocratic and
Tyrannical Elitist "Operation Choke Point"

Allowing His Elitist Club to Put Political Dissidents Our of Business

I n yet another dereliction of President Obama's duties to the American people and in another display of his complete obeisance to American plutocratic elitist tyranny, Operation Choke Point is an initiative of the United States Department of Justice that was announced in 2013 under fellow "club member" former Attorney General Eric Holder, which states that their purpose is "investigating banks in the United States and the business they do with payment processors, payday lenders, and other companies believed to be at higher risk for fraud and money laundering," but which instead is used as an openly unconstitutional weapon in the hands of tyrannical plutocrats behind the scenes within the US government and in the military-industrial complex security establishment to shut down, without warning or due process, any and all businesses deemed to be enemies of their political and militant agenda.

This operation, disclosed in an August 2013 Wall Street Journal story, has been accused of bypassing due process; the government is pressuring the financial industry to cut off the targeted companies' access to banking services without first having shown that the targeted companies are violating the law. As reported by the St. Louis Post-Dispatch, critics say, "It's a thinly veiled ideological attack on industries the Obama administration doesn't like, such as gun sellers and coal producers."

Ironically, while fellow "club member" Governor Andrew Cuomo has openly declared war on the anti-Israel economic boycott BDS movement in New York by disenfranchising them from business dealings and contracts with the state, encouraging others to follow in a complete and total violation of the First Amendment. No one seems to question or ask how corrupt elitists in America can now literally starve out, shut down, and cut off from credit anyone and everyone who pisses them off, for whatever reason under the guise of being a "high risk business."

Certain banks and merchant services are apparently shutting down credit card acceptance services of businesses all over the country accused of going after targeted businesses and individuals who are in competition with other favored businesses in their same locale so as to "cut out the competition" using the federal US government to do so.

Some merchant categories that the Federal Deposit Insurance Corporation (FDIC) had listed until July 2014 as being associated with "high-risk activity" include ammunition sales, cable box descramblers, coin dealers, credit repair services, dating services, debt consolidation companies, firearms sales, government grants, home-based charities, mailing lists / personal info, money transfer networks, payday loans (which actually help poor people in desperate times), pharmaceutical sales, pornography, "racist" materials, surveillance equipment (so as not to allow governmental competition), telemarketing, tobacco sales, travel clubs, and other individuals and businesses as "terrorist supporting."

Of course, this list can be added to at any time by anyone hidden within the "justice department" or US Treasury, headed by Jacob Lew, Adam Szubin, and David Cohen.

Frank Keating of the American Bankers Association complained that Operation Choke Point "is asking banks to identify customers" who are simply doing something government officials don't like (such as fighting for civil liberties, human rights, the US Constitution, and economic sanction movements). Banks then "choke off" those customers' access to financial services, "shutting down their accounts" without notice, warning, abruptly, and without any due process.

In August 2014, US Representative Blaine Luetkemeyer introduced a bill that would limit law enforcement's ability to restrict access to the banking system as a response against Operation Choke Point.

On April 8, 2014, the House Financial Services Committee held a hearing with the general counsels of the federal banking agencies regarding, among other things, Operation Choke Point. Committee members from both parties argued that Operation Choke Point is hurting lawful nonbank financial service providers by pressuring to eliminate access to the banking system and, in turn, the businesses unable to offer services to constituents.

The FDIC's Richard Osterman repeatedly asserted that Operation Choke Point is a justice department operation, and the FDIC's participation is limited to providing information and guidance upon request. Mr. Osterman also asserted that the FDIC is not attempting to prohibit banks from offering products or services to nonbank financial service providers operating within the law.

Similarly, Amy Friend, of the Office of the Comptroller of the Currency (OCC), stated that the OCC wants to ensure that banks conduct "due diligence and implement appropriate controls," but that the OCC is not prohibiting banks from offering services to "lawful" businesses. On May 29, 2014, the US House of Representatives Committee on Oversight and Government Reform published a highly critical staff report that concluded: "Forceful prosecution of those who defraud American consumers is both responsible and admirable."

However, Department of Justice initiatives to combat mass-market consumer fraud must be legitimate exercises of the Department's legal authorities, and must be executed in a manner that does not unfairly harm legitimate merchants and individuals. However, that was where it stopped, and nothing really happened after that point. Operation Choke Point fails both these requirements.

The department's radical reinterpretation of what constitutes an actionable violation under § 951 of FIRREA fundamentally distorts congress's intent in enacting the law and inappropriately demands that bankers act as the moral arbiters and policemen of the commercial world. In light of the department's obligation to act within the bounds of the law and its avowed commitment not to "discourage or inhibit" the lawful conduct of honest merchants, it is necessary to disavow and dismantle Operation Choke Point.

On November 21, 2014, William Isaac, the former chairman of the FDIC from 1981 to 1985, wrote a scathing opinion piece in the Wall Street Journal entitled "Don't Like an Industry? Send a Message to Its Bankers":

> With Operation Choke Point, the justice department's targets have included vendors of firearms and fireworks stating that he believed that the agency acted in bad faith.
>
> On March 24, 2015, a hearing was held before the Subcommittee on Oversight and Investigations of the House Financial Services Committee. Subcommittee chair Sean P. Duffy said at the outset, "I fear that activists at the DOJ and the FDIC are abusing their power and authority and are going after legal businesses and, in effect, they are weaponizing government

to meet their ideological beliefs." The FDIC and the Department of Justice (DOJ) have launched investigations into the operation, but of course since those agencies are staffed and run by elitists, this will of course go nowhere.

The FDIC's inspector general, Fred Gibson, said he would review the conduct of agency personnel to find if the "actions and policies of the FDIC were consistent with applicable laws, regulations and policy," as well as the regulator's mission. Gibson said he would investigate allegations that FDIC General Counsel Richard Osterman provided false testimony to Congress earlier this year when discussing his organization's activities. Osterman was testifying to the Representatives House of member when he rejected assertions that the FDIC wanted to cut off legitimate businesses' use of the financial system.

CHAPTER 5

Devil Comes Full Circle: Evisceration of America's Bankruptcy Laws and March toward a Debt-Slavery State

Very rarely in human history have the traitors to a nation and its people literally affixed their signatures to their work, said traitors usually preferring to work in the shadows, out of the public eye, and without consequence to their damnable behaviors and activities. However, in the case of US Bankruptcy Law, America's greatest traitors, as was the case with the drafting and enactment of the Violent Crime Control and Law Enforcement Act (VCCLEA) and Violence Against Women Act (VAWA), which literally gutted the US Constitution and incarcerated 1/3 of all American blacks, 1/6 of all Latinos, and 1/13 of all whites since Bill Clinton and Joe Biden ushered it into law in 1994 or through the drafting and enactment of the Federal Reserve Act of 1913 or the ushering of the federal income tax, or even the confiscation of all US gold by Franklin Delano Roosevelt or the drafting and enactment of the Glass- Steagall repeal separating the "mom and pop" savings accounts from the bloodthirsty greedy coffers of ruthless investment bankers who invested their hard-earned savings into risky investments or loaned them to foreign banks and debtors or other hideously draconian statutes which, often generations later, revealed their de jure and de facto negative effects on the American people and their freedoms.

However, the bankruptcy laws in America also have those same telltale signs.

The Founding Fathers literally fought their revolutions against the British Crown and their Deep State Banker backers in order to found a new republic, free and unfettered from their debt slavers in Europe. Countless people fought and died to get away from this banking enslavement, to establish a new world, the United States of America, which boasted of "no taxation without representation" and "live free or die," or "don't tread on me" as their mantras.

Bankruptcy law was explicitly drafted and enacted to protect those poor American citizens who found themselves on the receiving end of catastrophic bad luck or sometimes purposeful targeting by enemies to drive them into that bleak financial point. It was enacted to give a chance to the debtor to obtain a new start on life, free from the slavery, debt, and encumbrances of the past, as a fundamental basis and concept integral to basic human rights, civil liberties, and constitutional protections.

However, the concept of bankruptcy law, with its ability to discharge debts, incensed, outraged, and angered the powers that be, the Deep State Freemasonic bankers, who instead preferred that the debtor become a debt slave, indentured servant, rather than a "new man" as envisioned by the bankruptcy laws of the United States.

So as they usually say, these Deep State bankers proceeded to chip away, eat at, and degrade the federal bankruptcy laws in this country by lobbying for and getting elected traitorous senators, congressmen, presidents, judges, and others both public and private to begin to enact a series of clandestine and secretive amendments, statutes, repeals, and changes to the existing bankruptcy laws in order to further eviscerate and render quite useless the US bankruptcy laws, laying countless legal landmines throughout the bankruptcy statutes, which not even seasoned attorneys can understand or figure out in order to destroy or blow up those hapless debtors who dared to venture into the arena of bankruptcy law and protection.

Bankruptcy in the United States is governed under the United States Constitution (Article 1, Section 8, Clause 4), which authorizes congress to enact "uniform laws on the subject of bankruptcies throughout the United States." Congress exercised this authority by adopting the Bankruptcy Reform Act of 1978, as amended, codified in Title 11 of the United States Code and commonly referred to as the Bankruptcy Code (Code). The Code has been amended several times since, with the most significant recent changes enacted in 2005 through the Bankruptcy Abuse Prevention and Consumer Protection Act of 2005 (BAPCPA). Some law relevant to bankruptcy is found in other parts of the US Code. For example, bankruptcy crimes are found in Title 18 of the US Code. Tax implications of bankruptcy are found in Title 26 of the US Code (Internal Revenue Code) and the creation and jurisdiction of bankruptcy courts are found in Title 28 of the US Code. The current Bankruptcy Code enacted in 1978 by § 101 of the Act became effective on October 1, 1979, and was introduced in the House as HR 8200 by Don Edwards (D-CA) on July 11, 1977. The current Code completely replaced the former Bankruptcy Act of 1898, sometimes called the Nelson Act (Act of July 1, 1898, ch. 541, 30 Stat. 544), because it was named after Knute Nelson, also known as Knud Evanger (February 2, 1843-

April 28, 1923) a non- American, foreign-born, Deep State Freemasonic banker representative and Norwegian-American attorney and politician active in both Wisconsin and Minnesota. It was significantly amended by the Bankruptcy Act of 1938 (Introduced in the House as HR 8046 by Walter Chandler (D-TN) and signed into law by President Franklin D. Roosevelt on June 22, 1938. The current Code has been amended multiple times since 1978. (See Bankruptcy Abuse Prevention and Consumer Protection Act of 2005.)

The BAPCPA of 2005 was without a doubt the worst and most draconian amendments of the US Bankruptcy Laws, the Bankruptcy Abuse Prevention and Consumer Protection Act of 2005 (BAPCPA) (Public Law 109-8, 119 Stat. 23, enacted April 20, 2005), and was a legislative act that made several significant changes to the US Bankruptcy Code. Referred to colloquially as the New Bankruptcy Law, the Act of Congress attempts to, among other things, make it more difficult for some consumers to file bankruptcy under Chapter 7; some of these consumers may instead utilize Chapter 13. Introduced in the Senate as S. 256 by Chuck Grassley (R-IA) on February 1, 2005, it was passed by the 109th United States Congress on April 14, 2005, and signed into law by President George W. Bush on April 20, 2005. Most provisions of the act apply to cases filed on or after October 17, 2005.

Senator Chuck Grassley and George W Bush's 2005 BAPCPA made changes to American bankruptcy laws, affecting both consumer and business bankruptcies. Many of the bill's provisions were explicitly designed by the bill's congressional sponsors to make it "more difficult for people to file for bankruptcy." The BAPCPA was intended to make it more difficult for debtors to file a Chapter 7 bankruptcy, under which most debts are forgiven (or discharged), and instead required them to file a Chapter 13 bankruptcy. The debts they incurred are discharged only after the debtor has repaid some portion of these debts. According to George Packer in his book *The Unwinding*, Joe Biden (the scurrilous author of the abovementioned VCCLEA and VAWA), Chris Dodd and Hillary Clinton helped pass this bill. Of the three, however, only Biden voted for the final bill. Dodd voted against, and Clinton did not vote. The bill was supported by President George W. Bush. Tom DeLay also championed the legislation. The bill passed by large margins, 302-126 in the House and 74-25 in the senate, and it was signed into law by the clueless President George W. Bush.

It is widely known that support for the 2005 BAPCPA mostly came from Deep State Freemasonic bankers, credit card companies, and other creditors.

Since banks, credit companies, and other creditors are the ones who must bear the losses for debts discharged through bankruptcy, their lobby power was a great supporting factor to eventually prevailing and forcing legislatures to pass the Bankruptcy Abuse Prevention and Consumer Protection Act of 2005. It was widely claimed by advocates of BAPCPA that its passage would reduce losses to creditors, such as credit card companies, and that those creditors would then pass on the savings to other borrowers in the form of lower interest rates. These claims turned out to be false. After BAPCPA passed, although credit card company losses decreased, prices charged to customers increased, and credit card company profits soared.

The 2005 bankruptcy bill was opposed by a wide variety of groups, including consumer advocates, legal scholars, retired bankruptcy judges, and the editorial pages of many national and regional newspapers. While criticisms of the bill were wide-ranging, the central objections of its opponents focused on the bill's sponsors' contention that bankruptcy fraud was widespread, the strict means test that would force more debtors to file under Chapter 13 (under which a percentage of debts must be paid over a period of three to five years) as opposed to Chapter 7 (under which debts are paid only out of existing assets), the additional penalties and responsibilities the bill placed on debtors, and the bill's many provisions favorable to credit card companies. Opponents of the bill regularly pointed out that the credit card industry spent more than $100 million lobbying for the bill over the course of eight years. There has also been significant criticism of BAPCPA's changes to Chapter 11 business bankruptcies. Harvey Miller, one of the most prominent bankruptcy attorneys in the country (particularly in terms of representing corporate debtors) has described BAPCPA as ill-conceived.

One of the primary stated purposes of the 2005 BAPCPA bankruptcy bill was to "cut down on abusive or fraudulent uses of the bankruptcy system." As Congressman F. James Sensenbrenner Jr. (R-Wis), one of the bill's key supporters in the House, argued, "This bill will help restore responsibility and integrity to the bankruptcy system by cracking down on fraudulent, abusive, and opportunistic bankruptcy claims." Opponents of the bill argued that claims of bankruptcy abuse and fraud were wildly overblown and that the vast majority of bankruptcies were related to medical expenses and job losses. Their arguments were bolstered by an in-depth study by Harvard University medical and legal scholars, which found that more than half of bankruptcies cited medical issues as a contributor to bankruptcy.

Perhaps the most controversial provisions of the bill were the strict means test it established to determine whether a debtor's filing under Chapter 7 of the bankruptcy code would be considered as an "abuse" and therefore subject to dismissal. This decision was previously made by a bankruptcy court judge, who would evaluate the particular circumstances that led to a bankruptcy. Critics of the means test, which is triggered if a debtor makes more than their state's median income, argued that it ignored the many causes of individual bankruptcies, including job loss, family illnesses, and predatory lending, and would force debtors seeking to challenge the test into costly litigation, driving them even further into debt.

Besides the stricter means test, opponents of the bill also objected to the many other obstacles the bill creates for individuals seeking bankruptcy protection. These included more detailed reporting requirements, higher fees, mandated credit counseling, and the additional liability placed on bankruptcy attorneys, which critics argued would drive up attorneys' fees and decrease the number of lawyers willing to help consumers file. These criticisms have been borne out in the months following the new law, as lawyers have reported that the bankruptcy process has become significantly more arduous, forcing them to charge higher fees and take fewer clients.

One criticism of the law was that the law made the discharge of liability for medical bills more difficult.

The many provisions beneficial to credit card companies were also a major target of the bill's opponents. In particular, critics objected to the extension to eight years from six to the time before which debtors could liquidate their debts through bankruptcy and requirements that those who file for multiple bankruptcies pay previous credit card debt that would have been forgiven under the old law. The bill's opponents were especially critical of provisions that expanded exemptions to the discharge of credit card debt, forcing spouses-owed alimony to compete more often with credit card companies and other lenders for their unpaid child support. More broadly, the bill's critics argued that the legislation did nothing to curtail the predatory practices of credit card companies, such as exorbitant interest rates, rising and often hidden fees, and targeting minors, and the recently bankrupt for new cards. The bill's critics pointed out that these practices are themselves significant contributors to the growth of consumer bankruptcies.

Global Financial Crisis of 2008

With the (now-realized) pre-planned economic crash of 2008, due to the Bill Clinton-era repeal of Glass-Steagall and the Housing and Urban Development (HUD) lowering of credit requirements for people to purchase homes, otherwise known as the Global Financial Crisis of 2008, the die was cast. Millions of Americans found themselves in complete and total debt slavery by the theft of the elites but found themselves unable to, prohibited, or threatened/intimidated into NOT filing for bankruptcy protection, or they could face jailtime or other sanctions by the convoluted, oppressive, and land-mine-like new legal provisions of the 2005 BAPCPA described above. However, also based on the 2005 BAPCPA, investment bankers, hedge funds, and other Deep State Freemasonic bankers actually BENEFITED from this 2005 law change, wherein as noted during the fall of 2008, "the 2005 changes made clear that certain derivatives and financial transactions were exempt from provisions in the bankruptcy code that freeze a failed company's assets until a court decides how to apportion them among creditors."

This radically altered the historic process of paying off creditors and did so just a few years prior to trillions of dollars in assets going into liquidation as a consequence of bankruptcies following from the global financial crisis of 2008. Some observers argued that this contributed to the financial crisis of 2008 by removing the incentive that creditors would normally have to keep a borrower out of bankruptcy. Institutions who provided short-term funding to financial firms such as Bear Stearns and Lehman Brothers through repo lending could abruptly withdraw that funding even if it risked pushing the firms into bankruptcy, because they did not have to worry about tying up their claims in bankruptcy court due to the new safe harbor provisions of BAPCPA.

Therefore, the Deep State Freemasonic bankers' circle of evil and debt slavery, while evading the consequences of their own greedy actions, was now complete.

The Devil, using his minions described above within the US government, literally won the entire game while trampling the people of the United States under his feet.

CHAPTER 6

Correlation between 1994 Violence Against Women Act (VAWA) and Epidemic of Female Violence and Criminal Behavior in America Today

Today's news headlines showcase the most heinous, violent, depraved, sick, and twisted crimes increasingly featuring women and girls as perpetrators, because for the past twenty years since the enactment of VAWA, the lesson taught to American women and girls was that they could do no wrong-that in fact, violence, criminal activity, and sexual depravity were the exclusive province and fault of men and boys-and that the female sex was always the victim of "male predatory nature."

Since the inception of the Violence Against Women Act (VAWA) in 1994, written by then Senator Joseph Biden and ratified by then President Bill Clinton, as part of their sweeping and draconian Violent Crime Control and Law Enforcement Act (VCCLEA), the rates of incarceration of innocent men skyrocketed to the tens of millions, targeting mostly African-Americans, Latinos, and other minorities, often without any evidence or probable cause, selectively enforced by purposefully recruited racist, low-intelligence, discriminatory police officers all throughout the country.

Bill Clinton would later declare twenty years later, in May 2015, that the enactment and implementation of the VAWA and VCCLEA laws were the "biggest mistakes of his career" as president and directly caused the mass incarceration of 1/3 of all black males, 1/6 of all Latinos, and 1/13 of all white males born into the United States of America.

An added horror of his ill-advised federal crime law was the complete and total abrogation of the First, Second, Fourth, Fifth, Sixth, Thirteenth, and Fourteenth Amendments to the US Constitution because, as was stated above, in order to arrest and convict someone under this law, evidence and even probable cause is not a requirement, and mandatory arrests took the power of discretion away from an already aggressive police force, thus literally creating a nightmarish Lavrentiy Beria-style society, which as Jozef Stalin's secret police chief famously stated, "Show me the man, and I will show you the crime."

This horrific situation also called into mind the famed criminal defense lawyer Harvey Silverglate's famous declaration that the average American commits at least three felonies per day, just by living their daily life.

Tens of millions of American families were destroyed one by one, tens of millions of children grew up fatherless. Tens of millions of mothers went on welfare, and the national fabric of America was forever torn asunder.

But one of the most neglected and rarely discussed effects of Joe Biden and Bill Clinton's Frankenstein monster of a federal law was also the least expected the mass and asymptotic escalation and increase in violent criminal and sexual depraved behavior of women and girls in the United States.

Today's news headlines showcase the most heinous, violent, depraved, sick, and twisted crimes increasingly featuring women and girls as perpetrators, because for the past twenty years since the enactment of VAWA, the lesson taught to American women and girls was that they could do no wrong-that in fact, violence, criminal activity, and sexual depravity were the exclusive province and fault of men and boys-and that the female sex was always the victim of "male predatory nature."

After twenty years of unbridled coddling and encouragement of the misconduct of women and girls, is it any wonder that the United States has seen an unprecedented sharp rise in females committing sexual assaults, statutory rapes, violent crimes, such as stabbings, gang beatings, murders, child and animal abuse, suicides, and lesser crimes, such as harassment and stalking, than at any other time in this nation's (or the rest of the world's) history?

It seems that the lunatic feminist and progressive forces that forced America to accept that men and boys had a propensity for violent crimes and sexual misconduct while women and girls were supposedly devoid of such behavior or tendencies, allowed the proverbial "brush" of female criminal activity to grow into a relative "jungle," now unmanageable, out of control, sociopathic, and nearly impossible to correct.

In other words, twenty years of VAWA has bred an entire generation of tens of millions of hardened female criminals who are just as fearsome and dangerous as any of their male counterparts.

Sociopathic and dangerous behavior in females has been swept under the rug as they were all deemed to be perpetual "victims" in a hitherto male-dominated society, and so their latent and hidden pathologies were allowed to grow, fester, develop, and sprawl completely unfettered, unpunished, and untreated.

In fact, due to the heavy progressive and feminist influence in the popular media, music video, and film industry, criminal behavior and conduct in females was actually applauded, encouraged, and fostered, especially for the past twenty years since the enactment of this horrific and cursed VAWA law.

Does anyone really think it would be a stretch for these kinds of women to lie or deceive in order to get an innocent man arrested for any reason?

This sick conundrum is the gift and contribution to humanity of Joseph Biden and Bill Clinton's horrific VAWA and VCCLEA law of 1994, and the damage it has wreaked on American society must be reversed, and soon, or this country will further implode and destroy itself.

CHAPTER 7

Transformation of America into De Facto Apartheid State

Because of this de facto American-style of segregation, not open and state- sanctioned, it has outlived the openly de jure segregationist state of South Africa, which had an official governmental policy of apartheid and, because of its open and explicit state action, made it vulnerable to local and global anti-segregationist forces.

The difference between de jure and de facto legislation is not one of semantics—if a law is discriminatory on its face, it is called de jure. However, if an enacted law has the effect of being discriminatory, it is called de facto.

Most de jure laws are thankfully illegal in the United States; however, de facto discriminatory legislation is rampant throughout this country, with the effects often not seen for years, if not decades, on the populace. This means that if a president or sitting legislature passes a bad discriminatory law, the damages usually aren't seen until a long time in the future, long after that leader has left office, usually after he has made millions if not billions in the private sector, using his past laurels as an American politician. This is the ultimate mark of a true scoundrel-and unfortunately characterizes the vast majority of our political leaders.

The combined effect of this morass of discriminatory laws, regulations, and ordinances, coupled with the actual encouragement of police departments to recruit low IQ racist applicants while rejecting higher-scoring ones, or the awarding of complete and total immunity for unethical, dishonest, or politically motivated prosecutors and judges who selectively prosecute and punish based on racial, ethnic, or political grounds, whether federal or state, ensures a Josef Stalin-style police state more reminiscent of the days of the SS/Gestapo NAZI political dragnet targeting political dissidents and minorities than what the Founding Fathers probably envisioned. As famed criminal defense lawyer Harvey Silverglate aptly stated, "The average US citizen now commits at least three felonies per day unknowingly." And as Lavrentiy Beria, Stalin's secret police chief said, "Show me the man, and I will show you the crime." Adding to this mix are recent admissions by FBI Chief James Comey that racist organizations have been infiltrating police departments for decades. Or that FBI agents have been lying for decades in order to falsely convict people who may be innocent.

Because of this de facto American-style of segregation, not open and state-sanctioned, it has outlived the openly de jure segregationist state of South Africa, which had an official governmental policy of apartheid and, because of its open and explicit state action, made it vulnerable to local and global anti-segregationist forces.

For example, when past Housing and Urban Development Commissioner Andrew Cuomo passed sweeping legislation reducing the credit requirements for people to buy or mortgage a home, this allowed tens of millions of minorities and poor people who could not afford to buy a home to buy into a financial albatross trap around their neck, and when the economy started to sputter in mid-2008, the vast majority of those people who couldn't afford a house anyway began to default and then a huge avalanche of defaults ensued, causing the housing bubble to burst. Investment banks like Goldman Sachs actually bet against the people and set up "credit swap derivatives" based solely on the cynical prediction that this housing mortgage bubble crisis would occur, and then they sickeningly made money off this.

Adding insult to injury, then President Bill Clinton, bowing to pressure from ex-Goldman Sachs bigwigs Robert Rubin, Larry Summers, and Gene Sperling, who were in his cabinet at the time in "government service," repealed the Glass- Steagall Act in 1999, thus dissolving the wall between private checking/savings accounts of the people, and the wild and crazy gambling antics of the investment banks. This allowed these big banks to place high-stake, high-risk global investments using the American taxpayers' hard- earned money. But of course, even though Bill Clinton dissolved Glass-Steagall in 1999, the American people of course did not feel its after- effects until December 2008. And Andrew Cuomo was involved with HUD from 1993 to 2001, a full seven years before his housing bubble mortgage crisis hit the fan.

Similarly, the Violence Against Women Act (VAWA), written by then Senator Joe Biden and passed by then President Bill Clinton in 1994 seemed harmless, if not helpful, to battered women at that time, but the Trojan Horse of this very bad legislation allowed corrupt and racist local law enforcement, con-artist women, activist corrupt judges, money-and-power-hungry feminist women's groups, and others with a political agenda in the district attorney's office, to use the federal law's ability to summarily suspend anyone's First, Second, Fourth, Fifth, Sixth, Thirteenth and Fourteenth Amendment Rights whenever a complaint was made that someone engaged in some type of domestic dispute, even if no violence or evidence was found, arrest and charge that person, and then throw them into the abyss of the criminal justice system, where dishonest and unethical prosecutors or activist judges "on the take" from various special interests and lobbying groups could selectively prosecute or dismiss the case at their whim, with little to no recourse or remedy for the accused. This means that after twenty years, marriage is at an all-time low, more domestic violence has taken place, more children are growing up without parents, the child protective services have grossly enlarged and are now being accused of being vehicles for child abduction/abuse/sexual trafficking, and other horrific crimes. Furthermore, the very fabric of the American family has been broken down into damaged components while the "state machinery" operates to keep couples apart even if they want to reconcile, thus further breaking down families and exposing innocent children to the wolves of providence and predators.

Bill Clinton also passed the newly amended federal Child Support Enforcement Act in 1994, which also summarily tossed good men into jail without a trial or inquest, suspending their drivers and professional licenses even if they missed a few child support payments due to disability, loss of a job, bankruptcy, personal tragedy, or other unforeseen event. The effects of these two above laws reinstituted the Debtors' Prison in America, and many would argue that slavery was in fact reinstituted as well, in violation of Abraham Lincoln's greatest triumph, the Thirteenth Amendment prohibiting indentured servitude and slavery. Many a con artist in American society has taken advantage of these two laws with the full force and brute power of the state against that targeted individual. The same story applies to the Violent Crime Control and Law Enforcement Act of 1994, sponsored by US Representative Jack Brooks of Texas, which bill was also originally written by then Senator Joe Biden of Delaware, passed by congress and signed into law by then President Bill Clinton. And again, these laws target racial minorities much harder than their white counterparts.

Bill Clinton recently admitted in April 2015, more than fifteen years after he left office, that mass incarceration on his watch "put too many people in prison." He went on to further state that poor whites and minorities in America were victimized as a result of America's unparalleled rate of imprisonment due to the horrific laws that he enacted. More than 2 million people are still held in captivity in prisons and jails, giving the country 25 percent of the world's prison numbers despite having only 5 percent of its overall population. Bill Clinton's drug enforcement laws of 1994 created a crime bill that laid down several of the foundations of the country's current mass incarceration trends vowing to be "tough on crime" with his "triangulation" policy of creating incentives to individual states to build more prisons, put more people behind bars, and keep them there for longer, introducing a federal three- strikes law that brought in long sentences for habitual offenders, creating "truth in sentencing" states, which sentenced people to long terms in prison with no chance of parole being rewarded with increased federal funds, and the Clinton COPS program, i.e., the community-oriented policing services, where federal money was provided to states to allow them vastly to increase the number of police officers on the streets and consequently resulting in more arrests and convictions of poor whites and minorities.

In terms of real estate, buying homes and leases of property, the real estate market is notorious for working with local, city, state, and federal "urban planners" to literally, under the color of law and authority, "zone entire areas" to create the de facto result of segregating whites and other minorities from living, working, or going to school together.

This is according to the seminal study "Spatial Segregation and Neighborhoods" Nightingale: by Carl

> During the 1890s, the word segregation became the preferred term for the practice of coercing different groups of people, especially those designated by race, to live in separate and unequal urban residential neighborhoods. In the southern states of the United States, segregationists imported the word originally used in the British colonies of Asia to describe Jim Crow laws, and, in 1910, whites in Baltimore passed a "segregation ordinance" mandating separate black and white urban neighborhoods. Copy-cat legislation sprang up in cities across the South and the Midwest. But in 1917, a multiracial team of lawyers from the fledgling National Association for the Advancement of Colored People (NAACP) mounted a successful legal challenge to these ordinances in the US Supreme Court-even as urban segregation laws were adopted in other places in the world, most notably in South Africa. The collapse of the movement for legislated segregation in the United racial States occurred just as African Americans began migrating in large numbers into cities in all regions of the United States, resulting in waves of anti-black mob violence. Segregationists were forced to rely on non-statutory or formally nonracial

techniques. In Chicago, an alliance of urban reformers and real estate professionals invented alternatives to explicitly racist segregation laws. The practices they promoted nationwide created one of the most successful forms of urban racial segregation in world history, rivaling and finally outliving South African apartheid. Understanding how this system came into being and how it persists today requires understanding both how the Chicago segregationists were connected to counterparts elsewhere in the world and how they adapted practices of city-splitting to suit the peculiarities of racial politics in the United States.

These neosegregationists escaped allegations of housing discrimination due to the relative lack of interest and enforcement of civil rights laws by the local, state, and federal government. Some claim that organizations like the NYS Division of Human Rights often do nothing more than provide an illusion of enforcement while simply notifying or tipping off the offender so that they can cover themselves and then retaliate against the complainer. In 2008 by a bipartisan federal commission on housing equity found that in the United States, only about twenty thousand out of an estimated four million acts of housing discrimination receive any official attention in any given year.

As was described above, when in 1999 Bill Clinton repealed the Glass-Steagall Act dissolving the wall between investment banks and the people's hard-earned money, three de facto racially discriminatory and apartheid-causing results occurred: predatory "subprime" loans to poor minorities, mortgage-backed securities consisting of predatory loans bundled with other loans and resliced into highly lucrative "tranches," and "credit default swaps" meant to insure the mortgage-backed securities.

These three apartheid-spawning spiderwebs trapped huge numbers of minorities and poor people into bad mortgages using grossly fraudulent practices with guaranteed defaults.

Furthermore, according to Nightingale, black people were more than two to three times as likely as white people of the same income to be steered into subprime loans even though two- thirds were eligible for standard mortgages that on average cost $100,000 less over the life of the loan. The resulting racial disparities in housing foreclosures widened the large inequalities in wealth on either side of the American color line. Ibid. Furthermore, according to Nightingale, "in 2008, as the American mortgage bubble burst, bringing on a global recession, US whites possessed a staggering ten times more wealth on average than blacks of equal income, largely because of segregation in the American housing market. Four years later, as Obama finished his first term, the black-white wealth gap had doubled to twenty to one."

Reflecting on the above, it is no stretch of the imagination to conclude that the United States of America, through the de facto manipulation of its laws, especially in the last twenty years, in the laboratory-like settings of the family, criminal, and civil courts, both federal and local, as well as in its House of Representatives and senate, and capped off by the executive branch, has devolved into a fully functional apartheid state. Not on its surface, but in its practice. And this is the essential difference between a de jure apartheid state and a de facto one.

And as Johann Wolfgang von Goethe so eloquently stated, "None are more hopelessly enslaved than those who falsely believe they are free."

CHAPTER 8

Poetic Justice or Karma:
How Abandonment of Noblesse Oblige by
Wealthy and Privileged Class Ensures Own Demise

The people have spoken—they want wealth redistribution because the über- wealthy of America won't share it anymore, and if they won't share it or give back in some way, well then, the people will TAKE IT BACK.

Change is coming to America, but not the kind of change that the wealthy and privileged classes necessarily want. That change is revolution—not a violent one but a peaceful gathering of like-minded protestors who are growing weary and tired of the growing chasm between the super obscenely wealthy and the poor, with the complete and total evaporation of the middle class.

While the super-wealthy across America take to bragging in graphic detail about their extraordinarily opulent lives on social media applications such as Instagram, tripping the light fantastic on their private jets, partying in the most exclusive nightclubs with rows of champagne bottles of the highest pedigree, openly blowing cocaine and promiscuously bedding the most beautiful models night after night, sometimes in pairs or groups, and throwing around millions (if not billions) of dollars on flashy cars, fabulous restaurants, watches, luxury purses, and other accessories, the 99 percent of Americans watch, wait, and plot.

And they plot.

Their allies are groups like Anonymous, who pledge social justice and are the self-appointed guardians of social justice in a world gone truly amok and where the wealthy and privileged simply don't give a damn about them.

Bernie Sanders was a frontrunner of the Democrat side, and Donald Trump is a hero of the Right. Regardless of what the major media says, Jeb Bush and Hillary Clinton, who implicitly or explicitly promised to protect and safeguard the astronomical wealth and liquid cash of the super- elite in America, the millennial generation of America promises to come out in full force and effect in this upcoming 2016 election, and they will not allow the paid-for political pundits of CNN or Fox News to deter them in their course. They want change, and they have all resoundingly declared that power and wealth redistribution, in the manner described by either Democrat Bernie Sanders, an open and avowed Socialist, or Republican Donald Trump, an open and avowed political anarchist, is what they want. Either one promises and ensures the death knell for the super-wealthy and increasingly sociopathic class of America.

Once upon a time, the wealthy and privileged classes inculcated in their young the concept of noblesse oblige. That is, "the inferred responsibility of privileged people to act with generosity and nobility toward those less privileged."

America's former robber barons and old- moneyed families alike used to respect this concept. Great self-made men like Andrew Carnegie, John D. Rockefeller, Henry Ford, JP Morgan, and countless others spent their enormous wealth and invested their time into building institutions used to better their fellow citizens-hospitals, schools, universities, charities, symphony halls, and other charitable organizations-because even ruthless robber barons respected their responsibility as a wealthy segment of the American system of capitalism, and they also recognized that capitalism would fall and their fortunes alongside of it if the masses ever rose up against them to protest if they didn't somehow share their prosperity and give back to the national community.

But today's billionaires have completely forgotten about the concept of noblesse oblige and therefore have also abandoned the implicit rules of capitalism. They want to party themselves to death and burn out in a selfish self-inflicted inferno of earthly hellfire.

The people have spoken. They want wealth redistribution because the über-wealthy of America won't share it anymore, and if they won't share it or give back in some way, well then, the people will TAKE IT BACK.

CHAPTER 9

How Power Elite Rolled Back
Constitutional Protections for Masses

Various federal statutes and laws such as the Violent Crime Control and Law Enforcement Act (VCCLEA), the Violence Against Women Act (VAWA), the US Patriot Act, the National Defense Authorization Act (NDAA), Civil Asset Forfeiture, and various other federal, state and local laws enacted by congress at the behest and pressure of the power elite has acted to virtually destroy our freedoms and the protections afforded to Americans by the US Constitution by eliminating or removing the protections afforded by the First Amendment, Second Amendment, Fourth and Fifth Amendments, Sixth, Thirteenth and Fourteenth Amendments.

E ven though the United States was founded on the basis of a Constitution, enumerated with all its fundamental rights contained within the Amendments and Bill of Rights, as the country prospered, the wealthy became wealthier, and after the transformation of the nation after World War II into an oligarchic, plutocratic, NAZI- infiltrated land brought on by Operation Paperclip and into the national security state, which we recognize today, the Power Elite, Establishment, or "shadow government" as some conspiracy theorists like to call it, began to realize that the constitutional protections afforded to Americans was proving to be a massive impediment and drag on their ability to rule freely, easily, arbitrarily, and control the masses with impunity.

So, they set about destroying all these amendments and constitutional protections in order to streamline their rule and make it easier to arbitrarily and easily murder, incarcerate, detain, or take out of society anyone who stood in their pathway of tyrannical rule.

Various federal statutes and laws, such as the Violent Crime Control and Law Enforcement Act (VCCLEA), the Violence Against Women Act (VAWA), the US Patriot Act, the National Defense Authorization Act (NDAA), Civil Asset Forfeiture, and various other federal, state, and local laws enacted by congress at the behest and pressure of the Power Elite, has acted to virtually destroy our freedoms and the protections afforded to Americans by the US Constitution, by eliminating or removing the protections afforded by the First Amendment, Second Amendment, Fourth and Fifth Amendments, Sixth, Thirteenth, and Fourteenth Amendments.

In the wrong hands, the combined effects of these various statutes have rendered the average American even less free and more prone to arbitrary detention, arrest, prosecution and conviction than in the vast majority of countries around the world, even the so-called despots and tyrannical governments that we constantly hear about on CNN or Fox News.

The worst part about this is that all of these deprivations of life, liberty, pursuit of happiness, and property are carried out and done under the color of law and authority, as official actions, usually meted out by equally and thoroughly corrupted federal and state judges, who operate with complete and total immunity as they are protected from scrutiny or investigation by the Younger v. Harris case or by the "separation of powers" doctrine, whereby one branch of the three governmental entities (judicial, legislative, executive) are generally unable or are powerless to interfere with the illegal or unethical actions of the other.

The first step in fixing a problem is to acknowledge that it exists. Hopefully, Americans will begin to take the necessary steps to correct this out-of-control shadow government power elite's destruction of the American governmental fabric.

CHAPTER 10

Human Legal Experimentation in America

Today we must remember that the intrusive and unconstitutional bodies of legislation that created the TSA, Patriot Act, 24/7 total NSA surveillance, the National Defense Authorization Act (NDAA), the Violent Crime Control and Law Enforcement Act (VCCLEA), the Violence Against Women Act (VAWA), the Rockefeller Drug Laws, the Civil Assets Forfeiture Act, and other openly, blatantly criminal, and unconstitutional laws and behaviors of the federal and state governments, were enacted like a "thief in the night," and first used against our nation's most vulnerable and helpless members and inhabitants, and no one cared or did anything about it.

L ed by NGOs started by the likes of International Financier, suspected CIA asset, and alleged self- professed NAZI George Soros, human legal experimentation is well underway in the United States of America, often experimenting and preying on our nation's most vulnerable inhabitants, such as documented and undocumented immigrants, people entrapped within the criminal justice system, racial and religious minorities, and accused "terrorists," many of whom were set up completely from beginning to end by openly racist federal and state law enforcement agents.

Human experimentation is only decried by the mainstream citizenry when it affects them directly, or when they know that those threats will approach their doorstep anytime soon.

But what happens when that human legal experimentation is performed in secret, out of the public eye, clandestinely, performed on people that mainstream America not only does not care about but is actively programmed by the mainstream media and societal infrastructure to view with suspicion, hatred, and disdain?

The answer is that it will be allowed to proceed, unfettered, uninterrupted, until the final goal of getting unconstitutional laws on the books of the common law and judicial-created law that is the mainstay of American jurisprudence is achieved.

It is therefore no different with the enactment, enforcement, and interpretation of laws in this country. The most unconstitutional, tyrannical, unjust and intrusive newly enacted laws are first tested on the above-described "undesirables" in our society, because people will not complain, but once it becomes mainstream, then Americans wonder how the hell they got enacted in the first place.

It is very important to be vigilant about the legislation that our congress/senate, executive, and judicial branches promulgate, because often the "devil is in the details."

It is also equally important to scrutinize the backgrounds of the federal and state judges that take the bench, just as we must do with our elected legislature and executive branches, because sometimes those judges' backgrounds will reveal memberships in extremist or hate groups, left-wing or "progressive" institutions, which act to undermine the US Constitution or are at odds with the philosophies and goals of the Founding Fathers when they enacted the Bill of Rights, Constitution, and Declaration of Independence from tyrannical England.

Today we must remember that the intrusive and unconstitutional bodies of legislation that created the TSA, Patriot Act, 24/7 total NSA surveillance, the National Defense Authorization Act (NDAA), the Violent Crime Control and Law Enforcement Act (VCCLEA), the Violence Against Women Act (VAWA), the Rockefeller Drug Laws, the Civil Assets Forfeiture Act, and other openly, blatantly criminal, and unconstitutional laws and behaviors of the federal and state governments, were enacted like a "thief in the night," and first used against our nation's most vulnerable and helpless members and inhabitants, and no one cared or did anything about it.

Now that mainstream America has woken up to find that they too are subject to these draconian unconstitutional laws and regulations, perhaps they can start to roll back and unwind these problematic and liberty-constraining rules, and bring back America to the freedom we used to enjoy before the advent of these NAZI-like infiltrations and programs were imported to our shores after World War II with the arrival of card- carrying NAZIs in Operation Paperclip, who then proceeded to transform our country from the inside, armed, supported, and bankrolled by the Federal Reserve Central Bank and NATO.

Martin Niemöller was a German Lutheran pastor and theologian born in Lippstadt, Germany, in 1892. Niemöller was an anti-Communist and supported Adolf Hitler's rise to power at first. But when Hitler insisted on the supremacy of the state over religion, Niemöller became disillusioned. He became the leader of a group of German clergymen opposed to Hitler. In 1937 he was arrested and eventually confined in Sachsenhausen and Dachau. He was released in 1945 by the Allies. He continued his career in Germany as a clergyman and as a leading voice of penance and reconciliation for the German people after World War II. His statement, sometimes presented as a poem, is well-known, frequently quoted, and is a popular model for describing the dangers of political apathy.

He said, "First they came for the Socialists, and I did not speak out, because I was not a Socialist. Then they came for the Trade Unionists, and I did not speak out, because I was not a Trade Unionist. Then they came for the Jews, and I did not speak out, because I was not a Jew. Then they came for me and there was no one left to speak for me."

We must always be vigilant on the enactment, enforcement, and legal experimentation on our most vulnerable inhabitants of this nation, and both the de jure and de facto results of these laws as observed, otherwise Martin Niemöller's words will have no meaning, and history will continue to keep on repeating itself until we are all in the concentration camps.

CHAPTER 11

Why Socialism Can't Work in America

Human beings are human beings, but if some are given the ultimate power over life, liberty, and property for the "good of the state," then they WILL use that power indiscriminately, routinely, and often against others in the state that do not have that power, for selfish or improper reasons, and with complete and total impunity.

Everyone who has a conscience wants some type of wealth redistribution, income equality, or minimum wage so that everyone has the bare necessities of life, isn't starving, has adequate healthcare, and is otherwise not living on the streets and homeless.

And the argument that Socialism works in countries such as Norway, Sweden, Denmark, and Finland has been played out repeatedly, again and again.

But those countries mentioned above are all relatively homogeneous with regards to race, religion, ethnicity, culture, and value systems. It seems that these countries, because they are so low-conflict anyway, would probably thrive and be stable even if they had a theocracy or, God forbid, a constitutional republic capitalist style of government, like ours in the United States of America.

But what about in a high conflict, racially/ethnically/religiously diverse and varied country that is internally balkanized and divided, where conflict is a daily occurrence due to racial tensions, sexual tensions, wealth tensions, religious tensions, and other tensions?

It appears that if the US government was given magnified power by Socialism, where anything and everything that individual government workers did was protected, sanctioned, and safeguarded if it was for the "betterment of the state," or for "state national security," then all of our current underlying imperfections, conflicts, civil liberties, and human rights violations committed by say, police officers, judges, congressmen, senators, presidents, feds, child protective service workers, taxing authorities, and any other member of our governmental bureaucracy would become equally magnified and stronger, but this time, there would be no constitutional rights or separation of powers in order to either sue, seek, redress, or achieve justice.

This is precisely what happened in Jozef Stalin's Soviet Russia, in Hitler's NAZI Germany, in Mussolini's Fascist Italy, in all of those South American banana republics, in Pol Pot's Cambodia, and countless other Socialist nations, where the welfare and security of the state were paramount as a means to "better care for the people," but where hundreds of millions of people in total were "lost" or "disappeared," murdered, jailed, tortured, harassed, assaulted, beaten, or otherwise persecuted for any reason or whim that any government official willed it to be so.

And no one could sue or seek redress for such an assault on such basic human rights and civil liberties because of the government's Socialist nature, if it could be shown that said violation was for the "good of state," which could be supported for literally any reason at all.

Can you imagine that kind of governmental power vested in today's American police officers who are often caught beating, torturing, or even killing innocent young black men, but this time with no legal redress, consequences, or punishment?

Maybe these types of constant, internecine types of conflicts do not occur or are relatively non-existent in such homogeneous nations such as Norway or Sweden as mentioned above, but they are a constant, day to day, hour to hour reality in modern day diverse and "melting pot" America.

Human beings are human beings, but if some are given the ultimate power over life, liberty, and property for the "good of the state," then they WILL use that power indiscriminately, routinely, and often against others in the state that do not have that power for selfish or improper reasons and with complete and total impunity.

Lord John Dalberg-Acton said, "Power tends to corrupt, and absolute power corrupts absolutely."

If the United States of America becomes Socialist, it will make the 100 million murdered in the not-as-divided/balkanized former Soviet Union look like a minor skirmish.

The United States needs to figure out a better way.

CHAPTER 12

The Feminist Mafia

Because the Feminist Mafia operates under the fictitious guise of being "in the best interests of women and children," as first coined by NAZI Adolf Hitler, behind a closed Star-Chamber in the Family Courts not open to public scrutiny, this organized criminal entity can accomplish each and every evil act that the other organized criminal entities could achieve, but the difference is this: they can never ever be shut down, prosecuted, or investigated even when they do so much harm to their host nations, people, children, families, economy, moral fiber, and national security.

I f there was an organization created, owned and funded by the deep state plutocratic elite, which routinely engaged in black operations, threats, intimidation, subversion of the US Constitution, corruption of the courts, judges, senators, congress, the executive branch, blackmail, bribery of government officials with sexual favors and money, tax evasion, obstruction of justice, extortion, perpetrating fraud on the courts, murder, witness intimidation and tampering, illicit human organ trafficking, reduction of the moral fiber of a nation, child abuse / kidnapping / sex trafficking, and other federal and state crimes, then surely the US government, acting through the US Department of Justice (DOJ) and the Federal Bureau of Investigation (FBI), would aggressively go after it, investigate it, dismantle it, charge its members, arresting each and every single one of them, focusing on the leaders all the way down to its foot soldiers and agents.

These people would be prosecuted under the Racketeering-Influenced Corrupt Organization Act (RICO), and each and every single one of them would face dozens of years, if not a lifetime, behind bars in a federal prison. In fact, this is exactly what the DOJ and FBI already did when it took on the Italian Mafia and the Ku Klux Klan (KKK) in America and for the exact same reasons.

And it should also be noted that both the Italian Mafia and the KKK were created and founded by 33rd Degree Level Freemasons, Giuseppe Mazzini, and Albert Pike respectively (as was the FBI, which was created and founded by 33rd Degree Freemason J. Edgar Hoover). So why then is there an organization that openly engages in all of the above enumerated federal, state, and local criminal activities within the United States, and abroad, in the guise of international nongovernmental organizations (NGOs), sometimes collaborating with US Foreign and Domestic Intelligence, to destroy people, families, and children in the name of money, power, and a political agenda?

Which organization is this? Well, it can loosely be described as the Feminist Mafia.

But the reason this sprawling criminal organization has been able to grow in size, influence, power, political, and economic strength, even at the expense of men, children, AND women, is because apparently, each and every single law enforcement agency, whether state, federal, or local, as well as each and every member of congress, senate, or city council, and each and every federal or state judge, is AFRAID to take them on, investigate them, or prosecute them for fear of being branded a misogynist, women hater, abuser, or whatever horrible anti- women appellation one can think of. This is the same type of tactic that another Freemasonic deep state plutocratic elite creation, Zionism, uses against Jews and non-Jews alike, to quiet down dissent over their policies. Israel's Founding Fathers all the way from David Ben Gurion to Benjamin Netanyahu are all 33rd Degree Freemasons, loyal to Freemasonry rather than the Jewish or Israeli people.

This is why the International Oligarch Billionaires (mostly men) openly fund and empower these Feminist Mafia groups, because they know that they can use them in broad daylight, in the open, to achieve and accomplish many of their goals of global governance, destruction of political dissidents, abrogating targeted individuals' civil liberties and human rights as guaranteed by the US Constitution, steal property, generate trillions of tax-free dollars in revenue through state and federal child support collection units, populate their international sex trafficking, prostitution, and human trafficking businesses, as well as control each and every one of the above referenced government officials, lock, stock and barrel.

These puppet master deep state plutocratic elite/oligarchs have learned the hard way, after watching the destruction by the US government of their formerly useful tools the Mafia and the KKK, that having a moral authority is the only way to prevent a criminal organization from getting investigated, charged, indicted, and prosecuted by federal, state and local law enforcement authorities, getting targeted for congressional and senatorial hearings for investigation, outright war declared on them by the executive branch, or being ruled against by judges on the federal and state level.

In other words, because the Feminist Mafia operates under the fictitious guise of being "in the best interests of women and children," as first coined by NAZI Adolf Hitler behind a closed Star-Chamber in the Family Courts not open to public scrutiny, this organized criminal entity can accomplish each and every evil act that the other organized criminal entities could achieve, but the difference is this: they can never ever be shut down, prosecuted, or investigated even when they do so much harm to their host nations, people, children, families, economy, moral fiber, and national security.

So perhaps it will take someone who is from the inside, someone who is immune from the nonsensical insults, threats, and intimidation by the Feminist Mafia to take them down, perhaps a strong-willed woman who is either a US attorney, FBI agent, or a member of congress or senate, just like the Italian Mafia was taken down by Italian-American Rudolph Giuliani or how the KKK was infiltrated and taken down by White Anglo-Saxon Protestant men working as undercover agents for the FBI. Perhaps this is the only way that this feminist organized criminal entity will ever be taken down by a strong and independent woman or group of women working within the US government to expose their evil and then relegate them to the dustpan of history, just like the Mafia and the KKK were.

CHAPTER 13

New York District Court Judges Have No Respect for Civil Rights, Human Rights, or US Constitution

The goal is to cow-tow and beat into submission the people of New York City to accept their oppression by their ruling oligarchs/plutocrats, who both want and need the ability to squash the people's hopes and dreams, and for them to willingly accept slavery and indentured servitude.

I t is very well known that the federal judges of the US District Court Southern District of New York (US SDNY) have been handpicked over the last ten to twenty years to ensure that they are all either Freemasons or controlled by the Freemasons and are explicitly told that civil rights cases being brought under 42 § 1983 must be thrown out / dismissed as soon as they are filed, without even any formal answers or responses filed by the defendants/oppressors.

This is to dissuade the people from thinking that they even have any civil rights to protect.

The goal is to cow-tow and beat into submission the people of New York City to accept their oppression by their ruling oligarchs/plutocrats, who both want and need the ability to squash the people's hopes and dreams, and for them to willingly accept slavery and indentured servitude.

The federal courts in America and, most importantly, in New York City, are working alongside the Freemasonic power establishment in this country to openly and flagrantly transform the American people into peasants, with no situational awareness of their human rights or civil liberties supposedly protected by the US Constitution, denying the people their due process rights or the ability to appeal unfair/unjust/illegal lower court decisions.

Acting in concert with the legislative and executive branch, the judiciary is now fully stocked with civil liberties-hating judges who now openly lambast, ridicule, humiliate, and blaspheme the US Constitution and the plaintiffs who bring such cases and then proceed to sweep even the most egregious civil rights claims under the rug, unless of course it has some political value tending to benefit the perverted and sick Luciferian establishment (see for example Judge Paul Engelmayer's rulings allowing sex workers to sue for tips and overtime and Pamela Geller's lawsuit allowing her to post hate speech and anti- Muslim ads all over New York City). These federal judges, who are now openly chosen from large law firms whose clients were international banks and mega-corporations, are either willfully out of touch or simply don't care about the trials and tribulations of the average American citizenry.

However, if you are a member of any of the truly downtrodden and oppressed members of American civil society and if you wish to seek redress or appeal to the federal courts, particularly in New York City, well then you are quite simply out of luck.

Reform (and awareness) is needed now.

CHAPTER 14

How Case Doctrine of Younger v. Harris Stifles Civil Liberties, Human Rights, and Encourages Backwater Corruption and Organized Crime in State Courts and Judicial System

It is high time that the federal judiciary, executive, and legislative branches of the US government take a long and hard look at the case of Younger v. Harris, and analyze in a serious fashion the efficacy and long-term harmful effects of its use on a daily basis by federal judges and their courts to get rid of those cases which, if brought to federal judicial attention, would shed much needed light and analysis of state-sanctioned corruption, organized criminal conduct, judicial misconduct, and other harmful activities which cause the American people to angrily accept the reality that American courts ARE in fact corrupt, and justice is NOT the goal of these courts. Rather, the pursuit of MONEY is the only endgame.

The seminal case Younger v. Harris, 401 US 37 (1971), which stands for the principle that federal courts will not entertain appellate review or removal of pending state court actions, is constantly used and thrown down as a proverbial gauntlet by federal judges whenever they want to quickly dismiss or get rid of a case which smacks of blatant violations of civil liberties, human rights, and US Constitutional rights, whenever a poor hapless litigant in any state court finds himself surrounded by thoroughly corrupted state court judges, their law clerks, court appointed expert witnesses, state employees and prosecutors, or any other state-oriented governmental employees, who often work hand in hand with organized crime elements operating within the city or state where the grievance takes place.

The sad reality of most state courts and their judges in the United States is that most of them are ill-equipped or poorly versed, either purposefully or not, about the US Constitution or the law in general, that they often make decisions from the hip, without sound legal reasoning or a full appreciation of the legislative or historical intent of the statutes and laws that they are supposedly interpreting or enforcing.

The doctrine of Younger v. Harris most often comes up as a knee-jerk and automatic defense by state-appointed lawyers hired to defend criminally corrupted judges, prosecutors, and other state court employees even when there is flagrant, blatant, evident, obvious and glaring documentary and physical evidence of corruption, criminal behavior, or judicial misconduct in the state court, and the vast majority of federal judges, rather than exploring the case and evidence to probe whether or not wrongs were in fact committed, normally capitulate to their aggressive and shortsighted law clerks and staff, and quickly "punt" the case into the ether, back to the state court, which invariably results in severe retaliation and devouring by the former state court judges and employees who are predictably outraged and angered by the fact that the case was removed or appealed by the abused litigant to the federal court in the first place.

Since American law and jurisprudence has gradually devolved into a Talmudic-style body of law over the last hundred years, and further away from the US Constitution, ever since the placement of Louis Brandeis onto the US Supreme Court aided by his minions and followers in the federal and state courts throughout the United States, mostly in the urban and progressive states and locales in America, such as New York, California, Florida, Washington DC, and to some extent, Chicago and Texas, the result is even more troublesome considering that any judge can often find any reason to either incarcerate or destroy anyone who appears before them and for any reason.

Furthermore, the outright refusal of the Federal Bureau of Investigation or elected officials within the executive or legislative branch to get involved with the criminal and corrupted activities of the judiciary, either federal or state, by claiming the "separation of powers" doctrine, adds insult to injury to those few courageous litigants who seek to get a second, more sophisticated legal opinion and case adjudication from a federal judge, rather than their original state court judge.

The reality is that federal judges as a whole are naturally much more attuned to and acquainted with the actual sum and substance of the US Constitution simply because they deal with it each and every single day, as well as the fact that federal judges are usually selected from a much higher caliber of legal minds than their state counterparts, many of whom are not even lawyers to begin with, such as in the small-claims courts and civil courts scattered throughout the nation.

The inherent problem with the above issue is that the combined effect of using Younger v. Harris to prematurely and perfunctorily kick cases out of federal court or appellate review is to foster, create, and allow patently unjust adjudication of cases, massive violations of human rights, civil liberties, and constitutional rights all "under the color of law and authority" and provide a rubber stamp with the "seal of judicial approval" the most heinous of crimes, such as the kidnapping of children in the state family courts, the illegal incarceration or murder of innocents in the criminal courts, and the bankrupting and financial ruination of "unconnected" litigants in the state civil courts.

Judge Taking Bribe from Client

All the while, the parasitic underbelly of these state courts, with their hangers-on, such as thoroughly corrupted forensic examiners, law clerks, expert witnesses, law guardians, criminal and family court programs and research facilities, child protective service workers, court officers and others, are allowed (and encouraged) to openly partner up with organized criminal elements who can then together engage in criminal activity, all protected, sanctioned, and encouraged by the power of the presiding state court judge.

It is high time that the federal judiciary, executive, and legislative branches of the US government take a long and hard look at the case of Younger v. Harris, and analyze in a serious fashion the efficacy and long-term harmful effects of its use on a daily basis by federal judges and their courts to get rid of those cases which, if brought to federal judicial attention, would shed much needed light and analysis of state- sanctioned corruption, organized criminal conduct, judicial misconduct, and other harmful activities that cause the American people to angrily accept the reality that American courts ARE in fact corrupt and justice is NOT the goal of these courts, rather the pursuit of MONEY is the only endgame.

CHAPTER 15

Racist Problematic Concept
of Police Officer: Probable Cause

The entire concept of "probable cause" is problematic because it operates as a makeshift "shield" from any kind of liability, culpability, or ability for superiors of racist and malicious police officers who make an invalid or false arrest, thus ushering that targeted individual into the seemingly endless, bottomless, and hellacious world of the criminal justice system, which in this country often means being treated like you are already a convicted criminal, all the way from booking/fingerprinting, plea agreement, and trial. interrogation, arraignment,

T he power to arrest is the power to destroy and kill. One of the fundamental cornerstones of the criminal justice system is that a person can only be convicted if they have been found to be guilty "beyond a reasonable doubt."

However, that extremely rigorous standard of establishing a person's guilt is severely and utterly pushed to the brink, when police officers all across America are routinely and purposefully selected and recruited from the great hoards and legions of angry, racist, vengeful, and hateful white men across America. (See "FBI's Warning of White Supremacists Infiltrating Law Enforcement Nearly Forgotten" at TheGrio.com and "The KKK Has Infiltrated US Police Departments for Decades" at Alternet.org).

The entire concept of "probable cause" is problematic because it operates as a makeshift "shield" from any kind of liability, culpability, or ability for superiors of racist and malicious police officers who make an invalid or false arrest, thus ushering that targeted individual into the seemingly endless, bottomless, and hellacious world of the criminal justice system, which in this country often means being treated like you are already a convicted criminal, all the way from interrogation, booking/fingerprinting, arraignment, plea agreement, and trial.

And it does not help if you are non-white or a political dissident in this American criminal justice system, since statistics have already established that the likelihood of bad outcomes, unfair prosecutors and judges, goes up exponentially if you happen to be a person of color or political dissident.

To that end the racist police officer who initiates a person into this world of criminal justice, where your freedoms are taken away, you are jailed away from society, and you can easily be murdered within the system, needs to be heavily scrutinized, and his inherent power to arrest (destroy or kill) while being protected by this inherently problematic and institutionally racist concept of the defense of "probable case," consequently demands to be investigated, de- constructed, revamped, re-analyzed, cleaned, and then put back together, much like a decrepit or old outdated automobile engine when it breaks down.

And unfortunately, with the passage of then Senator Joseph Biden and then President Bill Clinton's purposefully unconstitutional 1994 Violent Crime Control and Law Enforcement Act (VCCLEA) which actually operated to make it much easier and more likely that Americans all across the board will be arrested, detained, prosecuted, targeted, and convicted through a forced/coerced plea agreement or rigged trial by biased prosecutors and judges, than ever before, the statistics now showing that since their 1994 enactment of this federal law, a horrid and unforgivable 1/3 of all African-Americans, 1/6 of all Latinos, and 1/12 of all whites in America have spent time under arrest or in jail/prison because of this purposefully designed "criminal justice system Venus flytrap" (see "Bill Clinton Admits His Crime Law Made Mass Incarceration Worse" found at msnbc.com and countless other articles substantiating this), which feeds to purposefully profit-making prison industry and jails for profit, not to mention the countless for-profit and myriad court ordered "treatment programs" for such issues as anger management, parenting classes, battery programs, drug programs, shoplifting programs, alcohol programs, which corrupted judges all across America, whether they are presiding over family, criminal, IDV, or civil court, invariably sentence and relegate millions of innocent men and women to every single day, with the sad truth that a great many of those corrupted judges stand to benefit financially from, if one digs or investigates deeply enough.

The concept of "probable cause" is defined in Black Letter Law in the legal dictionary on law.com at dictionary.law.com as "sufficient reason based upon known facts to believe a crime has been committed or that certain property is connected with a crime. Probable cause must exist for a law enforcement officer to make an arrest without a warrant, search without a warrant, or seize property in the belief the items were evidence of a crime. While some cases are easy (pistols and illicit drugs in plain sight, gunshots, a suspect running from a liquor store with a clerk screaming "help"), actions

45

"typical" of drug dealers, burglars, prostitutes, thieves, or people with "guilt written across their faces," are more difficult to categorize. Probable cause is often subjective, but if the police officer's belief or even hunch was correct, finding stolen goods, the hidden weapon, or drugs may be claimed as self-fulfilling proof of probable cause. Technically, probable cause has to exist prior to arrest, search, or seizure."

Cornell University Law School Legal Information Institute (LII) defines probable cause at raw.cornell.edu as "a requirement found in the Fourth Amendment that must usually be met before police make an arrest, conduct a search, or receive a warrant. Courts usually find probable cause when there is a reasonable basis for believing that a crime may have been committed (for an arrest) or when evidence of the crime is present in the place to be searched (for a search). Under exigent circumstances, probable cause can also justify a warrantless search or seizure. Persons arrested without a warrant are required to be brought before a competent authority shortly after the arrest for a prompt judicial determination of probable cause."

The Cornell LII goes on to further analyze the concept of probable cause in that from a constitutional basis: "Although the Fourth Amendment states that 'no warrants shall issue, but upon probable cause,' it does not specify what 'probable cause' actually means. The Supreme Court has attempted to clarify the meaning of the term on several occasions, while recognizing that probable cause is a concept that is imprecise, fluid and very dependent on context. In Illinois v. Gates, the Court favored a flexible approach, viewing probable cause as a practical, non- technical' standard that calls upon the 'factual and practical considerations of everyday life on which reasonable and prudent men [...] act.' Courts often adopt a broader, more flexible view of probable cause when the alleged offenses are serious."

Furthermore, the LII when discussing its application to arrests, states that "the Fourth Amendment requires that any arrest be based on probable cause, even when the arrest is made pursuant to an arrest warrant. Whether or not there is probable cause depends on the totality of the circumstances, meaning everything that the arresting officers know or reasonably believe at the time the arrest is made. However, probable cause remains a flexible concept, and what constitutes the 'totality of the circumstances' often depends on how the court interprets the reasonableness standard."

The LII goes on to state that "a lack of probable cause will render a warrantless arrest invalid, and any evidence resulting from that arrest (physical evidence, confessions, etc.) will have to be suppressed. A narrow exception applies when an arresting officer, as a result of a mistake by court employees, mistakenly and in good faith believes that a warrant has been issued. In this case, notwithstanding the lack of probable cause, the exclusionary rule does not apply and the evidence obtained may be admissible. Unlike court clerks, prosecutors are part of a law enforcement team and are not 'court employees' for purposes of the good-faith exception to the exclusionary rule."

The LII, when discussing its applicability to Search Warrants, states that "probable cause exists when there is a fair probability that a search will result in evidence of a crime being discovered. For a warrantless search, probable cause can be established by in-court testimony after the search. In the case of a warrant search, however, an affidavit or recorded testimony must support the warrant by indicating on what basis probable cause exists and a judge may issue a search warrant if the affidavit in support of the warrant offers sufficient credible information to establish probable cause. There is a presumption that police officers are reliable sources of information, and affidavits in support of a warrant will often include their observations. When this is the case, the officers' experience and training become relevant factors in assessing the existence of probable cause. Information from victims or witnesses, if included in an affidavit, may be important factors as well."

The LII goes on to state that "the good faith exception that applies to arrests also applies to search warrants: when a defect renders a warrant constitutionally invalid, the evidence does not have to be suppressed if the officers acted in good faith. Courts evaluate an officer's good faith by looking at the nature of the error and how the warrant was executed."

What should immediately strike absolute abject terror into the hearts of the reader of the above mini legal analysis should be the absolute abundance, amount, and flagrant use of the most abstract, non-defined, subjective, and loosely constructed words and phrases which undersigned has underlined, boldfaced, and italicized for added effect.

How in the world can we have a fair criminal justice system when the very gatekeepers (or entrappers), which are America's police departments, are granted complete and total immunity from investigation, prosecution, conviction, or civil liability legal retribution from the American public when the entire "shield from liability" is the hitherto gray concept of probable cause?

47

As was stated above, the power to arrest is essentially the power to destroy or, for that matter, kill.

And if the deck is stacked against minorities and political dissidents in America, wherein all these subjective concepts making up the definition of probable cause, already problematic since the founding of this nation as enshrined in the Fourth Amendment as the analysis above describes, then how can any minority or political dissident escape being arrested since the enactment of the 1994 VCCLEA and purposeful infiltration of America's police departments by racist organizations such as the Ku Klux Klan and others, as documented and verified by our very own FBI?

The fact remains is that in order to err on the side of caution, therefore, and because of the horrendously unfixable consequences of being brought into the criminal justice system and its lifetime effects on that individual, his family and loved ones, friends, career, personal and professional life, which can never be "cleansed" or "fixed," even after exoneration, that if the police have any reason to believe that the targeted individual for arrest is innocent, THEN HE MUST NOT BE ARRESTED AND BE RELEASED IMMEDIATELY.

Certainly, some guilty people will go free.

But that is inherently a lot better than sending millions of innocent people to jail or to their death.

Indeed, the Founding Fathers insisted on that outcome, because of the arbitrary arrests, incarcerations, and destruction of their freedom- loving cohorts in British England.

And this is why they sacrificed themselves at the altar of the War for Independence, dying heroically and bloodily in the process.

This concept was literally worth their lives, and it is still worth our lives today in the modern world.

To that end, if and when a police officer has been told by an alleged "victim of crime" that the accused party is innocent, then ALL INQUIRIES MUST CEASE, AND THE TARGETED PARTY MUST NOT BE ARRESTED, barring any other hardcore, physical, indisputable evidence to the contrary.

In other words, if there is no hard evidence to support or substantiate an arrest, then the targeted individual MUST BE LET GO AND NOT ARRESTED.

Unfortunately, in today's criminal justice system, police officers rampantly are arresting anyone and everyone, even when the alleged victim has recanted, admitted he or she lied, or fabricated the entire incident.

And in the case of domestic violence cases, rabid feminists are calling for the heads of these oftentimes innocent perpetrators even when the female has declared the innocence of the man arrested and being prosecuted, in complete and total contravention to the law, Fourth Amendment, and common human decency.

This is fundamentally un-American and unconstitutional and demands reform right now and immediately.

If the legislative or executive branches will do nothing about this, then it is incumbent upon the judiciary to do so, with a reinterpretation and setting down of new and fresh decisions and orders and analyses on the concept of probable cause, and defining exactly what the limitations must be, using hard concrete principles grounded in fairness, justice and equity, and not in "gray words and phrases" having no basis in certainty or science, rife and susceptible for abuse by the worst and most racist segments of American society within the police departments and prosecutors' offices.

The fact of the matter is that, owing to the purposefully vague, broad, and over- encompassing language used to describe the concept of probable cause by the legislature, the executive branch and the judiciary for the past two hundred years in this country's history, the issues touched actually directly affect each and every constitutional amendment, because of the "totality of the circumstances" approach to analyzing the concept of probable cause.

If police officers are allowed to justify their false arrests and racist or political targeting of innocent individuals defending themselves by declaring that they looked at the "totality of the circumstances" then we the people also have the right to grill and investigate them and their actions using the "totality of the US Constitution" and the "totality of the Bill of Rights" to make damned sure that they are being honest, not racist, politically neutral, fair, just, and responsible throughout, especially when they have been given this awesome and huge power to arrest and to kill us.

To that end, this is why this complaint cannot and will not be limited or excluded in terms of weaker or stronger constitutional amendment violations, which most assuredly should be an integral component in the calculation by the judiciary in determining whether or not a police officer's actions were lawful or just.

It is unacceptable and unforgivable that tens of millions of innocent men and women have been mercilessly arrested and killed by individuals over the past few hundreds of years who have escaped any degree of legal or equitable culpability and liability using outdated and cowardly "weasel words" as the above legal analysis demonstrates, and therefore, it is now incumbent and past due time for the judiciary to begin the process (if not complete) the definition of probable cause using concrete terminology, concise definitions, outline and delineate its scope and limitations, and go as far scientifically as possible to break it down to the fullest extent so that it is no longer dishonestly and casually thrown around and used as an all-purpose shield by dishonest or racist law enforcement (and prosecutors) to justify their crimes against humanity.

CHAPTER 16

Detecting Secret Government from Real One

We have a government that is a "fashioned" government-one that is structured as a "real government" and on the books and represented in our laws and administered by our three branches of government-the legislative, judicial, and executive branches.

T he ancient Chinese martial art of t'ai chi ch'uan has a basic tenet-distinguishing the "fashioned self" from the "real self"-i.e., the practice works on attempting to delink what we as humans have learned to project outwards to be accepted by society at large, and the person that we truly are.

The theory distinguishes the two selves because their claim is that true happiness can only be achieved by staying faithful to knowing and trusting in who we really are, rather than the fake persona we fashion for ourselves each and every day, reinforced and strengthened by society every time we act or behave in a manner which is not truly ourselves.

Similarly, we have a government which is a fashioned government-one that is structured as a real government and on the books and represented in our laws and administered by our three branches of government-the legislative, judicial, and executive branches.

If these three branches of government actually worked and functioned as they were meant to, the current problems we are facing as a nation should have absolutely no chance to grow and fester as they do now. They should in fact be curtailed and clipped by the checks and balances of the three branches of government, the separation of powers doctrine, and the self-correcting mechanisms that the Founding Fathers put in place to ensure that we do not slip back into the tyrannical monarchial bankster-controlled powers that they fought against to liberate themselves and their country from the yokes of England and the European banking cartels.

The problem is, the European-based bankers refused to let go. Instead, they slowly, over time, corrupted our leadership in all three branches of government with pure, unadulterated, unfiltered money power, blackmail, extortion, and coercion.

Sometimes this was accomplished through outright cash payments and gifts through straight- up bribery, but more often, especially with the advent of the severe criminalization of wanton and blatant acts of bribery/graft, instead this banking influence and corruption of our leaders occurred through a much more sinister and invisible spiderweb of banking and corporate corruption-so that now our leaders could be bribed through speaking tours, governmental appointments, lucrative financial deals both during and after they left office, cushy office jobs, television shows, sweetheart real estate deals, sexual bribery, pre-ordained successful book deals, university appointments, NGO chief jobs, interest-free or low-interest loans, and other modes and methodologies of encouraging our elected and appointed leaders to sell the American people out for the highest buck, leaving all of us to suffer in squalor, not being able to get justice, prevail in the courts, get specific legislation passed, burying all of us deeper and deeper into debt, obscurity, powerlessness, loss of our freedoms and self-determination, and oblivion.

It is very easy to detect our real government from our fashioned, fake government.

All one needs to do is read the newspaper and online headlines. An analysis and comparison of the news passed off from the mainstream media versus the real news emanating from the alternative media found mainly on the internet is an excellent source of determining what is real and what is not.

For example, while presidential candidate Ted Cruz wanders all across America, braying on news outlets such as CNN, Fox News, MSNBC, and in print journals such as the New York Times, Washington Post, and other periodicals about shrinking government, limiting government, getting rid of corruption, conservative values, fighting the Fed, it would help to note that the alternative media first reported and noted that Ted Cruz accepted a $1,000,000 interest-free loan from Goldman Sachs and then neglected to report it.

What does this example show?

It shows that no matter how much Ted Cruz yammers on and on about conservative or liberal values, he is in fact bought, paid for, owned, beholden, and controlled by international investment banking firm Goldman Sachs, and the leadership and actions of Goldman Sachs all around the world have been anything but conservative American Christian values. There are thousands more examples such as this with other elected and appointed leaders in America.

Follow the money, and you will find our fashioned government.

Our real government may be the structure and litmus test our leaders use to hide their tracks and obfuscate their shady dealings, but our fashioned government is the arena in which they actually operate.

And the ethics rules, which are invariably passed and enacted in almost every sphere of work and industry, are invariably placed out there in order to better hide our leader's unethical behavior and actions by creating millions of ethically sanctioned loopholes that, if there were no ethics rules, would never pass the "smell test" of the people that they govern and would invariably lead the vast majority of our leaders to jail, and certainly out of elected or appointed office.

The ethics rules and real government, therefore, add cover and structured protection for our leaders to engage in full-time unethical behavior and governmental administration "of the banks, by the banks, and for the banks."

Americans should once again return to the "smell test" of our Founding Fathers in the ranking and evaluation of our leaders if it "looks like a duck, walks like a duck, acts like a duck," then it's a goddamned duck.

A chart should be created to show the de jure and de facto actions and results of a leader. If it can be shown that during that leader's tenure certain things got worse, in whatever capacity, then that leader should be held accountable for it -regardless of whether or not their actions were legal, ethical, or in line and consistent with the roles and structures of our real government.

In other words, the "devil is in the details," and the true corruption and betrayal by our leaders occurs within the cracks and invisible crevices of our real governmental structures and ethics rules architecture, not in overt acts or omissions that are on their face illegal or unethical.

CHAPTER 17

Critique of American Justice System Pertaining to Race

It is only when the racial/religious minority enters that system, at whatever age, does he realize that in America, which was built on a legacy of slavery and indentured servitude, he is only a fraction of a human or citizen in the institutionalized eyes of the law.

T he most painful lesson a minority can experience is when he comes face to face with the American justice system, whether it be the criminal, family, or civil courts, or the law enforcement agencies which oftentimes feed them by dragging minorities before them.

It is only when the racial/religious minority enters that system, at whatever age, does he realize that in America, which was built on a legacy of slavery and indentured servitude, he is only a fraction of a human or citizen in the institutionalized eyes of the law.

Slavery was only abolished in the United States in 1865 while the Civil Rights Act (otherwise known as Title VII) was only enacted in 1964.

So, in essence this country only granted the rights (or perception) that all men are equal in the eyes of the law roughly fifty years ago, barely enough for two generations of Americans, and only 150 years since racial/religious minorities were literally enslaved and were not even considered human by their white European colonizers/owners.

Therefore, it should come as no surprise that the United States does indeed have a deeply entrenched race problem, where it can be hidden in the restaurants, bars, social circles, places of employment, universities, and other places where different races meet and congregate, but behind closed doors, white America still has not fully grasped the fact that non-white, non-European- based people are fully and 100 percent human as well.

Because of this deep-seated prejudice (if not hatred) and since the majority of law enforcement personnel and the courts are staffed with European-descended white Americans and because of the common law-based judicial made law that exists in this country, whenever there is any doubt about the guilt or innocence of the minority, this system almost always goes against that minority, and all this is committed under the color of law and authority, fully legal, and in the vast majority of cases, the lies often become the truth.

Even within interracial relationships, where one party is white and the other is not, that white individual will nearly always carry some remnant (however minuscule) that their partner is not fully human and therefore cannot fully be respected, so if a relationship goes sour or if an argument takes place, rather than respect the other party to work through it, the vast majority of white partners in that relationship will simply throw up their hands up and declare that it is not worth fixing anyway.

Why do they do that?

Well, because it is not possible to fully love and respect a "nonhuman" as an equal, deserving full respect normally accorded to a full-fledged 100 percent white human being.

And this is the saddest part of the truth and a lesson purposefully not taught in nursery, grammar, grade, high school, or even college, where teachers hope for a better future or don't want to ruin their pupil's hopes in their own future.

In fact, the exact opposite is taught, that all are equal in the eyes of the American justice system, like the fables of Santa Claus and the Easter Bunny, until that minority is one day shaken down to their very core, usually because of his experiences in the icy, cruel, sadistic, soulless American justice system, as described above.

There is unfortunately no quick fix to this problem, and sadly, it will go on for as long as it can run its course, but the fundamental truth must be acknowledged that America was built and assembled on the skulls and bones of the minority races, whatever their hue or religion, and white European-based Americans were the ones who stood on top of them.

This inherent institutionalized racism and discrimination goes to the very core and fabric of this country, and this is why so many minorities who come to these shores, looking for a better life, are so invariably heartbroken when they discover these eternal truths.

That they will always be an outsider. That they will never be able to fully develop true friendships or real love affairs with their fellow white citizenry. And that if ever there should be a disagreement or a conflict with one of them, at the end of the day, in the final analysis, the minority will always lose the battle, especially within the American justice system, normally without fail.

If you are in a courtroom with one of your white American counterparts, very often you will see the judge rule against you on nearly everything (denied motions, ex parte petitions granted in your absence, contempt motions against you freely signed and handed down against you by the judge while yours go unnoticed, unsigned, or disregarded, your opposition afforded rights and privileges not given to you, your opposition being tutored and counseled by the judge himself on how to defeat you, issues of doubt nearly always resolved in your opposition's favor, and other small but aggregated acts of institutionalized discrimination).

To that end, even if you are correct on the facts and law, the American justice system, given enough time and delay, will nearly always find you in the wrong.

In the criminal courts, this means jail time, probation, sanctions, and other horrific punishments, and in the civil system, this means bankruptcy, loss of money and property, loss of funds and livelihood, or other destructive edicts.

In the family court system, this means that you will most probably lose your own children even if you are the better parent, have them abducted and kidnapped right in front of you under the color law and authority, and you are rendered completely and utterly powerless to do anything about it.

The American police are also part of the problem, but what they make up for in a general lack of education in the law on par with the judge's ruling the courtrooms, they make up for in their brutal power to arrest, beat, detain, harass, surveillance, set you up with dishonest informants, eavesdrop, lie, cheat, and steal in order to destroy your life.

God forbid, you are a minority, and the police are white Americans, because they will also, under the color of law and authority, engage in the above acts, which are far worse and less respectful of your inalienable civil liberties and human rights than a judge could ever be.

Unfortunately, even if the minority is an attorney, litigant or defendant in the American justice system, born optimistic, driven, ambitious, highly organized, intelligent, and resourceful, he must finally acknowledge that there is no true real justice in America if you are a racial or religious nonwhite minority in the United States of America.

This is why 1/3 of all blacks, 1/6 of all Latinos, and 1/5 of all other racial and religious minorities have found themselves in jail, behind bars, or financially ruined in this country.

The American justice system is at its current state, a lost cause if you are not a white European-based person.

And it is a nightmare if you are not.

CHAPTER 18

Eleven Signs We Are Returning to Global Feudalist Society

All signs point to the clandestine and surreptitious herding of the American people into a neofeudal system designed to enrich the plutocrat/oligarch class at the expense of the masses.

1. arbitrary arrests and incarcerations without regard to individual human rights, civil liberties and constitutional protections brought on by Bill Clinton and Joe Biden's VCCLEA and VAWA laws
2. the ability of the international banking cartels to plunder the global population's personal bank accounts and savings through the repeal of Glass-Steagall Act by Bill Clinton
3. the increasing militarization of the police
4. the reinstitution of debtor's prisons by the jailing of poor people who cannot afford to pay filing fees or child support by out-of-control state and family courts
5. the arbitrary power to remove children from families by out-of-control corrupted child protective services
6. the privatization of prisons, making it profitable to arrest and incarcerate people even if they are innocent
7. the refusal of the three separate branches of government to watch each other, intervene during times of overreach, and all working for and loyal to the same powers international banking
8. the refusal of appellate or federal courts to review or investigate state court corruption, police corruption, judicial corruption, or unconstitutionality under the doctrine of the case *Younger V. Harris*
9. the refusal of government to punish or jail individual bankers or their employers for committing fraud or fleecing taxpayers to line their own pockets
10. the complete and total control of mainstream media by a few members of the corporate elite
11. the refusal of central bankers to inject capital into the markets for business loans, liquidity, and building infrastructure while removing and hoarding capital from the economy

CHAPTER 19

How Elite Use Family Court Industrial Complex to Quell and Quash Domestic Political Dissidents and Usurp US Constitution

Using the Hitlerian-coined phrase "best interests of the child," these family court industrial complex members proceed to deprive human beings of their God- given and constitutionally vested rights whenever they decide to do so.

While the same elite international banking and money powers use the "military-industrial complex," a phrase first coined by President Eisenhower, using the derogatory terms terrorist and insurgent to crush and quell the activities of foreign military and governmental power overseas, without the need to resort to the constitutional constraints imposed, enforced, and promulgated by the three branches of US governmental power embodied in the executive, legislative and judicial branches, this same power elite use the unconstitutional bodies of law and administration embodied within the Violent Crime Control and Law Enforcement Act (VCCLEA) and Violence Against Women Act (VAWA) to quell, control, quash, and destroy those they deem to be political impediments toward their grand vision of a New World Order using the "family court industrial complex."

Both of these methodologies have one common denominator-the appellation and labeling of a targeted individual or group with an emotional heart-pulling label, which therefore then allows the full force and power of the US government to skirt the US Constitution and the protections it affords to absolutely obliterate and destroy their intended targets.

Therefore, while the military-industrial complex focuses on destroying or disrupting those foreign impediments to the unbridled power of the international elite, the family court industrial complex, composed of bribed and corrupted judges, law clerks, child protective service workers, police officers, forensic evaluators, guardians ad litem, court appointed lawyers, and others intrinsically involved, act in concert to utterly destroy and silence those domestic individuals who represent a threat to their power within US borders.

Using the Hitlerian-coined phrase "best interests of the child," these family court industrial complex members proceed to deprive human beings of their God-given and constitutionally vested rights whenever they decide to do so.

In Khepri Rising's seminal book *The Family Court Industrial Complex and Post Traumatic Family Court Disorder*, the author describes how in the United States being a father means stepping into the heinous gladiatorial arena of the family court industrial complex. Men and their families have been pushed into the cattle cars of history with a disregard for the value of their lives. The criminals stand unaccused behind a veil of language and motives, which they purport are in the best interests of the child. Men wear the badge of "dead beats" and stand as thin Giacometti-esque caricatures behind a fence placed between themselves and their children, interred in a camp of illusions and false hopes given by a psychotic system that suffers from delusions of grandeur. *The Family Court Industrial Complex and Post Traumatic Family Court Disorder* conclusively establishes that child support and the savage nature of the family court system is evolutionary-based "male rape" and that many of the systems victims are suffering from an insidious malady known as post-traumatic family court disorder (PTFCD). For too long, man has laid dormant while the barbarian family court system has ravaged his home and decimated his family, and he emotionally too crippled to even put into words what lie submerged within a cavern of emotions too painful to even bear, let alone name or grieve. Khepri Rising's groundbreaking academic work published in 2012 "provides the groundbreaking foundation for the moral recognition and understanding of man's relationship to the kidnappers of his family."

The first step in abolishing your own slavery is to admit that it exists.

As Johann Wolfgang von Goethe said, "None are more hopelessly enslaved than those who falsely believe they are free."

It is time for the American people to wake up and face their enslavers and demand that their human rights, civil liberties, and constitutional protections be immediately restored.

CHAPTER 20

Institutional Racism and Rage of the Minority

The built-in bias, disparate treatment, and discrimination of American society manifests itself in many inconspicuous ways, from the rude treatment by the coffee barista at your local Starbucks to the cold manner in which the subway toll booth operator treats you when you buy a subway pass, to the outright hatred and mean-spirited words that bark from the mouth of the takeout deli worker, or any of the above.

O n a daily basis, racial minorities of both sexes are subjected to a barrage of subtle and not-so- subtle discriminatory acts and bias from the minute they leave their homes to the time they return at night.

The built-in bias, disparate treatment and discrimination of American society manifests itself in many inconspicuous ways, from the rude treatment by the coffee barista at your local Starbucks to the cold manner in which the subway toll booth operator treats you when you buy a subway pass to the outright hatred and mean-spirited words that bark from the mouth of the takeout deli worker or any of the above.

Most of these multiple acts of hostility and downright nastiness are below the radar-that is, they are not overtly blatant expressions of racial hostility or ethnic discrimination-but they are real and palpable enough to cause pain, humiliation, anger, and indignation in the minds of those minorities who are unfortunate enough to have to deal with it.

When minorities witness other mainstream majority races dealing with these same individuals, the contrast is stark-these same tool booth operators, coffee baristas, lunchroom counter employees, parking attendants, clothing store salespeople, restaurant and bar staff, and countless others are more noticeably kinder, gentler, friendlier, easy-going, and jovial.

This further reinforces and internalizes the rage and indignation that most minorities feel on a daily basis and is then internalized deep within to grow, fester, and gestate.

And it is not just racial majorities that do this to racial minorities either.

Racial minorities in positions of power often treat other racial minorities in a far worse, cruel, demeaning, and dismissive manner than their majority race counterparts, because they think that because they too are members of a racial minority group, they are somehow immune from the effects of the cruelty, bias, and discrimination that they inflict on others.

The latter are often the worst kind, because it makes racial minorities hate and detest other racial minorities, thus causing division and resentment from one minority race to another (see Asian-American deli owners versus African- American patrons, for example).

The real danger occurs when this sort of low- key, subtle, and covert form of racism and discrimination comes from someone with power in society over one's life, liberty, and pursuit of happiness-such as a police officer, court officer, judge, or any other member of society charged with determining if one literally lives or dies.

When this occurs, there is no hope and no relief.

There is no doubt that this type of human interaction is the major *casus belli* of the massive amounts of racial and ethnic minorities entrapped within the cycle of the prison system, poverty, despair, and hopelessness.

Majority white races and ethnicities simply do not have to go through this daily abuse (as much), so generally they see life through rose-colored glasses and generally do not understand the "minority rage" within their ethnic counterparts on society, having been internalized and reinforced day after day, month after month, year after year.

Majority races simply look on their minority counterparts as the "angry black male" or "angry black woman" or "angry Arab male" or "yelling Chinese woman," and dismiss them as crazy or unbalanced, further exacerbating the problem and driving that racial minority deeper into the hole of anger, rage, and frustration until it manifests itself in some other unhappy or negative way in society.

The first step in fixing a problem is to acknowledge that it exists and society's constant, daily, and rampant minute acts of cruelty and disrespect inflicted by one segment of society on another segment of society can and does have consequences on society as a whole.

It is high-time that Americans take a long and hard look at themselves and see where they fit into this horrific paradigm of continuous and systematic abuse from one group to another and the havoc it wreaks throughout society and in the country.

Perhaps if a dialogue of this issue enters our national conscience, if not sub-conscience, we can begin to heal, change, and alter our methods of dealing with people, and thus strive for a greater level of happiness and mutual respect within our communities.

It is difficult to not come to the conclusion that all this internecine conflict, with the white majority enjoying maximum daily life pleasure and lack of conflict and racial minorities suffering under the yoke and weight of institutional bias and discrimination, is by design.

That this is not on purpose, but it most probably is.

Additionally, the enactment of the Violent Crime Control and Law Enforcement Act (VCCLEA) in 1994 by then President Bill Clinton and written by then Senator Joseph Biden have criminalized this anger and made it possible to unconstitutionally arrest, prosecute, and incarcerate those victims of this daily barrage of institutional bias and racism, when they justifiably react and explode.

With the enactment of this unconstitutional law, which mandates that police officers must arrest an individual even with no real evidence or probable cause, has effectively brought back the "slaver's whip" of arbitrary arrest, beatings, incarceration, humiliation, and abuse once perpetrated by the original slaveholder owners that the United States of America was founded by.

The VCCLEA effectively reinstituted slavery and arbitrary arrest by denying all citizens their constitutional rights under the First, Second, Fourth, Fifth, Sixth, Thirteenth and Fourteenth Amendments.

And although this law was enacted against all US citizens and noncitizens alike, the data and history since its enactment in 1994 has shown an overall disproportionate effect on racial and ethnic minorities, with 1/3 of all African-Americans, 1/6 of all Latinos, and 1/13 of all whites having been arrested and incarcerated based on this Draconian and regressive racially discriminatory federal statute.

CHAPTER 21

Obama's Greatest Shame:
Refusing to Fix Broken Criminal
and Family Court Justice Systems

America's criminal justice and family court system was never designed to pursue justice or protect the "best interests of the child" but rather was enacted as an elaborate facade to conceal the satanic and evil conceit of complete and total societal control by a hidden, plutocratic, deep state elite.

In what could have been President Obama's greatest legacy, and indeed, what he was elected mainly for by the legions of hopeful Americans, young and old, black and white, male and female, gay and straight, was that he would use his own personal experiences as a black man, presumably oppressed and discriminated against his whole life, to inject some much-needed humanity and fairness into America's Draconian and foreboding criminal and family court systems, which in fact are the heir apparent to such luminaries as Adolf Hitler's NAZIs and other failed social engineers throughout history.

Indeed, America's criminal and family court systems are the only true, still existent, and living remnants of the nation's roots in abject slavery and genocide, wherein African-American and other minority slaves had their fathers ripped from their families to be murdered or disappeared, where children were wrested from the arms of their mothers or their fathers, where people toiled under the threat of the whipcrack to work for the state, i.e., their plantation masters, and if they missed a day of work, got sick, lost a limb, or were otherwise unable to "make their support payments," they were summarily executed or imprisoned without due process or trial.

The similarities between the criminal and family court justice systems in America with that of slavery are simply far too great to ignore, as the example of the Slave Patrol amply demonstrates, wherein this patrol was originally organized to pursue runaway slaves, and wherein their insignia was the copper star today used on every sheriff badge across the United States.

The 1994 Violent Crime Control and Law Enforcement Act (VCCLEA) written by then Senator Joseph Biden and enacted by then President Bill Clinton resulted in the wholesale mass incarceration of America to the tune of 1/3 of all African-Americans, 1/6 of all Latinos, and 1/11 of all whites (mainly poor whites). This Act further eroded, if not completely eradicated, the constitutional protections of the First, Second, Fourth, Fifth, Sixth, Thirteenth and Fourteenth Amendments and made an already bad situation even worse by transforming America into a veritable police state, with the Act also calling for one hundred thousand more police officers per state and more federal funding to mandatorily arrest and jail people without evidence or probable cause, coupled with a federal arrangement with the country's prisons to privatize our jails and make it profitable to lock people up.

One would think that President Barack Obama, after having squandered eight full years as the president of the United States, would have done SOMETHING about this, but alas, he did absolutely nothing.

Perhaps this is because his own Vice President Joseph Biden wrote the law, or perhaps his own Secretary of State Hillary Clinton pushed her husband to pass these criminal and family court laws, or perhaps because his own financial sponsor (some would argue the man that actually placed him into the White House) George Soros, born Gyorgi Schwartz in NAZI Germany, who allegedly betrayed his Jewish roots and helped the NAZIs to account for and confiscate his fellow Jews' property and money while allegedly turning in those Jews and other "undesirables" who were in hiding (Lewis, Michael [January 10, 1994], "The Speculator: What on Earth Is Multibillionaire George Soros Doing Throwing Wads of Money around in Eastern Europe?" New Republic. See also Kaufman, Michael T., Soros: The Life and Times of a Messianic Billionaire, Alfred A. Knopf: 2002, pp. 32-33).

George Soros reportedly has stated that those young NAZI years were for him, the "happiest time in his life." (Kaufman, Michael T., Soros: *The Life and Times of a Messianic Billionaire*, p. 37).

The social engineering and legal thicket created by our modern-day criminal and family court system literally has transformed our country into a Stalinesque police state, wherein Lavrenty Beria, who was Jozef Stalin's Secret Police Chief of the Cheka, famously declared, "Show me the man, and I will show you the crime."

Add to the mix that both the Stalinesque Communists of the former USSR and President Obama belong to the same secret society bent on global governance and the New World Order, the Freemasons. And for them, control of the people is of utmost importance, civil liberties and human rights be damned.

These plutocratic Luciferian megalomaniacs would rather that the masses literally live in a net- like thicket of laws, entangling the people daily so that they can selectively pick and choose just who exactly they want to take out of society.

As Frank Zappa once said, "America is a nation of laws-badly written and randomly enforced."

America's criminal justice and family court system was never designed to pursue justice or protect the "best interests of the child," but rather was enacted as an elaborate facade to conceal the satanic and evil conceit of complete and total societal control by a hidden, plutocratic, deep state elite.

The fact that Obama has refused to do a damned thing about any of this, except have a few talking-point and media-pleasing "conferences," is nothing but a betrayal of everything Americans thought that he would be, but more specifically to the legions of minority men and women, and poor white people, whose lives and families have been devastated and ravaged by the purposefully dysfunctional criminal and family court justice system in America.

CHAPTER 22

New Thug-Like Behavior
from Major Banks Becoming Norm

Since the big banks write the laws that regulate their own industry, which are then introduced and passed by their paid-for and bought-off congressional and senatorial "whores" in the US legislature, they clearly have the "home turf advantage" since many of their defense lawyers spent a significant amount of time on Capitol Hill as interns and representatives actually jamming through and enacting these unfair and immoral banking laws in the first place and are the only ones who know how to use all of the hidden and clandestine loopholes in the first place.

It seems that the veil of civility and professionalism hiding the criminal antics of the big banks is now coming crashing down in an open display of blatant fascism and tyranny backed up by violence and threats to the average consumer wronged by them on a daily basis.

It has been reported from all around the country that the big banks are now openly engaging in far-flung conspiracies geared and designed to increase their financial bottom line at their customers' expense, such as hitting people with finance charges and fees of sometimes $200 or more, orchestrating business client credit card chargebacks and debits withdrawing and removing tons of cash from their bank accounts without giving them enough time or due process to respond or provide proof of an authorized charge, coupled with credit card merchant services holding this type of ill-gotten cash for ninety days or more while allegedly collecting and keeping the ill-gotten interest skimmed thereon while it sits in their own escrow accounts, purposefully staffing their bank branches and customer service departments with untrained, uninformed, rude, belligerent, arrogant, and frankly stupid staff, literally designed to make small problems worse, failing to obey stop payments or ACH transactions even if you pay for them, freezing or blocking access to your own accounts even for routine debit card or banking transactions, forcing you to have a very limited dollar amount daily withdrawal on your own money and your accounts, coordinating with the federal and state governments to sometimes penalize or report you criminally for exercising your God-given right to access and use your own hard-earned money, summarily canceling or closing your account while blacklisting you or your business within their own bank if you protest but then also sharing any derogatory information with other banks even if the etiology of any problems with the bank was their own fault and otherwise treating their customers in an overly paternalistic and arrogant fashion with regards to their customers' own money, blocking and labeling them as "troublemakers" if they bother to complain or report their gross misconduct to the "relevant authorities" such as the Consumer Financial Protection Bureau (CFPB), whose high crimes and misdemeanors will be discussed later below in this article.

As was stated above, the CFPB was ostensibly created by the President Obama administration to protect banking customers from predatory behavior from these big banks, but upon further scrutiny, one finds that the most "bank protecting" administration in history under former Attorney General Eric Holder would never create an agency or entity that could actually "help" the people against the tyranny of the banks until you actually observe and watch how the CFPB handles complaints by the average banking customer, and why they are going after small pay- day loan companies which actually assist the poor to pay their bills and buy food and otherwise hang on for dear life.

When a pissed-off banking consumer files a complaint with the CFPB online, it immediately goes to the bank itself. That's when the magic happens. More often than not, the bank takes this complaint and proceeds to assign one of their countless high-powered, overly educated, obscenely paid in-house lawyers or big law firms to absolutely obliterate and destroy your complaint using all sorts of arcane and esoteric banking law terminology from both this country and others in order to absolutely blow your complaint out of the water.

They don't focus on what was morally, ethically, or even legally wrong about their conduct; they in fact simply regurgitate the countless myriad piles of unclear, inconclusive, and cleverly hidden banking laws and exceptions to show that, in fact, their unethical, immoral, and criminal banking behavior is completely and totally protected under the current state of the banking laws.

Since the big banks write the laws that regulate their own industry, which are then introduced and passed by their paid-for and bought-off congressional and senatorial "whores" in the US legislature, they clearly have the "home turf advantage" since many of their defense lawyers spent a significant amount of time on Capitol Hill as interns and representatives actually jamming through and enacting these unfair and immoral banking laws in the first place and are the only ones who know how to use all of the hidden and clandestine loopholes in the first place.

Crimes and acts which would, on their face, absolutely horrify and shock the average banking customer from anywhere around the world, such as the specific acts and actions described above, are simply laundered, cleaned, ironed, and pressed to present you with a nice, clean finished defense product, unfortunately without a nice little bow, and is evidently a governmentally sanctioned and approved criminal act.

You are expected to swallow their response and accept it and go away with your tail between your legs. To add insult to injury, this big bank then quietly etches and notates your full name, social security number, business tax ID number, address, and other confidential banking information and blackballs and blacklists you from ever doing business with their bank again and then proceeds to share this defamatory, slanderous, and libelous information with all the other banks, thus rendering you unable to obtain another bank account ever again.

You have now been relegated to bankers no-man's land, a stateless vile creature doomed to walk the earth, clutching filthy dirty dollars in your hand, dropping coins here and there while dodging the IRS and law enforcement as a potential "terrorist" who must pay for everything with cash, having no records for any of your transactions for tax reporting purposes or accounting, or being outright refused service from vendors who will only accept a debit/credit card or check as payment for their services and not cash.

This banking blacklist, akin to Dante's Inferno, is the hell you have been banished to forever questioning the banks and their outright and totally shameless plundering of you and your hard-earned money.

And if you are truly stupid enough to protest further, you will invariably be reported to their banking security "thugs" who will promptly take you aside physically if you dare to enter a bank branch or will call you on your personal cellphone from a blocked number, threatening you with any number of physical, emotional, or psychological threats designed to keep you afraid and keep you in line.

Such is the current state of the Rothschild Central Banking criminal empire, and it is only going to get worse so long as "whitewashing" entities masquerading as regulatory agencies such as the cowardly and traitorous CFPB are manning the gates.

Rinse, lather, and repeat for the FTC Antitrust Division and behemoth monopolies such as Google for whom they protect and interfere with investigation/prosecution for their alleged myriad criminal acts against the people with supposed search engine manipulation and other anti-trust violations, but that is another story and grist for another article.

CHAPTER 23

The Surreptitious Reincarnation of
COINTELPRO with the COPS Gang-Stalking Program

In Bill Clinton's COPS Gang-Stalking Program, civilian spies are recruited from every segment of society, and everyone in the "targets" life is made a part of this ongoing, continuous, and systematic form of control and harassment, with such actions that are specifically designed to control the target and to "keep them in line," like a Pavlovian Dog. These actions are also designed to mentally, physically, emotionally, spiritually, financially, socially, and psychologically destroy the target over years to make them appear to be crazy, leave them with no form of support whatsoever, and ultimately to drive the target to suicide.

In 1975 Senator Frank Church convened a joint senatorial/congressional inquiry into the egregious human rights and civil liberties violations of the Central Intelligence Agency (CIA), National Security Agency (NSA), as well as the Federal Bureau of Investigation (FBI) against people both foreign and domestic. Such blatant transgressions included the neutralization and elimination of political dissidents, enemies of the state, real or imagined threats to national security, and anyone else on the proverbial shit list of the military-industrial complex (MIC).

The Church Committee was the United States Senate Select Committee to Study Governmental Operations with Respect to Intelligence Activities, a US Senate committee chaired by Senator Frank Church (D-ID) in 1975. A precursor to the US Senate Select Committee on Intelligence, the committee investigated intelligence gathering for illegality by the aforementioned agencies after certain activities had been revealed by the Watergate affair.

Some famous examples that have since emerged include (1) the FBI sending letters to Martin Luther King Jr. encouraging him to kill himself or else they would tell the world about his sexual proclivities; (2) the planned or successful assassinations of foreign leaders such as Fidel Castro, Patrice Lumumba, and countless other South American, Middle Eastern or Asian leaders; (3) the wholesale undermining of entire foreign economies if they democratically elected someone at odds with the elite power structure deep state of the United States such as what occurred against Salvatore Allende of Guatemala; (4) the possible assassination of John F Kennedy; (5) revelations of Christopher Pyle in January 1970 of the US Army's spying on the civilian population; (6) the December 22, 1974, New York Times article by Seymour Hersh detailing operations engaged in by the CIA over the years that had been dubbed the "family jewels," involving covert action programs involving assassination attempts against foreign leaders and covert attempts to subvert foreign governments were reported for the first time; (7) efforts by intelligence agencies to collect information on the political activities of US citizens; and (8) countless other examples, both overseas and domestically.

The end result of the Church Committee hearings was the outright banning on CIA assassinations as well as the FBI/DOJ COINTELPRO gang-stalking programs. In 1975 and 1976, the Church Committee published fourteen reports on various US intelligence agencies' formation, operations, and the alleged abuses of law and of power that they had committed, with recommendations for reform, some of which were later put in place.

Among the other matters investigated were attempts to assassinate other foreign leaders such as Rafael Trujillo of the Dominican Republic, the Diem brothers of Vietnam, Gen. René Schneider of Chile, and Director of CIA Allen Dulles's plan (approved by President Dwight Eisenhower) to use the Sicilian Mafia to kill Fidel Castro of Cuba.

Under recommendations and pressure by this committee, President Gerald Ford issued Executive Order 11905 (ultimately replaced in 1981 by President Reagan's Executive Order 12333) to ban US sanctioned assassinations of foreign leaders.

Together, the Church Committee's reports have been said to constitute the most extensive review of intelligence activities ever made available to the public. Much of the contents were classified, but over fifty thousand pages were declassified under the President John F. Kennedy Assassination Records Collection Act of 1992.

The Church Committee learned that beginning in the 1950s, the CIA and FBI intercepted, opened, and photographed more than 215,000 pieces of mail by the time the program was shut down. The Church report found that the CIA was zealous about keeping the US Postal Service from learning that mail was being opened by government agents. CIA agents moved mail to a private room to open the mail or in some cases opened envelopes at night after stuffing them in briefcases or coat pockets to deceive postal officials.

On May 9, 1975, the Church Committee called CIA director William Colby. That same day, Ford's top advisers (Henry Kissinger, Donald Rumsfeld, Philip W. Buchen, and John Marsh) drafted a recommendation that Colby be authorized to brief only rather than testify and that he would be told to discuss only the general subject with details of specific covert actions to be avoided except for realistic hypotheticals. But the Church Committee had full authority to call a hearing and require Colby's testimony. Ford and his top advisers met with Colby to prepare him for the hearing.

The Ford administration, particularly Rumsfeld, was "concerned" about the effort by members of the Church Committee in the senate and the Pike Committee in the House to curtail the power of US intelligence agencies. It seemed that Rumsfeld et al. was comfortable giving the power to arbitrarily destroy anyone as "enemies of the state" by anyone working in the IC and MIC.

COINTELPRO (Counter Intelligence Program) was a series of covert and illegal projects conducted by the FBI aimed at surveilling, infiltrating, discrediting, and disrupting domestic "political dissidents."

FBI records show that COINTELPRO resources targeted groups and individuals that the FBI deemed subversive, including anti-Vietnam War organizers, activists of the civil rights movement or black power movement (e.g., Martin Luther King, Jr. and the Black Panther Party), feminist organizations, anticolonial movements (such as Puerto Rican independence groups like the Young Lords), and a variety of organizations that were part of the broader New Left.

FBI Director J. Edgar Hoover issued directives on COINTELPRO, ordering FBI agents to "expose, disrupt, misdirect, discredit, neutralize, or otherwise eliminate" the activities of these movements and especially their leaders. Under Hoover, the agent in charge of COINTELPRO was William C. Sullivan.

Tactics included anonymous phone calls, IRS audits, and the creation of documents that would divide their targets internally.

After the 1963 March on Washington for Jobs and Freedom, Hoover singled out King as a major target for COINTELPRO. Under pressure from Hoover to focus on King, Sullivan wrote: "In the light of King's powerful demagogic speech, we must mark him now, if we have not done so before, as the most dangerous Negro of the future in this nation from the standpoint of Communism, the Negro, and national security."

The Final Report of the Select Frank Church Committee blasted the behavior of the intelligence community in its domestic operations (including COINTELPRO) in no uncertain terms:

> The Committee finds that the domestic activities of the intelligence community at times violated specific statutory prohibitions and infringed the constitutional rights of American citizens. The legal questions involved in intelligence programs were often not considered. On other occasions, they were intentionally disregarded in the belief that because the programs served the "national security" the law did not apply. While intelligence officers on occasion failed to disclose to their superiors programs which were illegal or of questionable legality, the Committee finds that the most serious breaches of duty were those of senior officials, who were responsible for controlling intelligence activities and generally failed to assure compliance with the law. Many of the techniques used would be intolerable in a democratic society even if all of the targets had been involved in violent activity, but COINTELPRO went far beyond that the Bureau conducted a sophisticated vigilante operation aimed squarely at preventing the exercise of First Amendment rights of speech and association, on the theory that preventing the growth of dangerous groups and the propagation of dangerous ideas would protect the national security and deter violence.

According to attorney Brian Glick in his book War at Home, the FBI used four main methods during COINTELPRO:

1. Infiltration: Agents and informers did not merely spy on political activists. Their main purpose was to discredit and disrupt. Their very presence served to undermine trust and scare off potential supporters. The FBI and police exploited this fear to smear genuine activists as agents.
2. Psychological warfare: The FBI and police used myriad "dirty tricks" to undermine progressive movements. They planted false media stories and published bogus leaflets and other publications in the name of targeted groups. They forged correspondence, sent anonymous letters, and made anonymous telephone calls. They

spread misinformation about meetings and events, set up pseudo movement groups run by government agents, and manipulated or strong-armed parents, employers, landlords, school officials and others to cause trouble for activists. They used bad-jacketing to create suspicion about targeted activists, sometimes with lethal consequences.

3. Harassment via the legal system: The FBI and police abused the legal system to harass dissidents and make them appear to be criminals. Officers of the law gave perjured testimony and presented fabricated evidence as a pretext for false arrests and wrongful imprisonment. They discriminatorily enforced tax laws and other government regulations and used conspicuous surveillance, "investigative" interviews, and grand jury subpoenas in an effort to intimidate activists and silence their supporters.

4. Illegal force: The FBI conspired with local police departments to threaten dissidents; to conduct illegal break-ins in order to search dissident homes; and to commit vandalism, assaults, beatings, and assassinations. The object was to frighten or eliminate dissidents and disrupt their movements.

he FBI specifically developed tactics intended to heighten tension and hostility between various factions in their targeted groups and individuals, and this resulted in numerous deaths, among which were San Diego Black Panther Party members John Huggins, Bunchy Carter, and Sylvester Bell.

While COINTELPRO was officially terminated in April 1971, critics allege that continuing FBI actions indicate that post-COINTELPRO reforms did not succeed in ending COINTELPRO tactics.

Enter the COPS Federal and State Sanctioned Gang-Stalking Program

Community-oriented policing, is a strategy of policing that focuses on police "building ties and working closely with members of the communities," and originated in 1994 when then Senator Joseph Biden wrote and then President Bill Clinton enacted the Violent Crime Control and Law Enforcement Act (VCCLEA) establishing the Office of Community-Oriented Policing Services (COPS) within the US Department of Justice.

Community policing is supposedly a policy that requires police to engage in a proactive approach to address public safety concerns. It is a cornerstone of the Clinton administration gaining its funding from the 1994 Violent Crime Control and Law Enforcement Act.

Common implementations of community- policing include the following: (1) relying on community-based crime prevention by utilizing civilian education, neighborhood watch, and a variety of other techniques, as opposed to relying solely on police patrols; (2) restructuring the patrol from an emergency-response-based system to emphasizing proactive techniques such as foot patrol; (3) increased officer accountability to civilians they are supposed to serve; and (4) decentralizing police authority, allowing more discretion among lower-ranking officers, and more initiative expected from them.

In other words, federal and state sanctioned and approved GANG-STALKING.

Gang-stalking has been described as fascism, using East Germany-style Stasi tactics, a systemic form of control, which seeks to control every aspect of a targeted individual's life. Gang- stalking has many similarities to workplace mobbing but takes place outside in the community, where the target is followed around and placed under surveillance by groups of organized civilian spies/snitches 24/7, 365 days a year. Targeted individuals are harassed in this way for months or years before they realize that they are being targeted by an organized program of gang-stalking harassment. This is very similar to what happened to many innocent individuals in the former East Germany or activists and dissidents in the former Soviet Union. Many innocent people in the former East Germany would be targeted for these harassment programs, and then their friends, family, and the community at large would be used to monitor, prosecute, and harass them. In the former USSR, it was used by the state to target activists, political dissidents, or anyone that the secret police thought was an enemy of the state or as mentally unfit, and many were institutionalized or murdered using this form of systematic control.

In Bill Clinton's COPS Gang-Stalking Program, civilian spies are recruited from every segment of society, and everyone in the target's life is made a part of this ongoing, continuous, and systematic form of control and harassment, with such actions that are specifically designed to control the target and to "keep them in line," like a Pavlovian Dog. These actions are also designed to mentally, physically, emotionally, spiritually, financially, socially, and psychologically destroy the target over years to make them appear to be crazy and leave them with no form of support, whatsoever.

For the targets of this harassment, COPS Gang-Stalking is experienced as a covert psychological, emotional, and physical attack that is capable of immobilizing and destroying a target over time. For the state, it is a way to keep their targets in line, control them, or ultimately destroy them.

This modern-day systematic form of control is funded at the highest levels of government, just like it has in other societies where these similar types of harassment programs have been implemented.

Targets can be chosen for many reasons: (1) political views, (2) whistle-blowing, (3) political dissidence, (4) asserting rights at work, (5) making the wrong enemy, (6) too outspoken, (7) investigating something that the state does not want investigated, (8) signing a petition, (9) writing a letter, (10) being "suspicious" by a civilian spy/snitch, or (11) being a religious/ethnic/racial minority.

The goal of the COPS state sanctioned organized gang-stalking program is to isolate the target from all forms of support so that the target can be set up in the future for arrest, institutionalized, or forced suicide. Other goals of this harassment are to destroy the targets reputation and credibility and to make the target look "crazy" or unstable.

The process often involves sensitizing the target to everyday stimuli as a form of control, which is used to control targets when they get out of line. Targets of this harassment become vulnerable and destitute, and often become homeless, jobless, have a breakdown, are driven to suicide, similar to targets of the banned COINTELPRO. The government eliminates perceived "enemies of the state" in this manner.

When a target moves or changes jobs, the harassment continues.

Every time the target moves, the same defamation, lies, libel, and slander will be spread, and the systematic harassment will continue. Online defamation, libel, and slander on the internet has made this continuation of COPS gang-stalking a great deal easier.

People from all segments of society can be recruited to be the "eyes and ears" of the state, such as laborers, drug dealers, drug users, street people, prostitutes, punks, church groups, youth groups, your best friend, your lawyer, local policeman, doctor, emergency services, a neighbor, family, social workers, politicians, judges, dentists, vet, supermarket cashier, postman, religious leader, care worker, landlord, anyone.

Most of these recruited civilian spies/snitches do not understand or even care that the end consequence of this harassment protocol is to eventually destroy the targeted person and function as "useful idiots" of the state sanctioned COPS Gang-Stalking Program.

It has been reported that people participate in this COPS gang-stalking because it (1) gives them a sense of power, (2) is a way to make friends, (3) is something social and fun, (4) breaks down race/gender/age/social barriers, (5) is forced or blackmailed upon them by the state or police to take part, (6) is told to them that they are part of "homeland or national security" to help keep an eye on "dangerous" or "emotionally disturbed" individuals where they are "heroic spies for the state," (7) is used on local thugs or informants who are already being used for other activities where their energies are diverted into these COPS gang-stalking community spy programs, (8) is either a choice of spying for the state or police or else go to jail, (9) involves outright lies and slander about the target to get them to go along with ruining the targets life, (10) includes average citizens recruited by the state the same way citizens were recruited in the former East Germany and other countries.

Some techniques used against targets in this organized COPS Gang-Stalking Program include the following: (1) classic conditioning where a target is sensitized to everyday stimuli over a period of months and years to harass them in public to let them know they are constantly being harassed and monitored; (2) 24/7 surveillance following the target everywhere they go, learning about the target and where they shop, work, play, who their friends and family are, getting close to the target, moving into the community or apartment where they live, across the street, monitoring the targets phone, house, and computer activity; (3) isolating the target via defamation, libel, and slander campaigns, (e.g., people in the target's community are told that the target is a thief, into drugs, a prostitute, pedophile, crazy, in trouble for something, needs to be watched, false files will even be produced on the target, shown to neighbors, family, storekeepers); (4) constant or intermittent noise and mimicking campaigns disrupting the targets life and sleep with loud power tools, construction, stereos, doors slamming, etc.; (5) talking in public about private things in the target's life; (6) mimicking actions of the target and basically letting the target know that they are in the target's life; (7) daily interferences, not too overt to the untrained eye, but psychologically degrading and damaging to the target over time; (8) everyday life breaks and street theater such as flat tires, sleep deprivation, drugging food, putting dirt on targets property; (9) mass strangers doing things in public to annoy targets such as getting calls / text messages to be at a specific time and place to perform a specific action; (10) blocking targets path, getting ahead of them in line, cutting or boxing them in on the road, saying or doing things to elicit a response from the target; (11) "baiting" tactics where a surveillance operation can selectively capture evidence of a targeted person responding to harassment, and then that evidence could then be used to justify the initiation of more formal scrutiny by a government agency.

The COPS Gang-Stalking Program, as all other state-sanctioned/ approved gang-stalking programs, has always been funded by the government. They are the only ones with enough money, coordination, and power to keep such a system in place. These coordinated efforts then join hands with others for this systemic form of control and harassment.

Such operations have nothing to do with the target's criminality; they are led and perpetrated by federal agents and intelligence/security contractors, often with the support of state and local law enforcement personnel. Unofficial operations of this type are often private investigators and vigilantes, including many former agents and police officers, sometimes on behalf of corporate clients and others with connections to the public and private elements of America's security industry.

The goal of such operations is disruption of the life of an individual deemed to be an enemy (or potential enemy) of clients or members of the security state. Arguably, the most accurate term for this form of harassment would be counterintelligence stalking.

Agents of Communist East Germany's Stasi (state police) referred to this process as Zersetzung (German for decomposition or corrosion-a reference to the severe psychological, social, and financial effects upon the victim). Victims have described the process as no-touch torture-a phrase that also captures the nature of the crime: cowardly, unethical (and often illegal), but difficult to prove legally, because it generates minimal forensic evidence.

Tactics include online and personal slander, libel, defamation, blacklisting, "mobbing" (intense, organized harassment in public), "black bag jobs" (residential break-ins), abusive phone calls, computer hacking, framing, threats, blackmail, vandalism, "street theater" (staged physical and verbal interactions with the minions of the people who orchestrate the stalking), harassment by noises, and other forms of bullying.

Such stalking is sanctioned (and in some cases, orchestrated) by federal agencies; however, such stalking is also sometimes used unofficially for personal and corporate vendettas by current and former corrupt employees of law enforcement and intelligence agencies, private investigators, and their clients.

Since counterintelligence stalking goes far beyond surveillance-into the realm of psychological terrorism, as it is essentially a form of extrajudicial punishment. As such, the harassment is illegal even when done by the government. It clearly violates the US Constitution's Fourth Amendment, which prohibits unwarranted searches, and the Sixth Amendment, which guarantees the right to a trial. Such operations also violate similar fundamental rights defined by state constitutions. Stalking is also specifically prohibited by the criminal codes of every state in America.

As was stated above, organized stalking methods were used extensively by Communist East Germany's Stasi (state police) as a means of maintaining political control over its citizens. Although this is supposedly illegal in the US, the same covert tactics are quietly used by America's local and federal law enforcement and intelligence agencies to suppress political and domestic dissent, silence whistle-blowers, and get revenge against persons who have angered someone with connections to the public and private agencies involved.

Although Edward Snowden's revelations about the National Security Agency (NSA) in 2013 and 2014 generated a great deal of public discussion about mass surveillance, US domestic counterintelligence activities such as the COPS Program receive relatively little attention.

The FBI's COINTELPRO operation is still happening, involving even more advanced surveillance technology-and this program is none other than Joseph Biden and Bill Clinton's COPS Program.

US Department of Justice crime statistics from a 2006 survey indicated that an estimated 445,220 COPS gang-stalking victims reported three or more perpetrators (the only ones reported), and this number is growing exponentially on a daily basis.

In addition to being morally reprehensible, the COPS Gang-Stalking Program, just like the original version of the FBI's COINTELPRO operations, is very, very illegal. It violates criminal laws in all fifty states against stalking, as well as grossly violates the US Constitution's prohibitions against warrantless searches and extrajudicial punishment.

While the vast majority of Americans are never personally targeted by the Joseph Biden/Bill Clinton COPS Gang-Stalking Program, they should still be concerned about the existence of such operations.

Even if such activities were constitutionally legitimate (which they are not), they still have an enormous potential for abuse as a personal or political weapon by enemies currently employed or friendly with these governmental institutions.

Ending this cowardly and illegal practice by law enforcement agencies, intelligence agencies and their parasitic corporate and individual recruits will first require exposing what is happening to the public.

CHAPTER 24

Reverting toward Monarchy: How the Deep State Plutocrat Elite Are Subverting the Courts by Killing the Appeal and the Jury Trial

> Unfortunately, most people do not realize that the US courts and judicial system are just as important in the fight for human rights and civil liberties as any battlefield.

E ven in Ancient Rome, where violence, rape, pedophilia, criminality, and dehumanization were rampant on a daily basis, their legal system was better than ours than currently in the United States, where now the powerful forces of the deep state plutocrat elite are attempting to, with great success, kill our judicial and legal system by subverting the courts, destroying the appeal and jury trial process.

Prior to Ancient Rome, most early civilizations were ruled with an Iron Fist by the arbitrary edicts, orders, and judgments of kings or priests. Laws and the punishments for not obeying them were at the fickle word or whim of the despotic ruler. Then in Ancient Rome around 450 Bc, there was a violent revolt of the peasant class (plebeians) who fought and died because they believed that their civil liberties and human rights were ordained by God, and not by wealthy and corrupted men, to protect their freedoms and be able to interpret the code of laws and safeguard their civil liberties and human rights. The Twelve Tables were therefore established and a ten-man commission with extraordinary powers known as the *decemviri legibus scribundis* set forth the basis of law for all Roman citizens and comprised a complete *ius civile*. These laws covered the procedure that was to be used and followed for various crimes. These courageous plebeians forced the law to be open, transparent, and visible, and applicable to all people of Rome, including perfecting the appeal process and guaranteeing all people, regardless of socioeconomic status or class, the right to a trial by their peers with a jury. But as usual, the wealthy generally found ways to escape judgment.

Ancient Rome's greatest contributions to the modern legal system were therefore the right to appeal and the jury trial.

However, as of late, the deep state plutocrat elite, who view the appellate process, jury trials, and the "people seeking justice" as more of an impediment and nuisance in their ability to coldly dictate and delegate, view the people's assertion of their civil liberties and human rights in the courts as an enormous waste of time and a roadblock on their way to a streamlined global and despotic New World Order.

So, the deep state plutocrat elite have elected to experiment in the legal system on society's least popular residents-minorities, immigrants, enemy combatants, and terrorists. This is because few, if any, Americans will ever come to the aid or assistance of these disfavored members of the human race.

But like Pastor Martin Niemöller (1892-1984) famously stated about the cowardice of German intellectuals following the NAZI's rise to power and the subsequent purging of their chosen targets, group after group, "First they came for the Socialists, and I did not speak out because I was not a Socialist. Then they came for the Trade Unionists, and I did not speak out because I was not a Trade Unionist. Then they came for the Jews, and I did not speak out because I was not a Jew. Then they came for me, and there was no one left to speak for me."

The deep state plutocrat elite controlled US government has chosen to pick on the most vulnerable and unpopular segments of our society (all purposefully created) to engage in social legal experimentation in the US federal and state courts because they can get away with seriously and severely undercutting and abrogating humanity's civil and human rights, and by undercutting the appeals process (especially with immigrants who can be deported even if they have an appeal pending) and by targeting racial and ethnic minorities (who have historically for the past few hundred years been the object of abuse and ire by their host nation) and even more obscenely since 9/11 by the overt and open deprivation of human and civil rights against so-called enemy combatants and terrorists, whose ranks and definitions have now greatly expanded to include journalists and other "belligerents" by the Pentagon and the military-industrial complex, which are dominated by the deep state plutocrat elite, the foot-soldiers and recruits of the global worldwide central bankers of Europe.

The problem is that the American people, who grow more and more accustomed and apathetic to the blatant legal abuse, court-sanctioned torture, and flagrant violation of the civil liberties and human rights of people within their midst, end up like the proverbial frog that boils to death in a pot of slowly boiling water when they wake up and realize that the federal and state judges (often plucked from large law firms where their former clients were international central bankers and global financial denizens), and even the assigned prosecutors, feds, and police in their midst who are prosecuting them, are already accustomed to easily and without regret or remorse

83

systematically depriving and ignoring the countless legal protections afforded to people in America by the US Constitution and the Bill of Rights, so hard fought after the Founding Fathers penned the Declaration of Independence, fighting multiple bloody and countless wars to win their Independence from European Banker Bondage, Dictatorship, Tyranny, and Slavery.

Unfortunately, most people do not realize that the US courts and judicial system are just as important in the fight for human rights and civil liberties as any battlefield.

If those forums are subjugated and subverted successfully by these ruthless international banker forces, then we have reverted to a judicial and court system that is even worse than the Ancient Romans ever had, and we are on the road back to the system of the arbitrary rules and whims of kings or priests, however ruthless, cruel, deranged, misguided, or blood- thirsty they may be.

CHAPTER 25

Deep State Plutocrat Elite Use
"Protected Classes" to Do Their Dirty Work

George Soros, a known Rothschild International central banker agent and supposed CIA asset, is a great prototypical example of how the deep state plutocrat elite operate.

Since the essential nature and character of the deep state plutocrat elite are inherently cowardly and weak, they rarely, if ever, come out of the woodwork to do battle with their opposition and foes all around the world.

So, they purposefully fund and create "organizations" made up of certain "protected classes," such as women, blacks, gays, Jews, and others, in order to dispatch them to destroy, frame, set up, blackmail, extort, sabotage, and harass their opponents.

Alleged former NAZI George Soros, a known Rothschild International central banker agent and supposed CIA asset, is a great prototypical example of how the deep state plutocrat elite operate in this manner.

Examples of these types of organizations include various feminist organizations, black organizations, gay organizations, and Zionist organizations, the latter of which have proven to be the most useful and effective, because the Jewish people are inherently more well- educated, united, organized, clannish, mutually loyal, and supportive than the other protected classes.

"I am sometimes asked if I have any regrets about publishing our book. As of today, my only regret is that it is not being published now. After the humiliations that Obama has endured at the hands of the Israel Lobby and the Hagel circus, we would sell even more copies and we would not face nearly as much ill-informed criticism" (Stephen Walt, co-author of the book).

It is this same deep state plutocrat elite which has pressured and lobbied our legislators to give these "protected classes" extra and better civil liberties and human rights than anyone else, and which makes them even more powerful when they organize to target anyone whom the deep state plutocrat elite wants to neutralize.

So, if the deep state plutocrat elite want to target and destroy someone or something, they quickly go through their organizational Rolodex and pick out the best agent for the job.

None of these organizations have any idea who created and funded them, except for their highest echelons of power and leadership, who are literally sworn to secrecy on pain of death and destruction. Essentially, the leadership of these organizations are traitors to their own members, because their first duty of loyalty is to the deep state plutocrat elite and not at all to the people who pay their membership dues and attend their rallies.

If you have not noticed, most if not all of these organizations have the most expensive digs, offices, furniture, state-of-the-art technology, and sophisticated organization and structural makeup and hierarchy, and tons of well-paid employees and loyal staff with full benefits and privileges. Does one ever wonder how they can exist in such a high-level manner when their only form of sustenance is stated to be "donations" from the public at large? No, it is because these organizations are all gifted, funded, sustained, and beholden to the vast money power of the deep state plutocrat elite, and this is why they are so well funded and professional-looking.

Even in a bad economy.

If one digs further enough, they will find that the above aforementioned organizations, as well as other "successful ones," are literally funded and created by the same few families and people comprising the deep state plutocrat elite for the sole purpose of being their enforcement and character assassination arm, neutralizing and/or destroying their global targets and opposition using whatever means necessary.

These organizations, which always ultimately strive to increase the personal wealth and power of the deep state plutocrat elite, use these "protected class" organizations because if you attack or defend yourself against them for the trampling of your civil liberties, human rights attacks, and violations of law, then you are simply a disgruntled misogynist, racist, homophobe, anti-Semite, or whatever cruel and unusual derogatory appellation they choose to stamp you with, and you at once lose all your credibility while they continue to beat you down, hound you, sabotage your personal and professional life, jail you, bankrupt you, and ultimately, if you do not break down and comply, murder you.

CHAPTER 26

Hollywood Elite Obsession with Destroying Families, Encouraging Promiscuity and Dependence on State

Women (and men) in Hollywood are objectified as pure sex objects for exploitation, as is the message in their movies, but then the rulers of Hollywood return to their stable homes and enjoy a solid and satisfying family life.

A common theme in Hollywood movies, whether comedy or drama, seems to be a message from Satan himself: "Leave your family, your stable home life, and engage in sociopathic, irresponsible, immature, self- destructive, and community-destroying behavior."

While the bigwig Hollywood producers, directors, writers and moneyed elite are generally all married, with children, in their fancy homes in Beverly Hills driving their Rolls-Royces, shopping on Rodeo Drive, their message for the rest of the "unwashed masses" of the American populace encourages the exact opposite. Their goal is to stimulate instability, uncertainty, chaos, and rampant individualism, as then the masses can be better culled and controlled as if they were cattle.

Women (and men) in Hollywood are objectified as pure sex objects for exploitation, as is the message in their movies, but then the rulers of Hollywood return to their stable homes and enjoy a solid and satisfying family life.

This is directly in line with the deep state plutocrat elite goal of making women with children dependent on the state for their child support checks, eliminating the male father figure from the paradigm who would otherwise protect his family, and all in all forcing both sexes to turn to the state for stability and security. And of course, the Hollywood elite are part of the power structure that completely controls this "state."

It is much easier to control the masses when they are broken apart into fragments, when they cannot team up against your power and authority, and when they cannot trust each other so that they can figure out what you are up to, and plot together the demise of your power.

The deep state plutocrat elite realize that a stable, loving, and trusting family relationship is a key to personal and societal power—that a solid family unit is the building block from which all endeavors, goals, financial security, emotional health, and physical strength emanate-and the single life often leads to despair, loneliness, drug and alcohol addiction, and ease of manipulation by others.

That is why the Hollywood power elite nearly always stay married with children, and why their ruled over "peasants" are encouraged in their films and media to divorce, never get married, engage in dangerous and rampant promiscuity, drug and alcohol abuse, and other sociopathic behavior antithetical to a good solid family life.

CHAPTER 27

The Importance for the USA to Join Hands with the World

America should abandon their quest for global hegemony.

ZBIGNIEW BRZEZINSKI

N ow that former National Security Advisor Zbigniew Brzezinski has openly declared that the United States of America should abandon their quest for global hegemony, American leadership should take heed and amend their foreign policy objectives accordingly.

In his article entitled "Towards a Global Realignment," Mr. Brzezinski has declared that the United States should join hands with Russia and China, and India, to govern and establish order throughout the world.

While this declaration has no doubt invited consternation from America's neoconservatives, who blood-thirstily crave American dominance in all affairs globally, it is nonetheless a positive and healthy development for the following reasons:

1. America has failed miserably in foreign intervention, resulting in mass wanton death and destruction throughout the world with useless wars and clandestine paramilitary attacks and proxy wars using NATO, Saudi Arabia, Israel, and even Al Qaeda and ISIS on sovereign nations.
2. It is bankrupting the USA.
3. It has made the US much more hated than at any other time in history, thus making America and its citizenry even less safe.
4. It has ruined the value of our currency.
5. We have diverted precious resources from improving domestic infrastructure towards foreign expenditures and the military-industrial complex.
6. It has undermined American moral authority.
7. It has forced other formerly compliant and cooperative nations to group together for survival, and built an anti-American bloc in nearly every corner of the planet, thus effectively thwarting American everywhere, leaving the US isolated. influence
8. It is un-American to pursue empire.
9. It has affected US currency by forcing other nations to pursue the gold standard, rather than the petro-dollar.

10. It leaves all of our well-entrenched and loyal allies much weaker and more vulnerable to foreign intervention and attack.

It is vitally important that the US recognize that Russian President Vladimir Putin and China's Xi Jinping have consistently referred to America as their "partners," while the US has referred to them as "strategic competitors" and other such inherently loaded insults, which already starts the ball of negativity rolling.

The US should remain as a member of the International Monetary Fund and World Bank but should also place the other foot into the BRICS Bank and AIIB Paradigm in order to enjoy and share in both worlds economically and culturally.

If America truly believes in its "exceptionalism," then it should, with supreme confidence, enter the world as an active participant and not as a spoiled "bully in the schoolyard."

Only in this manner can America help to guarantee its current living standards, improve its economic engine of growth and progress, avoid unnecessary and destructive war and conflict, and move forward to a better future.

CHAPTER 28

Things That Bad Judges Do

There may be a pattern and practice of certain corruption and bad acts by that judge, and your notification of those authorities may not only help you and your case, but will also help the next hapless victim of that bad judge's behavior.

To paraphrase Thomas Jefferson, well-educated people are the ultimate safe-guarders of their own liberties.

What this means is that whenever the people see that their constitutional rights, civil liberties, and human rights are being violated, it is their responsibility to correct the situation.

The three branches of government (executive, legislative, and judicial) were set up supposedly to keep one another in check. However, as the decades have elapsed since the founding of the Republic, more and more members of those three branches have fallen into line with and been co-opted by the big banks, big corporations, and big money.

They all seem to be taking orders from the same deep state plutocratic elite, with none of them appearing to answer to or take care of the people they were meant to serve.

Even the supervisory bodies of these three branches of government appear to have been corrupted, so there is almost really nowhere to go for a person who has been wronged by a member of the US government.

No other branch of government is as powerful or imbues so much unfettered power to an individual judge, whether local, state, or federal.

This is because a presiding judge can literally hold the power of life, liberty, and the pursuit of an individual's happiness in the palm of their hand and can mete out justice (or injustice) at the drop of a hat, with a bang of a gavel, or with the issuance of a bad decision.

There is really no one in that courtroom that can check his or her power, or limit their decision, or question their conduct, like there is in a room full of legislators or within a Cabinet of executive leaders.

That is why it is so important to vet, screen, and watch like a hawk each and every member of our judicial branch, and to police them each and every single day for potential conflicts of interest, money trails, special interest links, judicial activism, bribery, corruption, bias, competence, and integrity.

However, if you find yourself on the other side of a judicial decision that did not favor you or your facts, it is wise to know some of the specific acts that bad judges engage in on a daily basis, and when you encounter one of them, you must march directly and file judicial misconduct complaints with your local or state judicial complaint bureau, with carbon copies sent to your local legislator, executive branch, as well as to the federal law enforcement agencies.

There may be a pattern and practice of certain corruption and bad acts by that judge, and your notification of those authorities may not only help you and your case, but will also help the next hapless victim of that bad judge's behavior.

For example, bad judges will often do the following:

1. Issue Ex Parte judicial orders even when the party affected has not received any notification or opportunity to defend his rights in the courtroom, and this can drastically and seriously affect the affected party's constitutional rights.
2. Give legal advice in the courtroom to your opposition while forcing you to fend for yourself in uncertain legal waters.
3. Unnecessarily and unfairly adjourning cases for months on end, thus prolonging your misery while forcing you to continue to pay your lawyer for legal services, extending their legal representation and keeping justice away from you. Martin Luther King Jr. once said, "A right delayed is a right denied," and this can be no better illustration of this type of judicial misconduct.
4. Be on the board of directors of members of certain organizations that routinely place their lawyers in front of them. For example, certain "nonprofit" organizations have legal wings wherein their lawyers literally help to pick and choose certain judges to be on the bench, lobbying for them or their opponents, and judges certainly know which side their bread is buttered, and will often bend over backwards to rule in their favor, even when they know that lobbying group lawyer's legal position is totally on the wrong side of the law.

5. Accept lucrative teaching positions, speech giving appointments, book deals, and awards ceremonies from certain special interest groups or non-profit organizations, who absolutely expect and demand judicial decision compliance, which simply amounts to outright and blatant bribery, although hidden and obfuscated by the pseudo-legal mechanism of the entire courtroom charade.

6. Since almost any judicial decision can be written in an outcome-determinative fashion, it is vitally important to note that a bad judicial order can and will consist of circular reasoning, circumlocutory prose, unclear syllogistic analysis, and convoluted decisions. This is again why it is important to vet and continue to investigate any and all judges sitting on the bench.

7. Allow their law clerks to write all their decisions, so definitely keep an eye on and investigate that judge's law clerk for the same type of special interest and nonprofit organizational linkages and corruptibility as described above.

8. Intimidate, threaten, insult, harass, and coerce you from the bench, and cow you into fear and submission, using vulgarity and other profanities to keep you in complete and total fear, humiliating you publicly to keep you in submission.

9. Cut off disfavored counsel in the courtroom, harass and badger them, not allow them to speak, trying to make them feel incompetent or idiotic, while allowing favored counsel or litigants to ramble on endlessly with little to no interruption, arbitrarily picking on each and every single statement or comment that comes out of the disfavored counsel or litigant's mouth while allowing the favored lawyer or litigant to bask in the glory of garrulous and unfettered free speech, thus totally skewing the outcome of the case and frustrating the disfavored lawyer or litigant to no end.

10. Instructing their law clerks, court officers, secretaries, and other court personnel to target, harass, defame, slander, libel, lose evidence of, annoy, or irritate a disfavored lawyer or litigant, while pretending that they had nothing to do with it.

11. Not accept the disfavored lawyer or litigant's submitted evidence or arguments while openly and in a biased fashion accepting literally every piece of evidence or argument from the favored lawyer or litigants in their courtroom, thus also skewing your case results and development.

12. Having sidebar or out-of-court conversations and communications with favored litigants or lawyers tending to influence or affect the case outcome. Again, this is normally done when the judge is linked to special interest or nonprofit lobbying groups that have lawyers on their staff and who often appear in that bad judge's courtroom.
13. Scores of other acts of judicial misconduct and bad behavior.

If a litigant or lawyer in any courtroom, whether local, state, or federal, experiences any of the above bad judicial acts, they should immediately write down their experiences and report it to their local or state judicial misconduct committee, but they should not just stop there; they should also notify their local legislator, congressman, senator, federal law enforcement authority, department of justice and district court civil rights and public corruption unit.

If enough complaints are filed, perhaps these bad judges will be thrown off the bench or thrown into jail, where they belong.

CHAPTER 29

The Importance of Educating
The People to Maintain Freedom

Thomas Jefferson believed that the most effective means of preventing the perversion of power into tyranny were to illuminate, as far as practicable, the minds of the people at large and more especially to give them knowledge of as many facts as possible in order to defeat the enemies of freedom.

At a recent speech given by American Elder Statesman Ron Paul, keeper of the flame of the US Constitution, civil liberties, and human rights, the audience was struck by his reminder that education was paramount in safeguarding and guaranteeing American constitutional rights and that the deep state plutocrat elite had spent the better part of the past seventy years purposefully dumbing down the American people to the point where they could not even recognize their own God-given constitutional rights if they even wanted to, through the restrictive, ineffective, inefficient, and contrived US Department of Education.

Dr. Ron Paul talked about Thomas Jefferson and his emphasis on educating the people in order to preserve the Union.

Thomas Jefferson said, "An enlightened citizenry is indispensable for the proper functioning of a republic. Self-government is not possible unless the citizens are educated sufficiently to enable them to exercise oversight. It is therefore imperative that the nation see to it that a suitable education be provided for all of its citizens."

Jefferson believed that there was no safer depositary of the ultimate powers of society but the people themselves, and if they were "not enlightened enough to exercise their control with a wholesome discretion, the remedy is not to take it from them, but to inform their discretion by education. This is the true corrective of abuses of constitutional power."

This was because he believed that "every government degenerate when trusted to the rulers of the people alone. The people themselves, therefore, are its only safe depositories. And to render even them safe, their minds must be improved to a certain degree."

Thomas Jefferson believed that the most effective means of preventing the perversion of power into tyranny were to illuminate, as far as practicable, the minds of the people at large and more especially to give them knowledge of as many facts as possible in order to defeat the enemies of freedom.

In one of his most pointed quotes, Jefferson said that "if a nation expects to be ignorant and free in a state of civilization, it expects what never was, and never will be."

He believed that no nation was permitted to live in ignorance with impunity and that "light and liberty go together."

He also believed that the study of science was invaluable, wherein its "value to a republican people, the security it gives to liberty by enlightening the minds of its citizens, the protection it affords against foreign power, the virtue it inculcates, the just emulation of the distinction it confers on nations foremost in it; in short, it has its identification with power, morals, order and happiness."

CHAPTER 30

Israeli Black Operations
in the USA—Operation Honeypot

They usually target anyone whom they deem to be antithetical
or non-supportive of Israeli domestic and foreign policy.

I t is well known that the Israeli Mossad using their Sayanim network in
the United States routinely engage in Black Operations (Black Ops)
against US citizens here in the United States.

They usually target anyone whom they deem to be antithetical or non-
supportive of Israeli domestic and foreign policy.

They routinely target senators, congressmen, politicians, celebrities,
CEOs, academics, intellectuals, journalists, diplomats, or anyone of relative
importance in American society.

Their favorite mode of operation against male targets is to hire prostitutes
to engage in "honey-pot" operations wherein that hooker links up with the
target romantically/ sexually, and then uses the VAWA laws enacted by Joe
Biden and Bill Clinton to ensnare that target in a false domestic violence case,
sexual assault case, extortion or blackmail case, or even worse, a false rape
allegation or even murder.

Once the male has been ensnared and entrapped, the Israeli/Zionist-
controlled media begins to blast, 24/7, 365 days a year, the defamatory,
slanderous, and libelous allegations against their target, effectively convicting
and destroying their target in the online and written press.

These women, considered protected and supported by society at large, are
then encouraged to destroy the target by various feminist groups, also on the
payroll and integrally intertwined with Israeli intelligence, and together they
prosecute and torture that target using Sayanim-friendly detectives, judges,
child protective workers, and prosecutors.

There is virtually no escape from this type of black op once a target has
been selected.

The Federal Bureau of Investigation (FBI) rarely if ever gets involved
because they are thoroughly infiltrated by Israeli intelligence from the top on
down, and 99 percent of the time, they actively support these clandestine
Israeli operations on US soil because of the tight grip Israeli lobbying has on

the jugular of the American legislative, executive, and judicial branches of the US government.

CHAPTER 31

The Double Standards of Criminality in America

Many of these white male perverts have been Department of Homeland Security bigwigs with security clearance.

Why is it that when a white Christian or Jewish man is arrested for criminality, no one cares, but when a Muslim man is arrested, it becomes a global terrorism case, with the full and awesome power and force of the US military-industrial complex, the fully owned US corporate mainstream media, and the US federal, state, and local police involved, coupled with the full unyielding support of the legislative and executive branches of the US government?

It is very well established that the vast majority of criminality in America derives and originates from white men, but the vast proportion of arrests are directed against minority men, i.e., black and Latinos.

The vast majority of sex crimes, including rape, pedophilia, incest, bestiality, child pornography, and other disgusting acts are committed by white men, not minority men. Many of these white male perverts have been Department of Homeland Security bigwigs with security clearance.

However, why is it that, whenever a violent crime is committed by a Muslim in America, it immediately becomes a global "terrorism" case, with the whole of white America going buck-wild, jumping on the bandwagon, and getting all excited?

Why is that the countless scores of white male violent criminality, even when attacking minority or black churches, or other such myriad crimes, is totally and virtually ignored by the mainstream media, the military- industrial complex, federal state and local police, and most, if not all, of middle white America?

The answer is that the Ku Klux Klan is alive and well in America, and the race war is in full effect from the top on down.

White America and white Males are essentially allowed criminal transgressions as momentary lapses of reason, while minority men are punished far more severely, while Muslim male criminality is on the even greatest extreme of treatment, i.e., global terrorism, with absolutely none of the constitutional and human rights protections afforded to even the lowliest dog or farm animal.

The fact that 99.99 percent of Muslims around the world have never even thought about engaging in criminal activity does not even matter.

If you are a Muslim and you are male and if you happen to engage in any type of criminality whatsoever, the white Christian and Jewish male world will absolutely fucking destroy you using all of its resources to do so.

How is that even okay?

CHAPTER 32

Clintons, Obama, and Biden Set Up
American Police State That Trump May Unwittingly Enforce

The loss of freedom often occurs like a "thief in the night."

T he price of liberty is eternal vigilance" (Thomas Jefferson, 1817).

Anyone watching the news today where Donald Trump has now openly praised the racist, apartheid, civil liberties and human rights violating practices and policies of the Israeli government should absolutely be freaking out right about now.

Where once Donald Trump appears to have offered a refreshing alternative to the American police state unwittingly (or purposefully) created by the unconstitutional and Draconian legislation and policies starting with then Senator Joseph Biden and then President Bill Clinton's Violent Crime Control and Law Enforcement Act (VCCLEA) of 1994, which Bill Clinton admitted caused "mass incarceration" in the United States, resulting in 1/3 of all blacks, 1/6 of all Latinos, and 1/10 of all (mostly poor) whites without due process or probable cause, resulting in 68 million Americans with criminal records—more than the entire population of France— (contrast that figure with Norway which has only seventy-four people in jail right now in the entire country), coupled with current President Barack Obama's refusal or inability to reform the horrifically biased criminal justice and family court system in America for the past eight years, all against the "backdrop" of the community-oriented policing (COPS) program of the US Department of Justice (also part of Bill Clinton 1994 VCCLEA law), which many argue is simply the reincarnation and resuscitation of the outlawed FBI COINTELPRO program, which sought to "disrupt and destabilize" political dissidents and other free thinkers, we as Americans may be in a lot of trouble.

These three shortsighted (at best) Democrats-Bill Clinton, Joe Biden, and Barack Obama-bowing to political and money pressure from the deep state plutocratic elite, have constructed and placed into normal American life, state-sanctioned surveillance "gang-stalking programs" and "terrorism programs," which have effectively over-criminalized Americans and have, in the words of famed attorney Harvey Silverglate, caused Americans to literally commit "three felonies per day" from the time they wake up in the morning to the time they go to bed at night.

As Buffalo Springfield once sang, "Step out of line, the man come and take you away."

And as Jozef Stalin's Secret Police Chief Lavrenty Beria once said, "Show me the man, and I will show you the crime."

Now that the technocratic infrastructure of the American police state is now firmly in place by these three Democratic and shortsighted politicians, all it is going to take is a knee-jerk, non-thinking, non-cerebral, loud-mouth megalomaniac to actually implement the full extent of this "prison planet," complete with FEMA Concentration Camps, arbitrary round-ups, firing squads, millions of American citizens being "disappeared," and other such horrific circumstances. Let's hope that Donald Trump does not become that man.

If people think that this could not happen in the USA, think again. If Americans truly wish to remain free, with their constitutional protections still in place, then as Thomas Jefferson once said, we need to be eternally vigilant and well educated/informed over our elected leaders and to watch and listen to every single word that they say—and to watch them like a hawk.

The loss of freedom often occurs like a "thief in the night," when the American people are neither looking nor watching. Just look at the enactment of the Federal Reserve Act during Christmas 1913 when 99 percent of our elected congressmen were at home celebrating the holidays.

In order to prevent another Adolf Hitler, Jozef Stalin, Pol Pot, or whatever dictator appears on the scene, we must never allow our leaders to make the kind of careless statements as Donald Trump made today. Freedom is not free, and we must be eternally vigilant to protect those freedoms.

CHAPTER 33

Zionists Have Been Hypocritically
Practicing "BDS" for Centuries

And all of these anti-BDS politicians and leaders are simply enabling this criminality and "chutzpah."

I n another blatant act of hypocrisy, Zionists from all over the world are hemming and hawing about the BDS (boycott, divestment, sanction) movement originating in university campuses and intellectual circles globally, which has a stated goal to "end international support for Israel's oppression of Palestinians and pressure Israel to comply with international law," according to the BDS movement website.

Organized Zionism seems to conveniently forget that the original creator of these types of economic boycotts, sanctions, and divestment programs to get other nations, individuals, or political organizations to comply with their demands, or bring them to their knees, began with the Zionists themselves.

There are countless examples throughout history where organized Zionism has literally declared economic warfare on their enemies or against entities whom they wanted to control and/or destroy with these methods, and the Palestinians (their current victims under Zionist heels) have merely learned from their oppressors to use their own economic boycott medicine against them.

Not only did the Zionists "declare an economic, boycott, and sanctions" war against Germany in the 1930s, they have also done so in the modern day against both Iran and Russia.

The real reason the GOP foreign policy elite prefer Hillary Clinton to Donald Trump—a Clinton win would mean more wars.

Furthermore, Zionist money is notoriously behind the modern-day American and European political leaders who are constantly waging a war of economic sanctions against any nation that pisses off Israel, such as against half of the Middle East or anyone else not bowing to their global or domestic political demands and this is only a precursor to their eventual lobbying for carpet bombing these "noncompliant nations into the stone age" if they don't cooperate or submit to their outrageous demands for complete and total domination.

Even more troubling, Zionist business owners are notorious for sabotaging, cutting off, disrupting, disorienting, and destabilizing other competing businesses in their midst, which are either in direct competition with their own businesses, either directly or indirectly, by using their vast Sayanim Network consisting of Zionist-friendly judges to rule against their competitors in the courts, corrupt police officers and federal law enforcement to make false arrests, greedy district and US attorneys to maliciously indict and charge their competitors, child protection workers to kidnap their enemies' kids, federal state and local taxing authorities to audit or roll up their competition, telecommunications and internet companies to summarily cut off their services, post office workers to lose their mail, landlords to harass or evict their business tenants, thugs and gangs to physically disrupt and break up their competitors businesses, and other surreptitious and disgusting methods to ensure that they, the Zionists, and only they, can stay at the top of any business area.

To that end, for the Zionists to now start getting up on their hind legs and bay at the moon simply because the poor, beaten-down Palestinians have finally learned what the Zionists have used for centuries to neutralize and destroy their competition in order to remain at the top is beyond hypocritical but is also in fact criminal.

And all of these anti-BDS politicians and leaders are simply enabling this criminality and "chutzpah."

CHAPTER 34

The Wholesale Co-Opting of International
Human Rights Organizations by Big Banks/Business

Any nonprofit organization that takes donations could be influenced by their donors.

One does not have to look very far into the money trails of the various mainstream "human rights organizations" scattered throughout the world to see that they usually wind up being funded, nurtured, strategized, and shaped by some of the greatest human rights violators the world has ever known.

This truism certainly has some serious side effects- for example, bona fide legitimate complaints of human rights violations reported all throughout the world often therefore go unanswered, uninvestigated, unprocessed, and therefore ignored for perpetuity.

Worse still, is that the originators of those human rights complaints and reports then often find themselves targeted and gang-stalked by local members of law enforcement, on orders by their federal overlords, who of course take their marching orders from their leaders who are all by and large servants of the big international banks and money power.

Human rights watchdog groups used to be staffed by individuals who had fire in their eyes, with a burning desire to right the wrongs of the past, bring to light oppression of civil liberties and rights, and would dedicate themselves to fighting to rectify situations wherein the victims either lacked the financial, educational, socioeconomic ability to help themselves. Now, these various international human rights organizations simply act like a "silent partner" who watches while their other "vocal partner" beats and abuses their victims.

Apparently, Human Rights Watch was given $100,000,000 by George Soros fairly recently, and Amnesty International is also a huge recipient as well. If one peruses the donor lists or founders of many of these so-called human rights organizations, the primary sponsors are also the world's greatest human rights violators, and this is the most sickening discovery that one can make, if one truly cares about human rights.

"Any nonprofit organization that takes donations could be influenced by their donors. Human Rights Watch is no different than any other non-profit,"

Independent Institute Center on Peace and Liberty Director Ivan Eland said in an interview.

Executive Intelligence Review editor Jeff Steinberg has previously stated that "Soros has been the number one funder of Human Rights Watch from its inception, and remember that Soros was a teenage Nazi collaborator in Hungary during the Nazi occupation, an experience he places great importance on in his learning how to profit off of tough times."

Organizations such as the ACLU seem obsessively preoccupied with LGBT rights rather than race relations or religious discrimination issues, simply because that's apparently what their wealthy white donors care more about, for example.

Even within the United Nations, the fact that the Saudi Arabian royal family, the greatest perpetrator of human rights violations both within their own country as well as outside their borders, regarding their bloody war and genocide in Yemen for example, have managed to "buy" the Human Rights Council chairmanship from UN Secretary General Ban Ki Moon for cold, hard, cash.

Ironically enough, Human Rights Watch has actively campaigned to get Saudi Arabia thrown off these human rights organizations, including Amnesty International. Saudi Arabia, as the leader of the nine-nation coalition that began military operations against the Houthis in Yemen on March 26, 2015, has been implicated in numerous violations of international humanitarian law, let alone the hundreds of thousands of heads they have chopped off in their own country since its inception for such things as stealing bread to feed ones starving family. Saudi Arabia has engaged in more than sixty-nine unlawful airstrikes as of June 2016, some of which may amount to war crimes, killing at least 913 civilians and hitting homes, markets, hospitals, schools, civilian businesses, and mosques. Nineteen attacks involving internationally banned cluster munitions, including in civilian areas have also been recorded.

International human rights organizations have also been co-opted and used to undermine governments, act as cover for intelligence operations and murder and even for *coups d' tat* of "unfriendly" governments by their donor nations. One only has to recall the CIA's involvement using the National Endowment for Democracy and its actions in Russia wherein they kept trying to undermine the Putin government or in India, where they used various "feminist organizations" and NGOs to blackmail, set up, and extort Indian elected leaders and diplomats such as Devyani Khobragade and Prabhu Dayal, with allegations of human trafficking and other nonsense.

It's a bloody joke that these same masters of chaos, death, and destruction can literally kill and destroy, enabling the rape and murder of countless millions of innocent men, women, and children, and then simply write a big check to these "human rights organizations" so that their high crimes and misdemeanors can be swept under the rug while these totally useless and impotent "human rights organizations" accomplish absolutely nothing on a daily basis, taking huge amounts of money from wealthy donors and banks and allowing countless millions of innocent men, women, and children to be beaten, starved, exploited, enslaved, raped, and murdered on a daily basis.

CHAPTER 35

Donald Trump Is Right:
America's Infrastructure Is Falling Apart

Talk about "auditing the Fed," but what about auditing the US Department of Transportation?

Over the past few weeks and certainly years, presidential candidate Donald Trump has been vociferously complaining that America's infrastructure—its airports, bridges, roads, tunnels, and train stations—are fast becoming more akin to a Third World country than to the standards that we are accustomed to in the United States.

Trump the builder!

And there is no one better suited and more knowledgeable to rebuild America's failing infrastructure than the master builder Donald Trump himself.

And now, what with the apparent massive train wreck on the NJ Transit System today involving the apparent derailing/slamming of a rush-hour train heading from New Jersey into New York City, killing one and injuring over one hundred people, this point could not have been driven home even further than it has.

The amount of money that the US transportation takes in every year, particularly within the tri-state area, is truly staggering. Some would argue that it is in the trillions of dollars per year with the obscene amount of tolls, taxes (federal state and local), as well as the other methods of raising revenue that should be earmarked for American infrastructure. The ultimate question is where the hell is all of this money going?

People constantly talk about "auditing the Fed," but what about auditing the US Department of transportation?

Why is it those other countries, just considered to be Second or Third World countries only a few years ago, are able to invest in and build world-class airports, buildings, roadways, interstate highways, bridges, and other state-of-the-art construction projects while America is lagging behind with the vast majority of our infrastructure dilapidated and falling part.

According to recent figures, the total amount of revenue generated from taxes and tolls in America, more notably in the major urban areas such as in

New York/New Jersey/Connecticut, Florida, California, and other major cities, is apparently exceeding trillions of dollars per year. The question is, where is all that money going, and who is stealing it? This is one of the most underreported and glossed-over questions in America today.

It is no secret that the psychological as well as physical effects of poor national infrastructure has corresponding effects on the overall productivity, sense of well-being, and general happiness of the nation's inhabitants and confidence in their own country, So perhaps this slow and steady decline in our national infrastructure is a purposefully designed degradation by certain "globalists" to subconsciously force Americans to accept that they are somehow merely a "cog in the wheel" of the international global New World Order and not "exceptional" as many Americans want to believe. Either way, it needs to be fixed.

Toll roads in some forms have existed since antiquity, collecting their fees from passing travelers on foot, wagon, or horseback, but their prominence increased with the rise of the automobile. Toll roads have existed for at least the last 2,700 years, as tolls had to be paid by travelers using the Susa-Babylon highway under the regime of Ashurbanipal, who reigned in the seventh century Bc. Aristotle and Pliny refer to tolls in Arabia and other parts of Asia. In India, before the fourth century Bc, the Arthashastra notes the use of tolls. Germanic tribes charged tolls to travelers across mountain passes. Tolls were used in the Holy Roman Empire in the Fourteenth and Fifteenth centuries.

River tolls were charged on boats sailing along the river. Many modern European roads were originally constructed as toll roads in order to recoup the costs of construction, maintenance, and as a source of tax money that is paid primarily by someone other than the local residents. In fourteenth-century England, some of the most heavily used roads were repaired with money raised from tolls by pavage grants. Widespread toll roads sometimes restricted traffic so much, by their high tolls, that they interfered with trade and cheap transportation needed to alleviate local famines or shortages.

Turnpike trusts were established in England and Wales from about 1706 in response to the need for better roads than the few and poorly maintained tracks then available. Turnpike trusts were set up by individual Acts of Parliament, with powers to collect road tolls to repay loans for building, improving, and maintaining the principal roads in Britain. At their peak, in the 1830s, over one thousand trusts administered around thirty thousand miles (48,000 kilometers) of turnpike road in England and Wales, taking tolls at almost eight thousand toll gates. The trusts were ultimately responsible for the maintenance and improvement of most of the main roads in England and Wales, which were used to distribute agricultural and industrial goods economically.

The tolls were a source of revenue for road building and maintenance, paid for by road users and not from general taxation. Most trusts improved existing roads, but some new roads, usually only short stretches, were also built. In the twentieth century, road tolls were introduced in Europe to finance the construction of motorway networks and specific transport infrastructure such as bridges and tunnels. Italy was the first European country to charge motorway tolls, on a fifty kilometers motorway section near Milan in 1924.

It was followed by Greece, which made users pay for the network of motorways around and between its cities in 1927. Later in the 1950s and 1960s, France, Spain and Portugal started to build motorways largely with the aid of concessions, allowing rapid development of this infrastructure without massive state debts. Since then, road tolls have been introduced in the majority of the EU member states.

That being said, it is high time that Americans demand the complete and total overall and rebuilding of our national infrastructure and to immediately investigate and determine just where the hell the enormous amounts of infrastructure money being raised is going in the first place.

CHAPTER 36

The Cowardly BRICS Bank Nations (Except Russia)

Except for Russia, who appears to be the only nation with balls enough to stand up to the enemy wreaking havoc on the innocents of the world.

I t seems that with every single day, both the mainstream and alternative media are reporting more and more innocent men, women, children, and little babies being blown to bits by bombs and artillery or drowning somewhere off the coast in some remote ocean off North Africa or Southern Europe on their way to flee from the bombed-out desperation and horror of NATO'S carpet bombing of Libya or from Western Intelligence and Saudi Arabia, Turkey, or Israel's proxy group ISIS and their collective attacks on Yemen, Syria, Iraq, and the Kurds.

With each and every additional single day of this mindless bloodshed, the world watches and wonders why it is being allowed to continue.

Vitaly Churkin, Russia's ambassador to the United Nations, speaks to the media on US Syria policy.

Why only Russia it seems is defending these people as best as it can, launching defensive strike after strike to counter the insane violence brought on by the United States, and its terrorist proxies ISIS, NATO, Saudi Arabia, Turkey, and Israel, who are bombing, droning, and murdering the daylights out of tens of millions of innocents for often what appears to be simply for gold, oil, heroin production, natural gas, total and utter greed.

For all of their pompous braying and photo ops showing a united BRICS Bank paradigm, with toothy grins from ear to ear of Brazil, Russia, India, China, and South Africa, showcasing all of their leaders Dilma Rousseff, Vladimir Putin, Narendra Modi, Xi Jinping, and Jacob Zuma, respectively, it appears that the only thing these leaders accomplished was a whole lot of nothing, joining hands and making trips to each other's nations presumably to boast, talk, and offer even more hot air and lavish praise upon one another.

The BRICS nations billed themselves in 2014 as a refreshing alternative to the out-of-control violence, bloodshed, exploitation, and debtor nation status being bankrolled and funded by the International Monetary Fund (IMF) and the World Bank, but to date, these five nations have done nothing but enrich their personal leadership coffers, and live the high life while the world still burns and its people get crushed further and further into debt slavery.

The mindless and out-of-control violence, bloodshed, carnage, and limitless death continues.

Yemen is burning, slaughtered, Palestinians are being Libyans are being drowned/murdered/raped, Iraqis are floundering and dying, Syrians are being blown to bits, refugee children by the tens of millions are being kidnapped/molested/disappeared, Kurds are being cut into pieces, and Ukrainians are being bankrupted.

And the BRICS Bank and its host nations do nothing but sit there and smile and take more pictures of themselves locked arm in arm in front of "flags."

Except for Russia, who appears to be the only nation with balls enough to stand up to the enemy wreaking havoc on the innocents of the world, Russia is standing up to NATO, to Saudi Arabia, to the out-of-control neoconservatives of the United States, to Turkey, to Israel, and to anyone else killing off innocent men, women and children in their Satanic lust for power, money, sex, and greed.

Architects of 'Regime Change'

We know what happened to Brazil; Dilma Rouseff was taken out in a Western-backed *coup d'état* and replaced with Michel Temer, their boy from Wall Street.

And Jacob Zuma has been embroiled in trumped up and falsified ethics charges back home in his native state of South Africa.

But what is China's excuse?

What is India's excuse?

Are they also afraid, based on their past legacy of colonialism and centuries-long beat-downs from Western European- and Saudi-brand Islamic colonization and subjugation, that they have lost their balls forever, never to stand up for what they know is the right thing to do?

To actually get up, and bray and yell and scream at the United Nations or wherever else they congregate, and demand that the senseless violence, killing, and death of millions of children must STOP?

Because Russia cannot do this all alone.

It's high time for India and China (and maybe even Brazil and South Africa) to get off their collective asses and do something to help stop the rivers of blood flowing in the Middle East now before it is too late.

CHAPTER 37

It's Time for the American People
to Rein in the Military-Industrial Complex

For some reason, neither John Kerry nor Barack Obama want to take on the MIC.

T
he news is steadily rumbling in, and each and every day, more and more American generals are coming out of the woodwork to make incredibly irresponsible and irrational declarations provoking World War III with Russia, China, Iran, and Syria, more akin to the behavior of Major Kong from the movie *Dr. Strangelove*, wherein he rides a nuclear bomb being dropped on the enemy, while maniacally waving his cowboy hat, hooting and hollering.

It is way past time for each and every American citizen who cares about their children, their home, their job, their family, their friends, and their way of life, to absolutely *INUNDATE* their local and state congressmen and senators with phone calls, emails, texts, and faxes, *DEMANDING* that congress or the senate (or both) call an emergency investigatory hearing and grill these out-of-control deep state Pentagon lunatics, and ask them, what do *they* know that the American people *don't* know?

Because both the mainstream and alternative media (rarely if ever in sync but this time they are) report that the United States is repeatedly violating mutually executed ceasefire agreements with Russia over the Syrian conflict and that apparently, the military-industrial complex (MIC), led by Defense Secretary Ash Carter, is *DELIBERATELY* undermining and going against the hard-fought and very sensitive diplomatic agreements and overtures being hammered out by Secretary of State John Kerry, as directed by President Barack Obama, in order to *AVOID* World War III.

Meanwhile, Russian Foreign Minister Sergei Lavrov and Defense Minister Maria Zakharova are exclaiming in an exasperated fashion, "Just who *IS* actually running America?"

If the unelected, unregulated, unsupervised, and unaccountable to the American people and media, closed-off military-industrial complex is now openly overriding, undermining, and sabotaging the duly elected and accountable executive, legislative, and judicial branches of the US government, selected and placed into office by the American people, then it is now truly, *only* the American people who can drag those responsible out of their armchairs at the Pentagon, and duly interrogate them using the congress and senate, to determine just what *exactly* it is that they seem to know and are so unreasonably aggressive about.

Russian President Vladimir Putin still respectfully refers to America as a "partner." China seems to just want to grow its economy and feed its people, and Iran appears to just want to grow its economy after forty years of cruel economic sanctions, a US/UK-backed bleeding war with Iraq and other sabotage financed and engineered by the US and the UK.

For some reason, neither John Kerry nor Barack Obama want to take on the MIC even when it is quite obvious to everyone in the world that the MIC doesn't seem to honor *anything* that the executive branch negotiates or does to avoid war in order to pursue peace.

Perhaps the executive branch is worried about the repercussions and retaliations that the MIC could take if they took the MIC on directly (e.g., a Venezuelan or Turkish-style *coup d' tat*).

But the American people are far too numerous, opinionated, and difficult to control and intimidate in this manner.

The American people must **DEMAND** an ad hoc, urgent, and emergency congressional/senatorial subpoena and investigation **IMMEDIATELY** of each and every decision-maker at the Pentagon and then report it back to the American people, watered down if necessary to avoid revealing legitimate state secrets or national security issues.

The prediction in 1961 by then president and decorated General Dwight D. Eisenhower has unfortunately come true; the MIC is now firmly in charge of the American ship, and are about to irreparably slam it into the proverbial iceberg of World War III, on purpose.

All of these MIC players have underground bunkers, weird **Occult** Freemasonic hiding chambers, fully stocked bank accounts full of gold, foreign islands, and countries that they can take off to at a moment's notice, thus protecting themselves and their kids/families from a "full on" nuclear war, while 99 percent of the rest of the American people have only their houses, socks, and blankets.

The MIC will be fine in a nuclear holocaust; it is the American people and their children, who will be burned to a crisp.

115

The MIC should no longer be allowed to conduct their warmongering and sociopathic behavior behind closed doors anymore under the "guise" of national security or whatever other opaque excuse that they provide.

If we Americans care about our country, kids, and way of life, we must contact our local congressmen and senators urgently and demand an investigation *immediately* before it is too late.

CHAPTER 38

Similarities by and between
Andrew Jackson and Donald Trump

Both are dedicated America-Firsters.

Aside from the obviously glaring physical similarities between one of the last, true-blue, and greatest US presidents in American history, Andrew Jackson, such as both of their honest, forthright2, direct, and straightforward verbal delivery styles as well as their flaming red fiery hair and piercing blue eyes, there are other, more subtle, but essential similarities as well:

1. Both are dedicated America-Firsters and care more about the welfare and condition of the United States and its citizenry than with stupid foreign wars and foreign entanglements designed to weaken and exploit America's money, troops, and good will.

2. Both are "pro-morality," grounded in Christian foundations and beliefs, rather than the Luciferian doctrines of progressivism, which seek to challenge and ridicule fundamental and common-sense American value systems, now apparently being defended today by only one other leader in the world, Russian President Vladimir Putin.

3. Both are being viciously attacked by international deep state bankers, wherein Andrew Jackson's greatest achievement and victory according to himself, was when he said, "I killed the banks," referring to his monumental accomplishment of not renewing in 1833 the Second Bank of the United States, the country's national bank, forerunner of the Federal Reserve established in 1913 by the same evil forces. Jackson used his executive power to remove all federal funds from the bank in the final salvo of what is referred to as the "bank war." Today Donald Trump is under siege and attack by these very same international bankers who desperately want to keep him out of office for fear that he will repudiate or renegotiate their usurious and inflated 23-trillion-dollar debt.

4. Andrew Jackson, the epitome of the frontiersman, objected to the bank's unusual political and economic power and to the lack of congressional oversight over its business dealings, and this is the same power structure that Donald Trump is railing against.

5. Andrew Jackson, known as obstinate and brutish but a man of the common people, called for an investigation into the bank's policies and political agenda as soon as he settled into the White House in March 1829. To Jackson, the bank symbolized how a privileged class of businessmen oppressed the will of the common people of America, and he made clear that he planned to challenge the constitutionality of the bank, much to the horror of its supporters. In response, the director of the bank, Nicholas Biddle, flexed his own political power, turning to members of congress, including the powerful Kentucky Senator Henry Clay and leading businessmen sympathetic to the bank, to fight Jackson. Today, the bankers employ the mainstream media and "useful idiot protected classes," such as organized and mafia-like extremist feminists, extremist Black Lives Matters groups, extremist minority groups, and extremist homosexual groups to blaspheme, attack, defame, slander, libel, entrap, intimidate, threaten, and harass Donald Trump, instead of the bankers using their previously bought off congressmen and senators (and presidents) to do their dirty work.

6. Both were victims of attempted assassination—Andrew Jackson with the physical attempt by a stupid ineffective gunman on the steps of the US Capitol and Donald Trump both physically as well as by the political character assassination in today's mainstream media using the false and hollow allegations that Donald Trump is somehow a racist, homophobe, anti-Semite, or anti-feminist misogynist, with all of these false attacks coming from, originating with, paid for, and funded by the very same elitist, hypocritical, deep state international bankers.

7. Both defended the honor of their wives after they were attacked. In 1806, Andrew Jackson killed a man in a duel over a matter of honor regarding his wife, Rachel, when they called her a bigamist, while Donald Trump aggressively defended the honor of his wife, Melania, when she was defamed, slandered, and libeled in the press as an illegal immigrant, a prostitute or whatever other character assassination they tried to use against her. Andrew Jackson said that he could forgive those who insulted him but that he would never forgive the ones who attacked his wife.

8. Both Andrew Jackson and Donald Trump enjoyed plurality in both electoral and popular votes against all major candidates, but both were undermined and attacked by the mainstream media

and members of the Congressional House of Representatives and the Senate owned by the international central bankers.

9. Both were heavily involved in purchasing land and making real estate deals. In 1794, Jackson formed a business with lawyer and planter John Overton "for the purpose of purchasing lands as well as those lands without as within military bounds". Donald Trump is arguably the most famous and well-respected real estate developer and land purchaser the world has ever known, and Andrew Jackson was one of the three original investors who founded the entire city of Memphis, Tennessee, in 1819.

10. In the midst of the rampant institutionalized racism and discrimination of his times, Andrew Jackson was actually considered a trailblazer in race relations and actually went against the grain to treat minorities with greater respect and freedom than his contemporaries while Trump also treats minorities very well within his Trump Organization as well, in stark contrast to the nonsensical and false attacks he receives on a daily basis by the mainstream media that he is somehow a racist.

11. Andrew Jackson is associated with Jacksonian Democracy, or the spread of democracy by passing political power from established elites to ordinary voters, and the Age of Jackson shaped the national agenda and American politics like Thomas Jefferson, such as "peace, commerce and honest friendship with all nations, entangling alliances with none," which further typifies Donald Trump's desires to work with Russian President Vladimir Putin and other nations to destroy ISIS rather than provoking them into World War III, also wishing to work with other nations to make America liked and the world a better place for all of earth's people.

12. Jackson advocated Republican values held by the Revolutionary War generation, and his presidency held a high moralistic tone with a limited view of the state's rights and the federal government. Jackson feared that monied and business interests would corrupt Republican values, and Donald Trump echoes these same exact sentiments in all his speeches.

13. Jackson believed that the president's authority was derived from the people and his choice of cabinet members. Instead of choosing party favorites or establishment types, he selected "plain businessmen." Trump also favors businessmen over career politicians and establishment figures.

14. Andrew Jackson was plagued by horrifically false and defamatory rumors that he was somehow misogynistic and "against women virtues" in such ridiculous scandals as the Petticoat Affair or Eaton Affair, and the organized extreme feminist conspiracy (owned and controlled by international bankers) attacking Trump is based on the same false and hollow types of character assassinations, designed to discredit both him and his candidacy.

15. Donald Trump famously has been declaring for nearly thirty years that "foreign nations need to pay their dues to the United States" for such things as military protection, as well as calling for them to honor better trade deals. In 1834, the nonpayment of reparations by the French government drew Andrew Jackson's ire, and he became impatient, and in his December 1834 State of the Union address, Jackson sternly reprimanded the French government for nonpayment, stating that the US federal government was "wholly disappointed" by the French and demanded that congress authorize trade reprisals against France.

16. Foreign nations were also routinely chagrined by Andrew Jackson's America-First policies and willingness to disparage and antagonize foreign countries "taking advantage of America," and feeling insulted by Jackson's words, the French people demanded an apology. In his December 1835 State of the Union Address, Jackson refused to apologize, just like Master Deal-Maker Donald Trump when irritating foreign nations such as the United Kingdom and Mexico with his America- First words, with Andrew Jackson stating that he had a "good opinion of the French people and his intentions were peaceful" but that he believed that the French government was purposely stalling payment. The French government accepted Jackson's statements as sincere, and in February 1836, American reparations were finally paid.

17. Both Andrew Jackson and Donald Trump have been viciously and falsely accused of having a quick temper. Of Andrew Jackson, a famous historian named Brands, said: "His audacity on behalf of the people earned him enemies who slandered him and defamed even his wife, Rachel he dueled in her defense and his own, suffering grievous wounds that left him with bullet fragments lodged about his body." However, other historians such as Remini stated that Jackson was in control of his rage and used it (and his fearsome reputation) as a tool to get what he

wanted in his public and private affairs. Brands also noted that Andrew Jackson's opponents were terrified of his temper: "Observers likened him to a volcano, and only the most intrepid or recklessly curious cared to see it erupt His close associates all had stories of his blood-curling oaths, his summoning of the Almighty to lose His wrath upon some miscreant, typically followed by his own vow to hang the villain or blow him to perdition. Given his record-in duels, brawls, mutiny trials, and summary hearings—listeners had to take his vows seriously." All of this could honestly have been written about Donald Trump himself.

18. As was said above, both cut dashingly tall and large figures, and both sported a shock of bright, unruly, and fiery red hair and deep-blue piercing eyes. Andrew Jackson was an imposing figure, standing at six feet, one inch (1.85 m) tall (very tall for that time period), and weighing between 130 and 140 pounds (64 kg) on average—Trump is virtually his twin.

CHAPTER 39

Just What DOES Federal Trade
Commission Antitrust Division DO Anymore?

When are we, the American people, going to begin to hold our elected (and non-elected but appointed) government leaders' collective feet to the fire?

I t appears that yet again, once more, Obama-appointee FTC Antitrust Chairwoman Edith Ramirez is asleep at her desk.

Previously, she was grilled about apparently not doing her job when it came to Google, wherein she was asked to address contradictions in testimony she gave to the senate judiciary committee regarding the FTC's dropping of an antitrust action against Google in 2013. The requests pointed to a variety of evidence obtained through open government laws that suggested that Ramirez and other FTC officials had unusually close relationships with Google and that those relationships may have helped the company avoid antitrust action.

Perhaps she is just the latest minority "protected class" member installed by the deep state plutocrat elite in order to do their dirty business, as usual, and given no power or mandate to effect or engage in any meaningful change for the benefit of the American people or the rest of the world.

The latest news broadcasts from up on high is that AT&T is about to buy Time-Warner Cable for a cool 85 billion dollars. And yet again, all we hear are crickets chirping from Edith Ramirez and the other FTC staff desks.

The Illusion of Choice: 90 Percent of American Media Controlled by Six Corporations

Do they not realize that yet again, **ANOTHER** huge media conglomerate is being swallowed and acquired by another huge media conglomerate to create another gargantuan media outlet in another consolidation of the enormous power, money, wealth, intimidation, conspiracy, and control of the American (and now global) media, which directly undermines and eviscerates the US Constitution, contained within the purview of the First Amendment?

The people have already spoken almost unanimously and screamed from the rooftops at the top of their lungs, that the media is controlled by only 6 major corporations and that the people literally have to scramble, scour the internet, subscribe to alternative media/news outlets, and otherwise sign up for "conspiracy theory" websites in order to get their much-needed and very necessary news and information about their country, the world, and current events, which directly affect their lives and their friends/family/children.

But FTC Chief Edith Ramirez, like she did during the Google investigations, says, and does nothing.

Could it be because she is somehow being told to "stand down" or is otherwise benefiting from this pyramid scheme-like media conglomeration?

Is she being promised a great job afterward, making millions of dollars at the American people's expense, like almost every other single revolving door government/private sector whore who puts in their time? See Goldman Sachs, Robert Rubin, Tim Geithner, Larry Summers, Gene Sperling, and others flitting around as US Treasury Secretary or Federal Reserve stooges or even former Attorney General Eric Holder's beeline back to his leather chair and cherrywood desk at über-elite bankster law firm Covington & Burling LLP after he essentially "whitewashed" the trillion-dollar international bankster crimes of 2008 during his tenure in the Obama administration, placing no one in jail, just hitting them all with fines of a few million dollars here and there, which really is just a "day's pay" for these banking behemoths and is otherwise just chalked up to the "cost of doing business" on their way to fleecing trillions of dollars from the American taxpayer and countless billions of people overseas, connected within the interlocking "keiretsu" banking system of the international central bankers?

When are we, the American people, going to begin to hold our elected (and non-elected but appointed) government leaders' collective feet to the fire?

When are we going to call them out for being the lazy, good-for-nothing, taxpayer-sucking crooks that they are, and demand that they actually do their jobs?

United States antitrust law is a collection of federal and state government laws that regulate the conduct and organization of business corporations, generally to promote fair competition for the benefit of consumers. (The concept is called competition law in other English- speaking countries.)

The main statutes are the Sherman Act 1890, the Clayton Act 1914, and the Federal Trade Commission Act 1914.

These Acts, first, restrict the formation of cartels and prohibit other collusive practices regarded as being in restraint of trade.

Second, they restrict the mergers and acquisitions of organizations substantially lessen competition. that could

Third, they prohibit the creation of a monopoly and the abuse of monopoly power.

The Federal Trade Commission, the US Department of Justice, state governments, and private parties who are sufficiently affected may all bring actions in the courts to enforce the antitrust laws.

The scope of antitrust laws and the degree to which they should interfere in an enterprise's freedom to conduct business or to protect smaller businesses, communities, and consumers are strongly debated.

One view, mostly closely associated with the Chicago School of Economics, suggests that antitrust laws should focus solely on the benefits to consumers and overall efficiency, while a broad range of legal and economic theory sees the role of antitrust laws as also controlling economic power in the public interest.

Preventing collusion and cartels that act in restraint of trade is an essential task of antitrust law.

It reflects the view that each business has a duty to act independently on the market and so earn its profits solely by providing better-priced and quality products than its competitors.

The Sherman Act §1 prohibits "every contract, combination in the form of trust or otherwise, or conspiracy, in restraint of trade or commerce."

This targets two or more distinct enterprises acting together in a way that harms third parties.

The American people and indeed the rest of the world need to pay closer attention to the assembling of the pyramid of oppressive global governance and New World Order infrastructure in their own midst, and in their own lifetime before they find themselves unable to escape the juggernaut and heavy machinery being built all around them in order to enslave.

CHAPTER 40

Similarities between Life under Former
USSR KGB, East German STASI, and US COPS Program

> The plutocrats, fearing the masses, pressured their governing leaders to institute more and more repressive policing systems so that it would be easy to marginalize, jail, incarcerate, and even murder any "troublemakers" living in their societies.

Even a cursory and abbreviated view of life and conditions of the people living under East Germany's secret police STASI, the former USSR's KGB, and under the modern-day United States after 1994 under Joseph Biden and Bill Clinton's community-oriented policing (COPS) program will demonstrate in a glaring and obvious fashion the similar living conditions under those repressive regimes.

All three of these systems of secret police governance, founded under the supervision and aegis of the country's secret society Freemasonic brotherhood, came during a time when a belief in God was at its all-time low and when the economy was purposefully destroyed by the plutocrats of its day in conjunction with their greedy central banker systems, who hoarded away cash and liquidity from the economy and its people so that they were left with very little, if anything to buy and sell goods with, or to just basically live, eat, and pay their bills and rent.

The plutocrats, fearing the masses, pressured their governing leaders to institute more and more repressive policing systems so that it would be easy to marginalize, jail, incarcerate, and even murder any "troublemakers" living in their societies.

This was obviously done to remove any threats or impediments to the continued looting, exploitation of, and enslavement of the nation's resources, people, and labor force.

East German STASI

For example, in East Germany's STASI headed by Markus Wolf, one of its main tasks was spying on the population, mainly through a vast network of citizens turned informants ("if you see something, say something" as per New York City's subway signs and scattered throughout all of the United States post-9/11) and fighting any opposition by overt and covert measures, including hidden psychological destruction of dissidents (*Zersetzung*, literally meaning "decomposition").

The STASI Ministry for State Security were responsible for (1) the surveillance of mail and telephone communications; (2) the reliability of the National People's Army (*Nationale Volksarmee, NVA*) personnel; (3) secret, unofficial networks of informants within the NVA; (4) protection against "sabotage" or "espionage"; (5) analyzing garbage for any suspect western foods and/or materials; (6) protecting high government and party buildings and personnel; (7) surveillance of foreigners—particularly from the West—legally traveling or residing within the country, including the diplomatic community, tourists, and official guests; (8) provided personal security for the national leadership and maintaining and operating an internal secure communications system for the government; (9) enforcing the political security of East Germany; (10) its own penal system, distinct from that of the Ministry of the Interior, comprising prison camps for political dissidents, as opposed to criminal offenders.

As was stated above, the Stasi perfected the technique of psychological harassment of perceived enemies, in a process called Zersetzung—a term borrowed from chemistry which literally means "decomposition" or "biodegradation."

The goal was to destroy secretly the self- confidence of people, for example by damaging their reputation, by organizing failures in their work, and by destroying their personal relationships.

The Stasi didn't try to arrest every dissident.

It preferred to paralyze them, and it could do so because it had access to so much personal information and to so many institutions.

It was recognized that psychological harassment was far less likely to be recognized for what it was, so its victims and their supporters were less likely to be provoked into active resistance, given that they would often not be aware of the source of their problems or even its exact nature.

Zersetzung was designed to sidetrack and "switch off" perceived enemies so that they would lose the will to continue any "inappropriate" activities.

Tactics employed under Zersetzung generally involved the disruption of the victim's private or family life.

This often-included psychological attacks, such as breaking into homes and subtly manipulating the contents, in a form of gaslighting-moving furniture, altering the timing of an alarm, removing pictures from walls, or replacing one variety of tea with another.

Other practices included property damage, sabotage of cars, purposely incorrect medical treatment, smear campaigns including sending falsified compromising photos or documents to the victim's family, denunciation, provocation, psychological warfare, psychological subversion, wiretapping, bugging, mysterious phone calls or unnecessary deliveries, even including sending a vibrator to a target's wife.

Usually, victims had no idea that the Stasi were responsible.

Many thought that they were losing their minds, and mental breakdowns and suicide could result.

One great advantage of the harassment perpetrated under Zersetzung was that its subtle nature meant that it was able to be plausibly denied.

It was Cold War policy for the KGB of the Soviet Union and the secret services of the satellite states to extensively monitor public and private opinion, internal subversion, and possible revolutionary plots in the Soviet Bloc.

During the Cold War, the KGB actively sought to combat "ideological subversion"-anti- Communist political and religious ideas and the dissidents who promoted them, which was generally dealt with as a matter of national security in discouraging the perceived influence of hostile foreign powers.

KGB dissident-group infiltration-featured agents provocateur pretending "sympathy to the cause" smear campaigns against prominent dissidents, and show trials. Once imprisoned, the dissident endured constant KGB interrogations and sympathetic informant cellmates.

Mikhail Gorbachev's glasnost policies lessened persecution of political dissidents.

United States Community-Oriented Policing (COPS) Program

Community policing, or community-oriented policing, is a "strategy of policing that focuses on police building ties and working closely with members of the communities."

In the United States, the Violent Crime Control and Law Enforcement Act of 1994 written by former Senator Joseph Biden and enacted by then President Bill Clinton established the Office of Community Oriented Policing Services (COPS) within the US Justice Department to promote "community policing," implemented by illegal and unconstitutional coordination by and between the Department of Homeland Security, the FBI, Immigration and Customs Enforcement, Customs and Border Protection, local police departments, and others.

Clinton Crime Bill

This has resulted in over 68 million Americans with criminal records, more than the population of France, with 1/3 of all blacks, 1/6 of all Latinos, and 1/11 of all whites in America having spent time under arrest and in prison, in violation of the US Constitution, without due process, without evidence, and without probable cause.

Community policing is a policy that requires police to inherit a "proactive approach" to address public safety concerns.

Community-oriented policing was a cornerstone of the Clinton administration and gained its funding from the 1994 Violent Crime Control and Law Enforcement Act.

Community policing is a philosophy of full-service personalized policing, where the same officer patrols and works in the same area on a permanent basis, from a decentralized place, working in a proactive partnership with citizens to identify and solve problems, i.e., extensively using gang-stalking and informants.

Community policing creates unconstitutional partnerships between law enforcement agencies and other organizations like government agencies, community members, nonprofit service providers, private businesses and the media.

Common implementations of community- policing include the following: (1) relying on community-based crime prevention by utilizing civilian education, neighborhood watch, and a variety of other techniques, as opposed to relying solely on police patrols, (2) restructuring patrol from an emergency response based system to emphasizing proactive techniques such as foot patrol, (3) increased officer accountability to civilians they are supposed to serve, (4) decentralizing the police authority, allowing more discretion amongst lower-ranking officers, and more initiative expected from them (extensive use of informants and gang-stalking techniques).

CHAPTER 41

Go Ahead, Sue the Government

When the people fear the government there is tyranny, when the government fears the people there is liberty.

Thomas Jefferson

Have you been wronged by someone who works in the US government, whether federal, state, or local?

A racist or violent local policeman? A disrespectful fireman? An overzealous child protective service worker? A rude absent-minded postal worker? Perhaps even a cruel arbitrary and capricious judge, such as in family, civil, traffic, or criminal court? Or a politically motivated, biased, and malicious prosecutor?

If so, don't get mad, get even by filing a civil lawsuit in federal district court.

Don't rely on simply filing a civilian complaint with that government worker's agency or his supervisor or even another branch of government (remember there are three—legislative, executive, and judicial) as they often tend to simply cover up for one another as they seem to all be sucking from the same international bankster/corporation teat.

Not that a civilian complaint won't make you feel better, it probably will, but it really should just be the opening salvo to the inevitable unleashing of the holy legal and equitable hell that you can and should provide by going ahead and filing a federal lawsuit in your local district court.

Now hold on, you say! File a federal lawsuit in my local district court? Won't that cost me an arm and a leg to pay those enormous attorney fees and costs? Even the filing fee alone is $400!

Well, the answer to that question is a resounding no.

The bottom line is that every single jurisdictional federal district court has a clerk within a unit called the *Pro Se Office*, a Latin phrase meaning "on behalf of themselves," which basically means advocating on one's own behalf before a court rather than being represented by a lawyer.

Pro Se is sometimes known as propria persona (abbreviated to *pro per*). In England and Wales, the comparable status is that of "litigant in person."

The beauty of all this is that you can literally walk down to that Pro Se clerk's office after locating your relevant district court near your address on the internet and proceed to fill out three forms—said forms which you can also pre-download online at your relevant district court's website—the (1) summons, (2) complaint form, and (3) civil cover sheet.

That's it.

Once you fill these three forms in, whether in your own handwriting or if you take the time to type it out, if you are suing a government worker who abused their authority under the color of law and authority, then your cause of action/claim would be listed as 42 § 1983, otherwise known as a Civil Action for Deprivation of Rights.

Just hand in those three forms to the Pro Se Clerk, pay $400, and he will stamp your documents with an index number, and you are now in business. Just serve the defendants and wait for them to answer and appear (twenty to thirty days). If you can't afford the $400 filing fee, simply fill in another form called *In Forma Pauperis*, which you can also either download from the district court website or request from that clerk.

If you are really creative, you can do some more research and perhaps throw a RICO claim in there (Racketeering Influenced Corrupt Organization Act) if there was a predicate criminal act or, if you are disabled, an ADA claim (Americans with Disability Act). You get the idea. But the main claim would be 42 § 1983, which basically states the following:

> Every person who, under color of any statute, ordinance, regulation, custom, or usage, of any State or Territory or the District of Columbia, subjects, or causes to be subjected, any citizen of the United States or other person within the jurisdiction thereof to the deprivation of any rights, privileges, or immunities secured by the Constitution and laws, shall be liable to the party injured in an action at law, suit in equity, or other proper proceeding for redress, except that in any action brought against a judicial officer for an act or omission taken in such officer's judicial capacity, injunctive relief shall not be granted unless a declaratory decree was violated or declaratory relief was unavailable.

Basically, any governmental worker that abused you and your civil liberties, human rights, or constitutional due process under the scope of their authority, can (and should) be sued under this statute for tens of millions of dollars in actual and punitive (punishment) damages.

If the American people just sit around and wait for their government to treat them better, they will wait for eternity, and things will only get worse as the criminals that often inhabit the vaunted positions of governmental power only get more and more comfortable, arrogant, cocky, and self- entitled, and their abuse and arbitrary exercise of power only gets more and more entrenched.

Do your part and legally and equitably knock them off their pedestal and force the US government to pay for lawyers to defend both them and their misconduct.

Perhaps your lawsuit will reveal that this particular government worker has one hundred other complaints, and yours will be the one to finally knock them off their perch, legally and equitably. Perhaps your lawsuit will also reveal that corrupt or abusive government worker's money, ideological, or paper trail, or help uncover a massive criminal conspiracy by and between enemies of the United States, both foreign and domestic, who need to be ferreted and routed out of the government.

This will also help to keep other abusive government workers in line and force them to adjust their behavior and respect the people that they work for, the people's taxes that they live off, and above all, the United States Constitution and all that it stands for.

People have died for this document for the past 250 years, and abusing it is a very serious offense.

"When the people fear the government there is tyranny, when the government fears the people there is liberty" (Thomas Jefferson).

CHAPTER 42

America Is Now at Greatest Risk of False Flag Attack

The neocons simply cannot be trusted as they work for the plutocrats who desperately want to hold on to their power.

N ever in America's history has she been in more danger of a "false flag" attack from her enemies, both foreign and domestic, than she is now.

The contemporary term *false flag* describes covert operations that are designed to deceive in such a way that the operations appear as though they are being carried out by entities, groups, or nations other than those who actually planned and executed them.

Historically, the term *false flag* had its origins in naval warfare where the use of a flag other than the belligerent's true battle flag before (but not while) engaging the enemy has long been accepted as a permissible *ruse de guerre*, by contrast, flying a false flag while engaging the enemy constitutes "perfidy."

Operations carried out during peacetime by civilian organizations, as well as covert government agencies, can (by extension) also be called false flag operations if they seek to hide the real organization behind an operation.

America has been thoroughly infiltrated by a mighty and wealthy foreign power and menace, while her people are suffering financially, and she is now poised to be sacrificed on the altar of history for a one world government headquartered overseas.

The neocon/Communist natives are restless; they desperately want their World War III, and they are wanting to move their wealth and power to their next world empire, which will be the final one in their sick deluded minds, unopposed and permanent.

Now that Hillary Clinton has been "theoretically re-indicted" by the FBI for the email scandals (although they are being obstructed by our very own US Department of "Justice" under Attorney General Loretta Lynch), this has effectively ruined her chances of becoming president through legal channels, so they only have one more option, and that is a false flag attack leading us directly into World War III in a nuclear war, using all their carefully placed traitors in the Pentagon, Department of Defense, Department of Homeland Security, Federal Bureau of Investigation, Department of Justice, and cooperative local police departments all throughout the United States, with a declaration of a state of emergency in both the United States and abroad.

This is why it is vitally important that all Americans, both in the private and public sector, start watching their government and elected leaders like hawks.

Americans need to use the neocon's mantra of "see something, say something" against them.

The neocon/Stasi/Communist's *Zersetzung*—organized gang-stalking under Bill Clinton's community-oriented policing (COPS) program—needs to be turned by the people against them, and the American people need to watch each and every single one of them like they would watch a lunatic holding an AK-47 in a mall.

The neocons simply cannot be trusted, as they work for the plutocrats, who desperately want to hold on to their power and will not willingly relinquish it to the people by way of Donald Trump and his populist revolt and uprising.

Some examples of real false flags throughout history having routinely disastrous results, wherein the "winners" rewrote history, include the following:

1. The 1914 Battle of Trindad fought between the British auxiliary cruiser RMS *Carmania* and the German auxiliary cruiser SMS *Cap Trafalgar*, which had been altered to look like *Carmania*.
2. World War II German commerce raider Kormoran, which surprised and sank the Australian light cruiser HMAS *Sydney* in 1941 while disguised as a Dutch merchant ship, causing the greatest recorded loss of life on an Australian warship.
3. Trial of Otto Skorzeny, who planned and commanded Operation Greif by a US military tribunal at the Dachau Trials included a finding that Skorzeny was not guilty of a crime by ordering his men into action in American uniforms.
4. The 1788 incident wherein the head tailor at the Royal Swedish Opera received an order to sew a number of Russian military uniforms to stage an attack on Puumala, a Swedish outpost on the Russo-Swedish border allowing King Gustav III of Sweden, who lacked the constitutional authority to initiate unprovoked

hostilities without the Estates' consent to launch the Russo-Swedish War (1788-1790).

5. September 1931 incident wherein Japanese officers fabricated a pretext for invading Manchuria by blowing up a section of railway.

6. Gleiwitz incident in 1939 involving Reinhard Heydrich fabricating evidence of a Polish attack against Germany to mobilize German public opinion for war with Poland.

7. November 26, 1939, incident wherein the Soviet army shelled Mainila, a Russian village near the Finnish border blaming Finland for the attack using the incident as a pretext to invade Finland, starting the Winter War four days later.

8. 1962 Operation Northwoods plot by the US Department of Defense for a war with Cuba involving scenarios such as fabricating the hijacking or shooting down of passenger and military planes, sinking a US ship in the vicinity of Cuba, burning crops, sinking a boat filled with Cuban refugees, attacks by alleged Cuban infiltrators inside the United States, and harassment of US aircraft and shipping and the destruction of aerial drones by aircraft disguised as Cuban MiGs to be blamed on Cuba and a pretext for an invasion of Cuba and the overthrow of Fidel Castro's Communist government.

9. Reichstag fire, which was an arson attack on the Reichstag building in Berlin on February 27, 1933, using as "evidence" by the Nazis that the Communists were beginning a plot against the German government, whereby Adolf Hitler, who was sworn in as chancellor of Germany four weeks before, on January 30, urged President Paul von Hindenburg to pass an emergency decree to counter the "ruthless confrontation of the Communist Party of Germany." And then with civil liberties suspended, the government instituted mass arrests of Communists, including all the Communist parliamentary delegates.

10. April 4, 1953, incident wherein the CIA was ordered to undermine the government of Iran over a four-month period, as a precursor to overthrowing Prime Minister Mohammad Mosaddegh by carrying out false flag attacks "on mosques and key public figures" to be blamed on Iranian Communists loyal to the government, code-named TP-Ajax, the tactic of a "directed campaign of bombings by Iranians posing as members of the

Communist Party" involving the bombing of at least one well-known Muslim's house by CIA agents posing as Communists.

11. The 2008 shooting of two minibuses carrying Georgians who lived in Abkhazia who wanted to cross the border so they could go and vote in the parliamentary election that day in a volatile area on the border of Abkhazia and the Republic of Georgia, wherein President Saakashvili indicated that the attack had been an attempt to disrupt the election, implying that it had been Abkhaz or Russian forces who had been behind it, providing a favorable opportunity for the president to focus the nation's attention on an external enemy, leading attention away from his domestic critics, as well as making use of his position as leader to rally the Georgians around his candidates in the election.

12. The assassination of Charlemagne Péralte of Haiti in 1919 after checkpoints were passed by military disguised as guerrilla fighters.

13. Mau Mau uprising in the 1950s, wherein captured Mau Mau members who switched sides and specially trained British troops initiated the pseudo-gang concept to successfully counter Mau Mau.

14. Algerian civil war in the middle of 1994 wherein death squads composed of *Département du Renseignement et de la Sécurité* (DRS) security forces disguised themselves as Islamist terrorists and committed false flag terror attacks.

15. Mexican wars of 1819 and 1846-48.

16. Spanish-American War of 1898 involving the surprise explosion of the battleship Maine at Havana, Cuba wherein the Hearst Press accused the Spanish and then the USA declared war on Spain, conquering the Philippines, Guam and Cuba.

17. World War I in 1914-1918 wherein a U- boat torpedo hit the ocean liner *Lusitania* near Britain and some 1,200 people, including 128 Americans, on board lost their lives, and subsequent investigations revealed that the major explosions were inside the Lusitania, as it was secretly transporting 6 million pounds of artillery shells and rifle ammunition, as well as other explosives on behalf of the Morgan Banking Corporation to help Britain and France.

18. World War II in 1939-1945 where a U- boat torpedo hit the ocean liner *Atheni* near Britain, with some 1,100 passengers, of which 311 were Americans.

19. US naval intelligence planning and suggesting "eight insults" to bring Japan into war with the United States, where President Roosevelt executed this plan immediately and also added some other insults, enraging Japan, such as a total blockade of Japanese oil imports, as agreed between the Americans, British and the Dutch—FDR also declared an all-out embargo against Japan and forbade them the use of the Panama Canal, impeding Japan's access to Venezuelan oil.

20. One of many incidents provoking Japan to attack Pearl Harbor some six months later

21. Korean War in 1950-1953, wherein South Korean incursions (e.g., the Tiger regiment) into North Korea (1949) led to contrary claims and into war. The cause of this war was covert action involving leaders of Taiwan, South Korea, and the US military-industrial complex (John Foster Dulles has been mentioned as an organizer of the hostilities).

22. Vietnam War in the Gulf of Tonkin Incident wherein the American destroyer Maddox was supposedly attacked twice by three North Vietnamese torpedo boats in 1964 in the Gulf of Tonkin-but which never happened.

23. Grenada invasion whereby the Grenadian leader, Maurice Bishop, who favored the left and invited Cubans to build infrastructure to accommodate long-range Soviet aircraft, was deposed and executed in October 19, 1983. Six days later, the United States invaded with the supposed reason that American medical students studying in Grenada were in danger due to a Cuban presence—and of course, the new leader supported by the US favored more traditional values and the right.

24. Panama invasion wherein an incident between American and Panamanian troops led to invasion and the earlier Carter administration plan to hand control of the canal over to Panama was cancelled.

25. US-Israeli sponsored wars between Iraq and Iran from 1980 to 1988.

26. Desert Storm War (First Gulf War) in 1991 wherein Saddam Hussein asked for permission from the United States (via their ambassador April Gillespie) to invade Kuwait and got an answer that the United States was not concerned with Arab quarrels. This was a trap, and after Saddam occupied Kuwait, George Bush Sr. mobilized a coalition of some forty nations to liberate Kuwait

and smash the recently built Iraqi military power base. This incident also involved a media hoax wherein the daughter of a Kuwaiti US Ambassador played a nurse on TV and then testified to "witnessing" Iraqi soldiers throwing babies out of incubators in Kuwait.

27. War on Terror launched by the Bush administration in October 2001—claimed to be the response to terrorism, especially the 9/11 incidents.
28. Operation Enduring (Afghanistan invasion). Freedom
29. Enduring Justice (Second Gulf War).
30. Countless others.

Paragraph 43 of the Field Manual published by the War Department, United States Army, on October 1, 1940, under the entry Rules of Land Warfare, states the following:

> National flags, insignias and uniforms as a ruse—in practice it has been authorized to make use of these as a ruse. The foregoing rule (Article 23 of the Annex of the IVth Hague Convention), does not prohibit such use, but does prohibit their improper use. It is certainly forbidden to make use of them during a combat. Before opening fire upon the enemy, they must be discarded.

The American Soldiers' Handbook states the following:

> The use of the enemy flag, insignia, and uniform is permitted under some circumstances. They are not to be used during actual fighting, and if used in order to approach the enemy without drawing fire, should be thrown away or removed as soon as fighting begins.

The 1977 Protocol Additional to the Geneva Conventions of August 12, 1949 (Protocol 1) states the following:

> Article 37—Prohibition of perfidy. 1. It is prohibited to kill, injure, or capture an adversary by resort to perfidy. Acts inviting the confidence of an adversary to lead him to believe that he is entitled to, or is obliged to accord, protection under the rules of international law applicable in armed conflict, with intent to betray that confidence, shall constitute perfidy. The following acts are examples of perfidy: (a) The feigning of an intent to

negotiate under a flag of truce or of a surrender; (b) The feigning of an incapacitation by wounds or sickness; (c) The feigning of civilian, non-combatant status; and (d) The feigning of protected status by the use of signs, emblems or uniforms of the United Nations or of neutral or other States not Parties to the conflict. 2. Ruses of war are not prohibited. Such ruses are acts which are intended to mislead an adversary or to induce him to act recklessly but which infringe no rule of international law applicable in armed conflict and which are not perfidious because they do not invite the confidence of an adversary with respect to protection under that law. The following are examples of such ruses: the use of camouflage, decoys, mock operations and disinformation.

Article 38—Recognized emblems. 1. It is prohibited to make improper use of the distinctive emblem of the Red Cross, Red Crescent or Red Lion and Sun or of other emblems, signs or signals provided for by the Conventions or by this Protocol. It is also prohibited to misuse deliberately in an armed conflict other internationally recognized protective emblems, signs or signals, including the flag of truce, and the protective emblem of cultural property. 2. It is prohibited to make use of the distinctive emblem of the United Nations, except as authorized by that Organization.

Article 39—Emblems of nationality. 1. It is prohibited to make use in an armed conflict of the flags or military emblems, insignia or uniforms of neutral or other States not Parties to the conflict. 2. It is prohibited to make use of the flags or military emblems, insignia or uniforms of adverse Parties while engaging in attacks or in order to shield, favour, protect or impede military operations. 3. Nothing in this Article or in Article 37, paragraph 1(d), shall affect the existing generally recognized law applicable to espionage or to the use of flags in the conduct of armed conflict at sea.

It is vitally important to note that while the United States may have these codes and regulations, her enemies, both foreign and domestic, are not bound by these rules.

The American people (and indeed the rest of the world) need to be exceptionally on guard and vigilant before the upcoming November 2016 election, and even many months afterward because the neocons/Communists may still try and get their World War III even if Donald Trump is elected.

After all, September 11, 2001, took place a full nine months after George W. Bush was sworn in at his Inauguration in January 2001, and this was blamed on Osama Bin Laden, who was a known CIA asset and who allegedly declared war on America in 1998. He might have been the neocons' insurance plan, cooked up during the eight-year Clinton Administration from 1992 to 2000.

And of course, 9/11 is what led to the wholesale bloodshed and regime changing wars for the past fifteen years, leaving the Middle East in flames, with countless millions of innocent lives and refugees lost forever, the greatest genocide and bloodbath the world has ever known.

And don't think that these crazed neocon psychopaths won't do it again, especially when there are only a few more countries left to "take out" now—Russia, Iran, and North Korea—as opposed to twenty.

CHAPTER 43

Federal Election Commission (FEC) Is
Another Example of a Lazy Corrupt Agency

FEC are refusing to even look into the rampant examples of election fraud plaguing the current Presidential Election, with Hillary Clinton and her operatives.

I n yet another dereliction of duty by a federal agency, the Federal Election Commission (FEC) has been noticeably silent, if not completely nonexistent, regarding the whirlwind of allegations pertaining to wide-scale election fraud, cheating, and active interference by the Democratic National Convention (DNC), the Foundation, Democratic Operatives Clinton Donna Brazile, John Podesta, and Debbie Wasserman Schultz, and countless others.

If Donald Trump had engaged in even a smidgen of the criminal conduct and behavior that has come to light both before and after the WikiLeaks revelations relating to Democrat-sponsored election fraud, he would be sitting in a federal prison or immediately disqualified from even running for the presidency and would be skewered 24/7 in 99 percent of the mainstream media and become a pariah overnight.

Indeed, Republican and Conservative Operative Dinesh D'Souza found out the really hard way, when he simply raised a little bit more money for a Conservative candidate at a family-based fundraiser when in January 2014, D'Souza was indicted by federal prosecutors for "campaign finance law violations." He was arraigned in a heavily leftist Clinton Foundation Territory US District Court for the Southern District of New York in Manhattan on January 24, 2014, and the two charges were for making $20,000 in illegal campaign contributions to the New York Senate campaign of Wendy Long and causing false statements to be made to the Federal Election Commission. In May 2014, D'Souza pleaded guilty to one felony count of making illegal contributions in the names of others. In September 2014, the court sentenced D'Souza to five years' probation, eight months in a halfway house (referred to as a community confinement center), and a $30,000 fine. He was also required to perform a day (eight hours) of community service each week during his probation and to undergo therapy on a weekly basis. D'Souza's attorney argued that D'Souza "did not act with any corrupt or criminal intent whatsoever" and described the incident as "at most an act of ... misguided friendship." His co-producers alleged that the indictment was a politically motivated retribution for the success of his 2012 movie 2016 *Obama's America*. D'Souza's claim of selective prosecution received support from some conservative media and commentators. According to liberal Harvard law professor Alan Dershowitz, "The idea of charging him with a felony for this doesn't sound like a proper exercise of prosecutorial discretion ... I can't help but think that [D'Souza's] politics have something to do with it... It smacks of selective prosecution." He went on to say such alleged campaign violations are common in politics. In May, United States District Judge Richard M. Berman rejected that contention, stating, "The court concludes the defendant has respectfully submitted no evidence he was selectively prosecuted."

This goes to show that it is not so much that America does not have the agencies/tools to combat the widespread and rampant corruption by the plutocrats/oligarchs in this country; it is just that they have been staffed and co-opted by members of the ruling class, who simply decide to "cherry-pick" and selectively investigate/prosecute "election offenders" within their jurisdictional arena.

The Federal Trade Commission (FTC) was previously shown to be an extremely biased and ineffective agency, choosing not to go after behemoths engaging in un-American and pro- cartel behavior in shutting out competitors and sabotaging healthy businesses by stacking the deck and allowing the plutocrat/oligarch class to grow even more powerful and unrivaled in their hegemonic power in whatever business they operate in.

Similarly, agencies like the FEC are refusing to even look into the rampant examples of election fraud plaguing the current presidential election, with Hillary Clinton and her operatives breaking nearly every rule, regulation, and law in the book, all to dismantle and destroy the campaign of Donald Trump or any of Hillary Clinton's opponents.

Apparently, examples of "electoral fraud" consist of one or more of the following:

1. Electorate manipulation
2. Manipulation of demography
3. Disenfranchisement
4. Voter intimidation
5. Vote buying
6. Distribution of false or misleading information in order to affect the outcome of an election

7. Misleading or confusing ballot papers
8. Ballot stuffing
9. Misrecording of votes
10. Destruction or invalidation of ballots
11. Tampering with electronic voting machines
12. Voter impersonation
13. other examples

Some of the examples of blatant election fraud by the Hillary Clinton camp and her allies that have turned up over the last few months include the following:

1. Democrat Operative and CNN Commentator Donna Brazile providing the election debate questions in advance to the Hillary Clinton campaign, so as to prepare her even better to debate Donald Trump unfairly.
2. The revelations that Debbie Wasserman Schultz, former DNC chairwoman, purposefully sabotaged Bernie Sanders's and other competitors from reaching their election goals.
3. The unexplained (and apparently uninvestigated) murder whistleblower Seth Rich. of DNC
4. Undercover video of Democrat operatives like Scott Foval admitting that they paid for, arranged, and "bussed in" various violent and disruptive factions into Donald Trump rallies to stir up violence, cacophony, and hatred to harm his campaign. "We manipulated the vote with money and action, not with laws," Democratic operative Scott Foval explained in one of the videos.
5. The clear overwhelming bias of the mainstream media against Donald Trump while being overwhelmingly pro- Hillary Clinton, wherein they absolutely refuse to cover any of the above types of allegations but instead bray 24/7 negative ad hominems and hatred against Trump.
6. The "firebombing" of the Donald Trump GOP Election Headquarters in North Carolina allegedly by DNC operatives (of course, there are no definitive answers as to who did this, because the FEC and other agencies are apparently simply not effectively investigating it).
7. Creating new Democrat voters out of dead people. Rudolph Giuliani was recently quoted on this rigged election phenomenon by declaring, "Dead people generally vote for Democrats."

8. Democrat Operative and Clinton Agent John Podesta in leaked emails discussing a "playbook for rigging polls through oversamples," discussed at http://www.zerohedge.com/news/ 2016-10-23/new-podesta-email-exposes-dem- playbook-rigging-polls-through- oversamples.
9. Allegations that the Google search engine is a deep state political actor working with the Hillary Clinton campaign to bury negative search results on her, but blasting negative search results against Donald Trump in order to sway the election.
10. Countless other examples.

Again, when are Americans going to hold our elected (and appointed) leaders' feet to the fire, make them get off their collective taxpayer-funded asses, and ***DO THEIR JOBS***?

CHAPTER 44

What Donald Trump Needs to Do

There has never been a better-suited and more experienced president when it comes to these issues.

N ow that Donald Trump has been elected president of the United States of America, there are a lot of things he needs to do.

He has seen firsthand the unseemly underbelly of the various deep state actors that have fought tooth and nail to both undermine and character assassinate him, as well as destroy him personally and professionally.

But Donald Trump is made of legendary stuff and not only endured these constant and underhanded attacks but also exposed and destroyed them all one by one.

However, the problems facing him and his administration still exist, and part of his mandate needs to not only "make America great again" but to also ensure that the cancers that plague American society are dealt with and destroyed once and for all.

The Media

Donald Trump needs to somehow dismantle and break up control of the American media by only 6 major corporations.

He needs to light a fire under the collective asses of the Federal Trade Commission (FTC) and force them to do their job.

No agency in the United States is so important but has been so asleep at the wheel than this one.

Problems with the FTC and its lack of teeth or motivation has resulted in some of the most heinous consolidations of illicit power in the hands of an evil greedy few devastating and hurting the American people and Donald Trump and his family as well.

Large behemoths such as the Hillary Clinton / deep state allies, such as Google, and the major media need to be first on the chopping/neutering block.

The Big International Banks

Similarly, the awesome power and monetary capital of the big banks, hedge funds, investment banking houses, and other financial institutions have also been left to their own devices, allowed to grow like a cancer without any FTC or Treasury oversight to the point where they literally threaten American democracy and its people on a daily basis. Indeed, they, just like the major media, got behind Hillary Clinton, even in the face of all her crimes and conspiracies, to unseat Donald Trump to ensure that he never got into presidential office.

This lesson Donald Trump should never forget—because as long as they are allowed to continue their domestic and global hegemony unchallenged, they will also pose an existential threat not only to the American people and their civil liberties/human rights/constitutional guarantees, but also to Donald Trump and his efficiency as President himself.

One of his first orders of business should be the reinstatement of the Glass-Steagall Act, previously repealed by Bill Clinton in 1998, which separates investment banking money from mom- and-pop checking/savings accounts so that risky investments by banking houses will and should result in their bankruptcy rather than being bailed out by the American taxpayer.

Many argue that this repeal, coupled with the forced reduction of credit standards of Fannie Mae and Freddie Mac by Bill Clinton through his HUD Director Andrew Cuomo to buy a home, created the mortgage crisis and crashed the American economy (some say deliberately) in 2008. Goldman Sachs sickeningly created a reverse credit swap derivative, betting on the impending housing mortgage crisis and made billions in the Glass-Steagall repeal that was pushed by their own Robert Rubin, Larry Summers, and Gene Sperling, when they were US Treasury Secretaries and Economic Policy Advisors under Bill Clinton.

Donald Trump also needs to take on the Federal Reserve, audit them, and if he finds any irregularities or shady behavior (which he most assuredly will), then he needs to immediately repudiate and/or renegotiate the insanely ridiculous 23 trillion dollars in American debt, delivering the American people from the yoke of financial and tax slavery by the central bankers of America, Europe, and overseas.

Optimally, he might consider issuing American currency from the US government rather than by a secret closed-off cabal of illicit and greedy private international citizens/corporations.

President Bill Clinton promotes NAFTA at the United States Chamber of Commerce in November 1993.

Bring Industry and Manufacturing Jobs Back to the USA

As Donald Trump so effectively and succinctly repeated while on the campaign trail over the past two years, the North American Free Trade Agreement (NAFTA) was singlehandedly one of the most devastating and disruptive treaties ever placed on the books of American jurisprudence, thus resulting in the mass loss of tens of millions of American jobs, industries, manufacturing facilities, revenue, and self-confidence of the American people.

Donald Trump needs to rebuild and reestablish American preeminence in industry, manufacturing, and hardcore goods for services, all made and manufactured in the United States of America.

Stupid Foreign Wars

Donald Trump has also echoed the American overwhelming cry of anti-neoconservative bloodlust by keeping America out of stupid foreign wars geared only for the benefit and power of a few, endangering the safety and welfare of the many.

To do this, Donald Trump must revamp and refresh the US Department of Defense, the Pentagon, the Intelligence Services, and the Military.

He must ensure that not one single drop of American blood be shed for another hopelessly stupid war—if the United States has become a national security state with its greatest source of income and revenue being the weapons, artillery, and products of the military-industrial complex (MIC) then he needs to find alternative and supplemental sources of revenue such as what was described above in terms of manufacturing and industrial jobs and factories being reestablished within the United States.

Section 60 of Arlington National Cemetery
Offers Tragic Testimony to America's Most Recent Wars

Donald Trump needs to value the heroism and self-sacrifice of American soldiers, military and veterans, and stop sending them on unnecessary stupid wars for the sake of the wealth and power of the deep state, and also to ensure that once our soldiers return home, that they are treated like the true heroes and privileged class that they are, and always should be (jobs, health care, benefits, and utmost respect).

No one has better described the predicament facing the American people in this regard than Dr. Paul Craig Roberts in his stellar work, *The Neoconservative Threat to World Order.*

This also means developing working and effective relationships with other great world powers, such as Russia, China, and India, in the spirit of mutual respect and friendship to jointly take on the world's problems and terrorists together based on mutual consultation and consensus, rather than with the United States "policing the entire world."

Reversing Divide and Conquer

One of the first things that Donald Trump said upon accepting his election as president was that he wanted to listen to everyone and bring everyone together under the fabric of the United States of America.

Right off the bat, he declared that he would be a uniter and not a divider.

To that end, he needs to now undo the "special protected classes," chock-full of con artists and whiners who use their protected class status to get special privileges, abuse others, trample on the right of others not lucky enough to be different, or oppress the constitutional, civil, and human rights of the rest of America.

From undermining the Second Amendment and influencing elections to sponsoring color revolutions in Eastern Europe and the Middle East, the ominous footprint of George Soros is everywhere.

These protected classes have been revealed to be the "henchmen" and agents of the deep state by the likes of such men as arch-manipulator and "color revolution" social engineer George Soros, who use these unwitting "protected classes" to do their dirty work in their ongoing assault on the American people with their "divide and conquer" rhetoric, pitting men against women, children against their own parents, gays against straights, minorities against majorities, and different races/religions against one another.

The only ones who benefit from this intra- American infighting have always been the ruling class deep state plutocrat elite, who have watched with smiles, rubbing their hands, as they kept the American people fighting among themselves so that the people are too busy fighting and killing each other to notice or challenge the crimes and conspiracies of the deep state elite themselves.

Criminal Justice and Family Court Reform

No single American industry has been so lucrative to the deep state elite and debilitating to the American people than the horrific butchering process known as the American criminal justice and family court system. Indeed, many would argue that the dismal state of race relations in America have their origins in the disparate treatment of racial and religious minorities by the state-sanctioned and wholesale criminality of the American police state as implemented by Bill Clinton and Joseph Biden's Crime Bill of 1994 and its corresponding Draconian legislation pertaining to the family and criminal courts and its privatized prison industrial complex.

All too often, fundamental constitutional rights and guarantees have been squelched and squashed by the American Stasi as formulated by the 1994 Crime Bill and its corresponding US Department of Justice state-sanctioned "community-oriented policing" gang-stalking program, resulting in 1/3 of all African-Americans, 1/6 of all Latinos, and 1/10 of all whites having been unfairly and without due process, probable cause, or evidence arrested, incarcerated, with families destroyed, resulting in over 70 million Americans with permanent criminal records (more than the entire population of France). Something is wrong here, and Donald Trump needs to do something about the fact that Biden and Clinton et al. have transformed our once great and proud country into a "nation of criminals."

Donald Trump needs to take the immediate measures and remedies to undo and reverse the American police state as described by John Whitehead in his seminal book and treatise *Battlefield America*.

Foreign Relations

As Donald Trump echoed while on the campaign trail, he is a subscriber to the Thomas Jefferson school of thought of "peace, commerce, and honest friendship with all nations—entangling alliances with none."

"I am sometimes asked if I have any regrets about publishing our book. As of today, my only regret is that it is not being published now. After the humiliations that Obama has endured at the hands of the Israel Lobby and the Hagel circus, we would sell even more copies, and we would not face nearly as much ill-informed criticism" (Stephen Walt, co-author of the book).

Donald Trump is an America-Firster and will not allow the United States to get embroiled and enmeshed in unnecessary foreign stupid wars, treaties, and other entanglements that tend to negatively affect American sovereignty, weighing us down like a rock around our collective necks. Foreign nations need to put their "big boy pants" on and deal with their own internal skirmishes, civil wars, financial problems, and other internecine conflicts on their own, without the constant hand-holding (and financial and military support) of the United States and its hard-working taxpayers.

Unless the sovereignty or security of the United States is directly at risk, the USA needs to stay the hell out of the world's problems and to focus on our own people, economy, and issues.

The sentiments echoed herein can be attributed to legendary libertarian statesmen such as Dr. Ron Paul and his protégé Daniel McAdams.

Re-injecting and Reinforcing American Moral Standards

No area of American life has been so undermined and impacted as the deterioration of fundamental American values, morals, and character in the past few decades of American society, disastrously affecting American individuals, families, cities, states, and eventually the nation itself.

This has been augmented and exacerbated by the constant, irresponsible, and disgusting messages in the American media, movie industry, Hollywood, by the undermining of organized religion in America and the disruption of common value systems as brought on by unregulated mass immigration and non-assimilation by various foreign elements.

A nation's moral health and compass is absolutely essential for it to be considered a "shining city on a hill" as described by legendary President Ronald Reagan himself.

For this, Donald Trump must use his "bully pulpit" as a leader to identify, isolate, target, and then take on the purveyors of common filth and disrepute by the American Hollywood movie and television industry, media, and other enemies of common human decency and morality.

American Infrastructure

As Donald Trump is the ultimate and consummate "builder," it will be awe-inspiring to watch him rebuild American infrastructure, such as our railroads, transportation systems, airports, roads and highways, hospitals, schools, buildings and cities.

There has never been a better-suited and more experienced President when it comes to these issues, and Donald Trump will not disappoint in this very important arena of America's pride, patriotism, self-confidence, and self-respect.

Cleanse the Judiciary

It is no secret that the last eight years of steady Obama appointments have stocked the American judiciary, federal state and local, with either deep state bankster agents, or their "protected class" useful idiot appointees who all report back to the same deep state oligarchy/plutocracy anyway.

The only thing these appointees have in common is that they generally have no respect for or understanding of the US Constitution or the Bill of Rights.

The direct deep state judicial appointees, usually hailing from the big law firms, who in turn represent the big banks/corporations, know exactly who their masters are, while the ambitious "protected class" judicial appointees are either imbalanced activists or too stupid to realize that their biased, unconstitutional judicial opinions serve the same deep state elite anyway, as they help to eviscerate and destroy the protections afforded and guaranteed by the US Constitution.

Either way, a major house cleaning is in order, and Donald Trump needs to restock the judiciary with learned, educated, and constitutionally minded judges in the federal and state courts all throughout America, beginning with the major cities first, "pruning the judicial tree" as he goes along.

Pardon and Assist Whistle-Blowers Such as Julian Assange, Edward Snowden, Jeffrey Sterling, Thomas Drake and Bradley (Chelsea) Manning

The above-mentioned whistle-blowers and countless more were the victims and recipients of the absolute and unbridled retaliation and rage of the full deep state plutocratic elite shadow government, spearheaded by Hillary Clinton and Barack Obama, and their information and heroically courageous leaks of outright and blatant government corruption and cronyism came with great personal sacrifice to themselves, their families, and their friends.

But in the true spirit of patriotism, they helped to open the eyes and minds of the American people (and the rest of the world) and helped to catapult Donald Trump into the office of the presidency.

Their legacies and memories should not be forgotten and were part and parcel of Donald Trump's "movement."

If Bill Clinton could pardon the likes of Marc Rich and others, then Donald Trump can and should pardon the heroic patriots and whistle-blowers who helped make his presidency and the American people's liberation from repressive oligarchy possible.

CHAPTER 45

Trump Cabinet:
He Is Not a Masochist

He may temporarily forgive, but he does not forget.

President-Elect Donald Trump is a seasoned businessman from New York City and is as tough as they come. His track record, statements, and past behavior indicate that he is a ruthlessly smooth businessman who believes in revenge (see Rosie O'Donnell and others) and never ever forgets. He may temporarily forgive, but he does not forget.

This rule of thumb has served him well in transforming his father's multimillion dollar but fledgling real estate company into the multibillion-dollar international real estate powerhouse that it currently is.

So, what gives in regards to the names of his Cabinet that are being floated around?

Mind you, some of the list below was gleaned from the *New York Times*, so a huge grain of salt should be taken before one delves into this analysis.

However, let's take a look-see at some of the names being bandied around to be installed in the President Trump White House, and let's see if they comport with his style, history, and personality.

The danger is that people who have either demonstrated disloyalty in the past or have shown lackluster support or were deep state members who stood against almost everything mentioned in Donald Trump's campaign and mandate would only serve to both undermine his chances for success and, worse, destroy and sabotage his vision to "make America great again."

Treasury Secretary

His top choices for Treasurer are Jamie Dimon, CEO of JPMorgan, or Steve Mnuchin, his finance chairman and former Goldman Sachs executive.

They don't bode well for moving away from the banking oligarchy, as Mr. Trump promised during his campaign.

In fact, JPMorgan Chase Chief Executive Officer Jamie Dimon did not support Republican Donald Trump's presidential campaign, yet some Trump advisers want America's most famous banker to become treasury secretary to calm nerves on Wall Street.

His campaign finance manager, Steven Mnuchin, is a former Goldman Sachs Group banker, but at least he has that much coveted loyalty factor going for him.

Regarding the treasury secretary position, Thomas Barrack Jr., founder, chairman and executive chairman of Colony Capital, private equity and real estate investor is both loyal as well as in agreement with Donald Trump, so he is a good choice.

And according to conventional wisdom, so does Jeb Hensarling, representative from Texas and chairman of the House Financial Services Committee.

Steven Mnuchin, former Goldman Sachs executive and Mr. Trump's campaign finance chairman also has the two requisite qualities as described above, but Ron Paul calls him a neocon infiltrator.

However, Tim Pawlenty, former Minnesota governor, as recently as August 2016 called Trump "unsound, uninformed, unhinged and unfit" to be president and dropped his support.

Attorney General

The former New York City mayor Rudy Giuliani may be slated for attorney general, and he has certainly demonstrated his loyalty to Trump, even going against his own daughter in the process-a truly Abraham-Isaac moment in Republican politics-but what about agreement with Trump's policies and vision? Rinse, lather, and repeat on both loyalty and agreement with policy.

Leslie Rutledge, first female and first Republican elected attorney general of Arkansas would be worth a consideration.

She also served as deputy counsel at the National Republican Congressional Committee before joining the Republican National Committee as counsel.

As US attorney general, the nation's top law enforcement official, they will have the authority to carry out Mr. Trump's "law and order" platform, including his threat to jail Hillary Clinton.

Another good choice for the US attorney general position would be Trey Gowdy, a no- nonsense, US Constitution-loving, extremely patriotic all-American prosecutor who enjoys a stellar reputation and respect from both sides of the aisle.

He has been tried, tested, and true on everything with balls of steel, from the IRS scandals to Hillary Clinton's email and Benghazi investigations, only having been hampered by out-of-control renegade Democrats who would support Hillary Clinton through anything, including egregious violations of federal and state law.

The nominee can also change how civil rights laws are enforced.

Chief of Staff

Trump apparently chose Reince Preibus for his White House chief of staff even though Republican National Committee chairman Reince Priebus condemned Donald Trump's comments about women in a curt statement: "No woman should ever be described in these terms or talked about in this manner. Ever."

Does this mean that if Trump is once again set up by the now-infamous Feminist Mafia led by Hillary Clinton et al. or if "new information comes to light," as it always does, that Reince will once again throw Trump under the bus?

Only time will tell, but Reince's disloyalty has already been shown.

Chief Strategist

The greatest and most perfect choice for Trump's inner *sanctum sanctorum* is for the chief strategist position in the form of Stephen K. Bannon.

No one has better encapsulated the necessary loyalty and policy agreements with Donald Trump than Mr. Bannon, his closest advisor and confidant.

Stephen Bannon is an exemplary choice because he is brilliant (Harvard and Georgetown graduate), highly patriotic (former naval officer), and no-nonsense.

It also helps his credibility that the ones castigating and smearing him the most are the exact same enemies of America who were voted out of office and who are the same individuals that relentlessly targeted Donald Trump both during and after his campaign.

Secretary of State

As is discussed below, Secretary of State John R. Bolton is a horrible idea.

Bob Corker, senator from Tennessee and chairman of the Senate Foreign Relations Committee, tried to distance himself from Trump in a statement and called Trump's remarks "inappropriate."

Newt Gingrich, former house speaker and a close adviser to Donald Trump, openly broke with Trump in August 2016 and endorsed Senator John McCain (R-Ariz.) for reelection against Trump's wishes, also calling him "unacceptable" at times.

There is simply not enough data on Zalmay Khalilzad, former United States ambassador to Afghanistan, but the fact remains that he was once a center of the storm in previous hardcore neoconservative administrations.

Stanley A. McChrystal, former senior military commander in Afghanistan, stated only as recently as July 2016 that "I would decline any role with Donald Trump."

So much for loyalty or policy agreement, and he also actively supported Hillary Clinton for president.

Others of his top Cabinet choices include ultraneocon reactionaries, such as Secretary of State Newt Gingrich, the neocon former house speaker who was even in Trump's top choice as running mate; and John Bolton, ultra-Zionist and former United States ambassador to the United Nations under George W. Bush.

Newt Gingrich is a true Republican gentleman and statesman and has never spoken ill of Trump on the record, even going so far as to knock out Trump's enemies on live television.

John Bolton is the most bizarre and truly cacophonous selection thus far, as he supports the lie that ISIS was not created by the United States, Saudi Arabia, London, Israel, and Turkey and other gulf states to wreak havoc in the Middle East and serve as a "boogeyman" in the US and Europe in order to usher in martial law.

He is the moral savage who brought shame on his country each day that he sat as America's ambassador (unconfirmed) at the UN and who had told the world that a dead Israeli civilian is worth a whole lot more in terms of moral outrage than a Lebanese one.

Furthermore, Bolton voraciously supports finishing up his fellow neocons, Rumsfeld, Wolfowitz, Feith and their cronies menu list of countries to preemptively "take out," such as Iran, Russia, North Korea among others. He is truly a dyed-in-the-wool neoconservative/Communist New World Order kook.

Trump should quickly and summarily eliminate him from the selection process, lest he lose support from the American people who believed in his promises when they voted for him.

John Bolton has also openly challenged Trump when in July 2016 he stated that he was "disturbed" by Donald Trump's suggestion that if a NATO country is attacked, it shouldn't necessarily expect help from the United States if it hasn't kept up with its financial obligations.

Bolton does not have either loyalty or agreement with the Donald Trump camp, so he too should be exiled from the Cabinet.

Defense Secretary

For defense secretary, the incoming secretary will shape the fight against the Islamic State while overseeing a military that is struggling to put in place two Obamaera initiatives: integrating women into combat roles and allowing transgender people to serve openly.

Both could be rolled back.

Kelly Ayotte, departing senator from New Hampshire and member of the Senate Armed Services Committee, lost her reelection bid precisely because the voters punished her for her openly disloyal statements about Trump and because she vocally withdrew her support for him in October 2016.

She would be a terrible choice for the Trump administration.

Lieutenant General Michael T. Flynn, former director of the Defense Intelligence Agency, is really the only sound, sane, and perfect choice for this position in the Trump Cabinet.

He has been steadfast and knowledgeable throughout since the beginning, of Trump and his vision, and has been exceedingly loyal and both are on the same page vis-à-vis foreign policy, defense and intelligence.

Stephen J. Hadley, national security adviser under George W. Bush, went to Yale Law School with Bill and Hillary Clinton. He advocates a degree of foreign policy continuity between administrations and was a centerpiece of foreign and defense policy under the ultra- neoconservative George W. Bush administration.

One does not need to be a rocket scientist to see how his appointment would be dangerous.

Although to Mr. Hadley's credit, he counseled diplomacy, not war with Iran, thus averting World War III.

This is a fifty-fifty choice.

But at least Michael Flynn is 100 percent.

No opinion or enough data about Jon Kyl, former senator from Arizona, but Jeff Sessions definitely is loyal to Trump, regardless of whether or not a Republican from New York and one from Alabama could possibly agree on anything.

Interior Secretary

Regarding the interior secretary position, this manages the nation's public lands and waters.

The next secretary will decide the fate of Obamaera rules that stop public land development; curb the exploration of oil, coal, and gas; and promote wind and solar power on public lands.

Jan Brewer, former Arizona governor, while she may be very supportive of Trump is also just plain belligerent and could alienate Hispanic Americans with her overtly racist tactics in arresting immigrants in Arizona. In short, she would not make Trump look good to 80 percent of the country, and Trump needs all the help and support of the country constituency as he can possibly get.

Not enough data on either Robert E. Grady (accused neocon by libertarian statesman Ron Paul) Gryphon Investors partner, Harold G. Hamm, chief executive of Continental Resources, an oil-and-gas company,

Forrest Lucas, president of Lucas Oil Products, which manufactures automotive lubricants, additives, and greases, but maybe that's a good thing.

Sarah Palin, former Alaska governor, is both loyal and in full agreement with Donald Trump's policies, and in any event, she is harmless anyway as long as she stays the hell away from foreign policy and international cultural issues.

Agricultural Secretary

The agriculture secretary oversees America's farming industry, inspects food quality, and provides income-based food assistance.

The department also helps develop international markets for American products, giving the next secretary partial responsibility to carry out Mr. Trump's positions on trade.

Sam Brownback, Kansas governor, has remained steadfastly loyal to Donald Trump throughout his campaign and will probably go along with Trump's vision.

So was Chuck Conner, chief executive officer of the National Council of Farmer Cooperatives, and Sid Miller (the man who tweeted the c-word at Hillary Clinton). Texas agricultural commissioner is also satisfactory on these two fronts.

Although Sonny Perdue, former Georgia governor, seems like a "wildcard" from the South and unpredictable thereon.

Commerce Secretary

The commerce secretary has been a perennial target for budget cuts, but the secretary oversees a diverse portfolio, including the Census, the Bureau of Economic Analysis, and the National Oceanic and Atmospheric Administration.

Chris Christie, New Jersey governor, is both loyal and in full agreement with Donald Trump. Why he gets little to no respect from Trump is a mystery, although the specter and shadow of the George Washington Bridge scandal may have something to do with it.

Chris Christie, New Jersey governor, is the obvious choice, but so is Dan DiMicco, former chief executive of Nucor Corporation, a steel production company, but Lewis M. Eisenberg, private equity chief for Granite Capital

International Group, has been negatively commented on where some conservatives were unhappy with him as the party's national finance chairman, saying things like "I have a big problem with Eisenberg," said prolife Texas RNC member Tim Lambert.

"My perception is he is only for Republicans who are leftofcenter."

Labor Secretary

The labor secretary enforces rules that protect the nation's workers, distributes benefits to the unemployed, and publishes economic data like the monthly jobs report.

The new secretary will be in charge of keeping Mr. Trump's promise to dismantle many Obamaera rules covering the vast workforce of federal contractors.

Not much is known about Victoria A. Lipnic Equal Employment Opportunity Commissioner and workforce policy counsel to the House Committee on Education and the Workforce.

Press Secretary

Laura Ingraham would be the best choice for press secretary.

Laura Ingraham is an American radio talk show host, best-selling author, and conservative political commentator. Her nationally syndicated talk show, *The Laura Ingraham Show*, airs throughout the United States on Courtside Entertainment.

Department of Health and Human Services

The Health and Human Services Secretary will help President Trump achieve one of his central campaign promises: to repeal, amend, or replace the Affordable Care Act.

The department approves new drugs, regulates the food supply, operates biomedical research, and runs Medicare and Medicaid, which insure more than 100 million people.

Here Dr. Ben Carson, former neurosurgeon and 2016 presidential candidate, is the obvious golden choice.

Mike Huckabee Former Arkansas governor and 2016 presidential candidate just doesn't make sense for this position, but Bobby Jindal, former

Louisiana governor who served as secretary of the Louisiana Department of Health and Hospital, makes a lot of sense as well.

Rick Scott, Florida governor and former chief executive of a large hospital chain, has openly talked smack about Trump, and that never helps.

Energy Department

Despite its name, the primary purview of the Energy Department is to protect and manage the nation's arsenal of nuclear weapons.

Legendary Libertarian Statesman Ron Paul has warned Trump about James L. Connaughton, chief executive of Nautilus Data Technologies and former environmental adviser to President George W. Bush as a major neoconservative/CFR infiltrator, as well as Robert E. Grady, Gryphon Investors partner, but has not said the same about Harold G. Hamm Chief executive of Continental Resources, an oil-and-gas company.

In fact, Ron Paul has also declared this about John Bolton, Stephen J. Hadley, Steven Mnuchin, and Lewis M. Eisenberg as well.

Education Secretary

Mr. Trump has said he wants to drastically shrink the Education Department and shift responsibilities for curriculum research, development and education aid to state and local governments.

Both Dr. Ben Carson and Williamson M. Evers, education expert at the Hoover Institution, a think tank, are great choices, although Carson would be better suited for the DHHS as described above.

Secretary for Veterans Affairs

The Secretary of Veterans Affairs will face the task of improving the image of a department Mr. Trump has widely criticized.

Mr. Trump repeatedly argued that the Obama administration neglected the country's veterans, and he said that improving their care was one of his top priorities.

Jeff Miller, retired chairman of the House Veterans Affairs Committee, hounded the agency for failing to enact meaningful changes to cut wait times and fire workers who hid delays. However, if selected, he will be the first secretary of Veterans Affairs who has never served in the military.

Homeland Security Secretary

The Homeland Security Secretary, formed after the attacks of September 11, 2001, has one key role in the Trump administration: guarding the United States' borders.

If Mr. Trump makes good on his promises of widespread deportations and building walls, this secretary will have to carry them out.

Joe Arpaio, departing sheriff of Maricopa County, Arizona, while entertaining, is too extreme for this sensitive role. David A. Clarke Jr., Milwaukee County sheriff, may not be knowledgeable or experienced enough. Rudolph W. Giuliani, former New York mayor, may be the best choice since he helped to found it. Michael McCaul, representative from Texas and chairman of the House Homeland Security Committee, could alienate Russia as he has bashed them and accused them of hacking even when Trump said he did not believe him, and maybe he is too aggressive for this role, and Jeff Sessions Senator from Alabama, who is a prominent immigration opponent, may be too culturally insensitive and *milquetoast* for the job.

Environmental Protection Agency

The Environmental Protection Agency Administrator, which issues and oversees environmental regulations, is under threat from the president-elect, who has vowed to dismantle the agency "in almost every form."

To that end, if that is his agenda, then anyone could theoretically qualify. Although Myron Ebell (climate change skeptic) may be the best choice, Robert E. Grady, Gryphon Investors partner who was involved in drafting the Clean Air Act Amendments of 1990, was previously negated as a neocon, and Jeffrey R. Holmstead, lawyer with Bracewell LLP and former deputy EPA administrator in the George W. Bush administration, seems to be a decent choice, although he could be a closet neocon as well.

US Trade Representative

The US Trade Representative will have the odd role of opposing new trade deals, trying to rewrite old ones and bolstering the enforcement of what Mr. Trump sees as unfair trade, especially with China.

Dan DiMicco, former chief executive of Nucor Corporation, a steel-production company and a critic of Chinese trade practices, is apparently the only choice for this role.

UN Ambassador

The UN ambassador, second only to the Secretary of State, will be the primary face of America to the world, representing the country's interests at the Security Council on a host of issues, from Middle East peace to nuclear proliferation.

Kelly Ayotte, departing senator from New Hampshire and member of the Senate Armed Services Committee, is a horrible choice because she already backstabbed and betrayed Donald Trump as was described above.

Openly gay activist Richard Grenell, former spokesman for the United States ambassador to the United Nations during the George W. Bush administration may be the right choice, and Giuliani likes him the best-but this is a close call.

CIA Director/Director of National Intelligence

The CIA director / director of national intelligence will serve when Mr. Trump takes over at a time of diverse and complex threats to American security.

The new CIA director will have to decide whether to undo a CIA "modernization" plan put in place this year by Director John O. Brennan and how to proceed if the president-elect orders a resumption of harsh interrogation tactics—which critics have described as torture—for terrorism suspects.

The choices that are the best for the reasons described above are Michael T. Flynn, former director of the Defense Intelligence Agency.

Peter Hoekstra, former chairman of the House Intelligence Committee, displayed disloyalty when he attacked Trump when he dressed down a biased Hispanic judge who was against him.

Mike Rogers, former chairman of the House Intelligence Committee, just resigned from selection.

Frances Townsend, former homeland security adviser under George W. Bush, signed a letter stating that Trump is "fundamentally dishonest" in an open letter, plus she has been tweeting pictures of her shoes for the past ten years. She is probably slightly out of touch and in the loop for the current changes and circumstances happening now, so clearly Michael Flynn is the only real true and logical choice here.

National Security Advisor

The national security adviser, although not a member of the Cabinet, is a critical gatekeeper for policy proposals from the State Department, the Pentagon and other agencies, a function that takes on more importance given Mr. Trump's lack of experience in elective office.

Once again, Michael T. Flynn, former director of the Defense Intelligence Agency, is the only logical choice, or someone exactly like him (or selected by him).

CHAPTER 46

Case for Trey Gowdy as US Attorney General

No other prospect for US attorney general has the same level of courage, integrity, respect for the US Constitution and drive to do what's right for America.

There is no other congressman in the United States who has demonstrated the necessary temerity, love, and respect for the US Constitution, no-nonsense attitude when it comes to prosecuting federal and state crime, who is most against government corruption and graft, is supported by the people, has bigger balls of steel, and is unafraid to speak truth to power than South Carolina's own Trey Gowdy. He literally is a hero of the people and must be appointed as US attorney general, as he is absolutely unfettered and non-corruptible to special interests, lobbyists, and other forces of political and monetary influence.

Benghazi Investigation

In 2014, Gowdy became chairman of a House Select Committee to investigate the 2012 Benghazi attack, where he demonstrated unbridled and fearless integrity, aggression, humor, and focus when no one else in congress had the gumption or confidence to take on the legal and corruption issues in front of him.

Gowdy ruthlessly and courageously questioned former Secretary of State Hillary Clinton about terrorist attacks on an American diplomatic compound in Benghazi, Libya, where his experience as a prosecutor blasted through.

Hillary Clinton Classified Email Leak Investigation

Trey Gowdy methodically questioned FBI Director James Comey on the definition of intent and how Hillary Clinton could possibly have evaded punishment with her email server scandal.

The exchange often got heated when Gowdy stated, "You and I both know *intent* is really difficult to prove. Very rarely do defendants announce, 'On this date, I intend to break this criminal code section. Just to put everyone on notice, I am going to break the law on this date."

IRS Targeting Conservatives Investigation

He is an outspoken champion of conservative principles.

He was relentless at looking for the truth about Internal Revenue Service (IRS) political operatives that used the color of law and authority of that bureaucracy to silence Tea Party conservatives.

University of Baltimore law professor Charles Tiefer was brought in by Democrats as an "expert" to help determine whether the House Judiciary Committee should appoint a special counsel to investigate the IRS scandal.

Gowdy was incensed that IRS's Lois Lerner referred to conservatives as "assholes."

At the hearings about IRS abuses, Gowdy offered Tiefer some "free litigation advice" when he refused to answer one of his questions that seemed very direct and unanimous.

Trey Gowdy freaked out in righteous anger at a House Oversight Committee held for the purpose of a determining whether to hold Lois Lerner in contempt.

The former IRS executive in charge of tax-exempt entities was at the center of the IRS Tea Party targeting scandal, but allegedly obstructed the investigation by declaring her Fifth Amendment right to silence, while making other statements in her defense.

Gowdy concluded his enraged speech with the angry statement that "the same Constitution that allows her the right, if she wants to, to sit there and say nothing, allows these groups the right to petition their government for redress."

Background

Harold Watson "Trey" Gowdy III was born on August 22, 1964, and was a successful American attorney, politician, and former prosecutor.

He currently serves as the US representative for South Carolina's fourth congressional district. He is a member of the Tea Party movement and the Republican Party. His district includes much of the upstate region of South Carolina, including Greenville and Spartanburg.

Before his election to Congress, Gowdy was the district attorney for the state's Seventh Judicial Circuit, comprising Spartanburg and Cherokee Counties. From 1994 to 2000, he was a federal prosecutor for the US attorney for the district of South Carolina.

He is the son of Novalene (née Evans) and Harold Watson "Hal" Gowdy, Jr., MD. He grew up in Spartanburg, where as a young man, he delivered newspapers for the local daily, and worked at the community market. Gowdy graduated from Spartanburg High School in 1982, earned a BA in history from Baylor University in 1986, and earned a JD degree from the University of South Carolina in 1989.

Gowdy married Terri (née Dillard) Gowdy, a former Miss Spartanburg and second runner-up for Miss South Carolina. The couple have two children, Watson and Abigail. Terri Dillard Gowdy is a teacher's aide in the Spartanburg School District.

There is no one with a more wholesome, healthy, and positive personal and home life than Trey Gowdy, and he is a role model and great American for all people, young and old.

Gowdy served as clerk for John P. Gardner on the South Carolina Court of Appeals as well as for United States District Court Judge George Ross Anderson, Jr. He then went into private practice before being selected as a US federal prosecutor in April 1994. Gowdy would later be awarded the Postal Inspector's Award for the successful prosecution of J. Mark Allen, one of America's Most Wanted suspects.

In February 2000, he left the United States Attorney's Office to run for Seventh Circuit Solicitor. He defeated incumbent Solicitor Holman Gossett in the Republican primary. He ran unopposed in the general election. Gowdy was reelected in 2004 and 2008, both times unopposed. During his tenure, he appeared in two episodes of "Forensic Files," as well as Dateline NBC and SCETV. He prosecuted the full set of criminal cases, including seven death-penalty cases.

When the state faced a budget crunch that forced many employees to go on unpaid furloughs, Gowdy funneled part of his own campaign account into the solicitor's budget so his staff could keep working. This is unprecedented in the annals of American history and proves that this man puts people over money any day.

In the summer of 2009, Gowdy announced that he would challenge incumbent Republican US Congressman Bob Inglis in the Republican primary for South Carolina's fourth congressional district.

In the run-off election, Gowdy defeated Inglis 70-30 percent. The fourth district was so heavily considered Republican that it was widely presumed

Gowdy was assured a seat in that class of congress. Gowdy defeated Democratic nominee Paul Corden 63-29 percent.

Gowdy ran for reelection to a second term against Democrat Deb Morrow, who was allegedly heavily funded by special interests and lobbyists. He would defeat his competitor Morrow 65-34 percent.

Gowdy ran for reelection again in 2014. His only opponent was Libertarian Curtis E. McLaughlin. He was reelected with 85.2 percent of the popular vote.

In the November 2016 election, Gowdy faced Democrat Chris Fedalei, a twenty-six-year-old attorney. Trey Gowdy easily defeated Chris Fedalei with 67.23 percent of the vote to retain his seat.

In August 2011 during the 2011 US debt ceiling crisis, Gowdy opposed Speaker John Boehner's debt limit bill, and he voted against the final debt ceiling agreement.

He heroically took on the military-industrial complex / national security state when he opposed the 2011 defense authorization bill, citing concerns about the prospect of Americans being detained without trial on national security grounds.

In December 2010, he told *Congressional Quarterly* that he would support a measure only if its sponsor could demonstrate that the Constitution gave the government the power to act in a particular realm, once again deferring to the United States Constitution before allowing any expansion of executive governmental powers to abrogate and vitiate human rights, civil liberties, and constitutional protections.

Gowdy has also worked on the Committee on Judiciary, the Committee on Oversight and Government Reform, and the Committee on Education and the Workforce.

In 2012, he received the Defender of Economic Freedom Award from the fiscally conservative 501(c)4 organization Club for Growth.

The award is given to the members of congress who have the year's highest ranking, according to the Club for Growth's metrics.

Gowdy scored 97 out of 100, and was one of 34 congressmen given the award.

An ardent social conservative, Gowdy considers himself "pro-life plus."

He not only believes "in the sanctity of life" but argues that "the strategy should be broader than waiting for the Supreme Court to revisit *Roe v. Wade.*"

Trey Gowdy signed the Contract from America, which aims to defund, repeal, and replace the Patient Protection and Affordable Care Act, limit United States Environmental Protection Agency regulations, enact a reform of the federal tax code, pass a balanced budget amendment, and end earmarks.

On March 4, 2014, Gowdy introduced the ENFORCE the Law Act of 2014 (HR 4138; 113th Congress) into the house. The bill would give the United States House of Representatives and the United States senate both the standing to sue the president of the United States in a federal district court to clarify a federal law (that is, seek a declaratory judgment) in the event that the executive branch is not enforcing the law, truly a grass roots movement designed to keep a check on out-of-control executive action in contravention to the US Constitution.

House Republicans argued that the bill was necessary because the Obama administration refused to enforce the laws. HR 4138 has passed the house but has yet to become law.

In total, Gowdy has sponsored eleven bills, including HR 1894, a bill to permit a guilty plea made by the accused prior to the announcement of the sentence in a capital offense trial before a military commission to form the basis of an agreement to reduce the maximum approved sentence, introduced May 13, 2011; HR 2076, a bill to allow the attorney general to assist with investigation incidents in which three or more people are killed or are targeted to be killed, introduced June 1, 2011, signed into law January 14, 2013; HR 6620, a bill to authorize the United States Secret Service to protect former presidents, their spouses, and their children under the age of sixteen, introduced November 30, 2012, signed into law January 10, 2013; HR 652, a bill to prohibit non-humanitarian relief foreign aid from being sent to countries that engage in state-sanctioned persecution of religious minorities, prevent equal access to education on the basis of gender, race, or ethnicity, or do not accept the return of nationals who have been extradited; HR 5401, a bill to prohibit Libyan nationals from engaging in aviation maintenance, flight operations, or nuclear-related studies or training inside the United States; and many others.

He has been on the Committee on Ethics, Committee on the Judiciary, Subcommittee on Immigration and Border Security (chairman), Subcommittee on Crime, Terrorism, Homeland Security and Investigations, Committee on Oversight and Government Reform, Subcommittee on Health Care, Benefits and Administrative Rules, Subcommittee on Government Operations, Select Committee on the Events Surrounding the 2012 Terrorist Attack in Benghazi (Chairman), and others.

In July 2015, Republican nominee Donald Trump named Gowdy as a possible nominee for attorney general in a Trump Cabinet.

In late December 2015, Gowdy endorsed Senator Marco Rubio for president, praising him as a rarity among elected officials for having kept his campaign promises.

Gowdy's endorsement strained his relations with Donald Trump's campaign and Trump said that Gowdy had "failed miserably on Benghazi."

Rubio withdrew from the race in March after losing his home state of Florida to Trump.

Two months later, on May 20, Gowdy endorsed Trump for president, admitting that while he was a "Rubio guy," he would support the presumptive Republican nominee.

CHAPTER 47

Ron Paul: The True and Essential Choice
for US Secretary of State

It is time to return to the basics and foundations of what made this nation great, in line with President-Elect Donald Trump's vision.

T he *Merriam-Webster Dictionary* defines the word statesman as "a usually wise, skilled, and respected government leader."

There can be no doubt that Ron Paul, hero of the Libertarian movement and follower of Thomas Jefferson, is at once unusually wise, skilled, and respected throughout all of the world.

The dictionary goes on to further break the term down as "one versed in the principles or art of government, especially one actively engaged in conducting the business of a government or in shaping its policies."

Ron Paul is also equally well-versed in this regard, having had a career in the US House of Representatives spanning nearly forty years.

Paul is also a senior fellow of the Mises Institute and has been an active writer, publishing on the topics of political and economic theory, as well as publicizing the ideas of economists of the Austrian School such as Murray Rothbard and Ludwig von Mises during his political campaigns.

Paul has written many books on Austrian economics and classical liberal philosophy, beginning with *The Case for Gold* (1982) and including *A Foreign Policy of Freedom* (2007), *Pillars of Prosperity* (2008), *The Revolution: A Manifesto* (2008), *End the Fed* (2009), and *Liberty Defined* (2011).

While a medical resident in the 1960s, Paul was influenced by Friedrich Hayek's *The Road to Serfdom*, which caused him to read other publications by Ludwig von Mises and Ayn Rand.

He came to know economists Hans Sennholz and Murray Rothbard well, and credits to them his interest in the study of economics.

When President Richard Nixon "closed the gold window" by ending American participation in the Bretton Woods System, thus ending the US dollar's loose association with gold on August 15, 1971, Paul decided to enter politics and became a Republican candidate for the United States Congress.

Wikipedia describes a *statesman* alternatively as "usually a politician, diplomat or other notable public figure who has had a long and respected career at the national or international level."

The statesman (Greek: *politikos*), also known by its Latin title, *Politicus*, is a Socratic dialogue written by Plato.

The text describes a conversation between Socrates, the mathematician Theodorus, another person named Socrates (referred to as Young Socrates), and an unnamed philosopher from Elea referred to as the Stranger (Xénos).

It is ostensibly an attempt to arrive at a definition of *statesman*, as opposed to *sophist* or *philosopher* and is presented as following the action of the sophist.

According to John M. Cooper in the seminal treatise "Introduction to *Politikos*," Cooper and Hutchinson (1997), the dialogue's intention was to clarify that to rule or have political power, called for a "specialized knowledge."

The statesman was one who possesses this special knowledge of how to rule *justly* and well and to *have the best interests of the citizens at heart.*

In each and every thing that Ron Paul has ever said or done in his career both inside and outside of government service, he has always, without fail or missing a beat, acted at all times both "justly," avoiding war and conflict, and while "having the best interests of the citizens at heart."

His nemesis enemies have been the warmongering neoconservatives, who have consistently misused the good will and heavy coffers of the US Treasury owned by its hard-working industrious American taxpayers to conquer, destroy, invade, rape, pillage and extort other nations around the world, only for the benefit of its imperial/plutocrat deep state elite.

Paul has been described as a conservative and libertarian.

According to University of Georgia political scientist Keith Poole, Paul had the most conservative voting record of any member of congress from 1937 to 2002 and is the most conservative of the candidates that had sought the 2012 Republican nomination for president, on a scale primarily measuring positions on the role of government in managing the economy—not positions on social issues or foreign policy matters.

Other analyses, in which key votes on domestic social issues and foreign policy factor more heavily, have judged Paul much more moderate.

The *National Journal*, for instance, rated Paul only the 145th most conservative member of the House of Representatives (out of 435) based on votes cast in 2010.

The foundation of Paul's political philosophy is the conviction that "the proper role for government in America is to provide national defense, a court system for civil disputes, a criminal justice system for acts of force and fraud, and little else."

He has been nicknamed Dr. No, reflecting both his medical degree and his insistence that he will "never vote for legislation unless the proposed measure is expressly authorized by the Constitution."

The *statesman* is presented that politics should be run by this specialized knowledge, or *gnosis*.

Those that rule merely give the appearance of such knowledge, but in the end are really sophists or imitators.

The neocons are great examples of rulers and not statesmen.

Paul's foreign policy of nonintervention made him the only 2008 Republican presidential candidate to have voted against the Iraq War Resolution in 2002.

He advocates withdrawal from the United Nations and from the North Atlantic Treaty Organization for reasons of maintaining strong national sovereignty, completely in line with President-Elect Donald Trump's philosophy.

The Secretary of State is a senior official of the federal government of the United States of America heading the US Department of State, principally concerned with foreign policy and is considered to be the US government's equivalent of a Minister for Foreign Affairs.

The Secretary of State is appointed by the president of the United States and is confirmed by the United States Senate.

The first American Secretary of State was Thomas Jefferson, who took office in March 22, 1790, and left office in December 31, 1793.

Secretary of State Thomas Jefferson lived and governed by one of his most notable statements of "Peace, commerce, and honest friendship with all nations entangling alliances with none" that he delivered at his inaugural address on March 4, 1801.

Ron Paul has consistently embodied and legislated with this fundamental precept, guiding his every word and act for as long as anyone can remember during his entire career, both public and private.

There has never been a better analysis and breakdown of the term's *peace, commerce, honest friendship*, and *entangling alliances with none* than that appearing in Laurence M. Vance's "Jeffersonian Principles" dated September 1, 2004, and appearing at https://www.lewrockwell.com/2004/09/laurence-m-vance/peace-commerce-and-honest-friendship/.

This methodical breakdown, using quotations from Thomas Jefferson's and other notables of politics and literature, clearly reveals that the best candidate and who typifies the true and essential nature for US Secretary of State is none other than Ron Paul.

The Secretary of State, along with the Secretary of the Treasury, Secretary of Defense, and Attorney General are generally regarded as the four most important cabinet members because of the importance of their respective departments.

Secretary of State is a Level 1 position in the executive schedule and thus earns the salary prescribed for that level.

The current Secretary of State is 2004 presidential nominee and former Massachusetts Senator John Kerry, the sixty-eighth person to hold the office since its creation in 1789.

The specific duties of the Secretary of State include the following: (1) organizes and supervises the whole community United States Department of State and the United States Foreign Service; (2) advises the president on matters relating to US foreign policy, including the appointment of diplomatic representatives to other nations and on the acceptance or dismissal of representatives from other nations; (3) participates in high-level negotiations with other countries, either bilaterally or as part of an international conference or organization, or appoints representatives to do so (this includes the negotiation of international treaties and other agreements); (4) responsible for overall direction, coordination, and supervision of interdepartmental activities of the US government overseas; (5) providing information and services to US citizens living or traveling abroad, including providing credentials in the form of passports and visas;

(6) ensures the protection of the US government to American citizens, property, and interests in foreign countries; (7) supervises the United States immigration policy abroad; and (8) communicates issues relating the United States foreign policy to congress and to US citizens.

The original duties of the Secretary of State include some domestic duties, such as the following: (1) receipt, publication, distribution, and preservation of the laws of the United States; (2) preparation, sealing, and recording of the commissions of presidential appointees; (3) preparation and authentication of copies of records and authentication of copies under the department's seal; (4) custody of the Great Seal of the United States; and (5) custody of the records of the former secretary of the Continental Congress, except for those of the Treasury and War Departments.

As the highest-ranking member of the Cabinet, the Secretary of State is the third-highest official of the executive branch of the federal government of the United States, after the president and vice president and is fourth in line to succeed the presidency, coming after the vice president, the speaker of the House of Representatives, and the president *pro tempore* of the senate.

Six secretaries of State have gone on to be elected president.

Others, including John Kerry, William Seward, Henry Clay, and Hillary Clinton have been unsuccessful presidential candidates, either before or after their term of office as Secretary of State.

Former Secretaries of State retain the right to add the title secretary to their surnames.

As the head of the United States Foreign Service, the Secretary of State is responsible for management of the diplomatic service of the United States.

The Foreign Service employs about 12,000 people domestically and internationally, and supports 265 United States diplomatic missions around the world, including ambassadors to various nations.

The nature of the position means that Secretaries of State engage in travel around the world.

The record for most countries visited in a secretary's tenure is 112 by Hillary Clinton.

Second is Madeleine Albright with 96.

The record for most air miles traveled in a secretary's tenure is 1.06 million miles by John Kerry.

Second is Rice's 1.059 million miles, and third is Clinton's 956,733 miles.

When there is a vacancy in the office of Secretary of State, the duties are exercised either by another member of the Cabinet or, in more recent times, by a high-ranking official of the State Department until the president appoints, and the United States Senate confirms, a new secretary.

The *Washington Post* in an article by Philip Rucker (November 19, 2016) recently declared in one of their headlines located at https://www.washingtonpost.com/politics/trump-mulls-a-secretary-of-state-clone-crusader-stat esman-or-clean-slate/2016/11/18/59669270-acee-11e6-977a-1030f822fc35 _story.html: "Trump mulls a secretary of state: Clone, crusader, statesman or clean slate?"

Ironically enough, they throw around names such as Rudolph W. Giuliani, John Bolton, Nikki Haley, Mitt Romney, Bob Corker, but nowhere do they even mention the ultimate statesman, who meets all the classic requirements, as Ron Paul.

This should be of no surprise, considering that many would argue that the *Washington Post*, like the *New York Times*, is simply a mouthpiece of the neoconservative movement of aggressive, warmongering government style, beating, threatening, and intimidating other nations, countries, and foreign leaders into submission ("*Washington Post* Editorial Board Goes Full Neocon," by Spandan Chakrabarti of May 28, 2014, at http://www.thepeop lesview.net/main/2014/5/28/washington-post-goes-full-neocon or "The *Washington Post*: The Most Reckless Editorial Page in America" by James Carden and Jacob Heilbrunn of December 15, 2014, at http://nationalint erest.org/feature/the-washington-post-the-most-reckless-editorial-page-am erica -11857).

Ron Paul endorses constitutional rights, such as the right to keep and bear arms and *habeas corpus* for political detainees.

He opposes the Patriot Act, federal use of torture, presidential autonomy, a national identification card, warrantless domestic surveillance, and the draft.

Paul also believes that the notion of the separation of church and state is currently misused by the court system: "In case after case, the Supreme Court has used the infamous 'separation of church and state' metaphor to uphold court decisions that allow the federal government to intrude upon and deprive citizens of their religious liberty."

Sometime within the same month but much after the event of authorities executing a lockdown in sequence to the April 2013 Boston Marathon bombing, Paul commented on the tactics used by governing forces into a harsh criticism that he has written as a "military-style occupation of an American city."

It is time to return to the basics and foundations of what made this nation great, in line with President-Elect Donald Trump's vision, and this means returning to what the Founding Fathers truly meant when they created these Cabinet Positions in the first place. And what better way to start than by installing a man into this position of Secretary of State than Ron Paul, who literally embodies the spirit and essence of the man who first held the position—Thomas Jefferson himself.

CHAPTER 48

Upcoming War on Alternative Media
from Deep State Mainstream Media

This declaration of war was typified by Google and Facebook.

The mainstream media (MSM), fully owned and co- opted by the deep state plutocrat/oligarch elite, are extremely unhappy that Donald Trump won the 2016 election.

They did not bank on this and were completely and totally confident that their trillions of dollars of money issued by the Federal Reserve and international central banks, control of the National Security State as represented by the military-industrial complex and bought and paid for representatives in the US legislature (congress and senate), executive branch, and judiciary would have ensured their victory.

So, what turned this election around to upset the proverbial apple cart and deliver the presidency to Donald J. Trump?

Even the MSM has openly and formally admitted that it was the tireless and "round the clock" work of the alternative media, but instead of giving the millions of independent investigators, whistle-blowers, independent journalists, and other patriotic Americans who respect and fought for the First Amendment of the United States Constitution the respect that they deserve, instead they declared "war" on all of them this past week by announcing that they would block, filter, drown out, and crush them all, as being purveyors of fake news.

This declaration of war was typified by Google and Facebook, who then tried to claim that they were not media outlets, but rather search engines or social media sites with a responsibility to ensure that fake news does not infect the political process.

Even President Obama was apparently coerced into joining this "bullshit bandwagon," when he went around Europe this past week during his latest speech tour, telling the media that he too supported outlawing fake news while wiping away fake crocodile tears, because he "cares so much" about the American people.

When and how these gargantuan media behemoths took it upon themselves, and arrogated unto themselves this right, is beyond anyone's comprehension or understanding, but it most certainly belies the supreme and total arrogance, bullying, intimidation, and coercion of the deep state plutocrat/oligarch elite, and must be resisted with the peaceful and nonviolent full force, might, temerity, and aggression of all of America's 300 million citizenry, tooth and nail.

For this promise, announced by the deep state MSM, is an outright threat to the First Amendment, by a purely private and sprawling commercial entity, and is no less dangerous than the threat of removing any other of America's other hard-won and hard-fought for Amendments.

The reason that it is the "First" Amendment, is because the Founding Fathers probably believed that it was the most important of all of them.

Since the MSM is not considered a governmental body, it might be able to crush and destroy this First Amendment with impunity, as the First Amendment only truly applies to public legislation issued by a government sponsored entity-indeed the text of the edict states that "*Congress shall make no law respecting an establishment of religion, or prohibiting the free exercise thereof; or abridging the freedom of speech, or of the press; or the right of the people peaceably to assemble, and to petition the government for a redress of grievances.*"

But what happens when the MSM has openly, flagrantly, and clearly infiltrated, dominated and has become synonymous with, the United States government?

CHAPTER 49

The Hidden Communist History
of the Neoconservatives (Neocons)

Neoconservatism fully began to rear its ugly head in the 1990s when they thoroughly infiltrated the once patriotic and pro-America Republican Party, also known as neocons.

Now that organized Communism has been revealed, mainly since the fall of the USSR in the late 1980s / early 1990s, to be simply a very well-hidden mechanism of total social control by a small group of paranoid, megalomaniacal "control freaks," the people are waking up to realize that they really do not want to have every single aspect of their lives, their families, or their friends dominated, manipulated, harassed, intimidated, threatened, or micromanaged by a small cabal group of psychotic plutocratic warmongering freaks who consistently maintain one set of rules and morals for themselves and another set for others.

There is a reason why their favorite mantra for themselves is "Do what thou wilt" and "God is according to my right [*Deus Meumque Jus*]."

Now that the former Soviet Union is dead and defunct, replaced instead by a wholesome, healing, green, and reinstated Christian state by Vladimir Putin after his installation of Patriarch Kirill, the country is starting to resemble the true, heartfelt patriotism of its people as America enjoyed prior to World War II, where men and women lived and died believing in the ideals and cultural values of their country.

But the United States has instead switched places with the control freak mechanisms and social control of the former USSR, and even NAZI Germany, because the same miscreant international banksters, have abandoned their German and Russian projects to exclusively focus on the American Project, i.e., the once free, proud, healthy, and strong United States of America.

At the helm of this nightmarish and Frankenstein-like transformation of the USA into something more akin to the former USSR and/or NAZI Germany is the national security state / military-industrial complex, spearheaded by the deep state plutocrat/oligarch elite, using their most effective "useful idiot" agents, the neoconservative (neocon) movement.

Neocon Architects of Iraq War

Each and every single neocon is by nature un-American, antithetical to personal freedom, addicted to stupid foreign wars and destroying foreign national sovereignty, obsessed with global Communist control of the world's people and resources, inherently anti-family or national borders, pro-central banker federal reserve *fiat* (paper) currency as opposed to gold or precious commodity backed currency, maniacally controlling all forms of the major media to brainwash Americans into their way of thinking, obsessed with remaining at the top and crushing under their boot-heels, everyone else not lucky or sociopathic enough to be in their club.

Each and every person and entity within their midst are simply a means to an end, and if their servants step out of line, they retaliate and destroy you with willful abandon using other "useful idiots," movements, entities, and agencies at their disposal and control in a "divide and conquer" mechanism and scenario.

The neoconservatives are also directly behind the new movement by the mainstream media to seek out and destroy all remaining free alternative media outlets in their campaign to go after fake news, i.e., media not controlled and dominated by the Communist movement found at http://www.veteransne wsnow.com/2016/11/19/the-upcoming-war-on-the-alternative-media-by-t he-deep- state-mainstream-media/).

Perhaps a "list" needs to be created of all active neoconservatives both within the government and without, just as they have done with their list of "fake news" websites, which clearly and transparently serve their own needs and attempt to quash their enemies and exposers, wherein they have tried to paint any media outlet which is anti-war, America-First, anti-neocon, and pro-human rights as a "Russian Propaganda" website. See http://www.zero hedge.com/news/2016-11-25/washington-post-names-drudge-zero-hedge-anti-clinton-sophisticated-russian-propaganda.

The super-compartmentalization of one group being positioned against another is completely and totally unknown and alien to those being manipulated, and sadly, these divided actors/nations/entities will kill each other off and won't even realize that they've been used and "had" for decades, if not centuries.

Neoconservatism fully began to rear its ugly head in the 1990s when they thoroughly infiltrated the once- patriotic and pro-America Republican Party.

They are the true Manchurian candidates of the modern age.

Their favorite modus operandi is to fund and support "useful idiot" protected classes in order to do their dirty work by turning them on their enemies and detractors with character assassination, labeling their targets as anti-Semites, misogynists, racists, or homophobes.

See http://www.paulcraigroberts.org/2016/11/11/the-anti- also trump-protesters-are-tools-of-the-oligarchy-paul-craig-roberts/and http://www.ve teransnewsnow.com/2016/08/29/deep- state-plutocrat-elite-use-protected-classes-to-do-their- dirty-work/.

The neocons are also behind the movement to disarm the people of the United States by destroying the Second Amendment in their agenda to ultimately arrest, incarcerate, and remove from society any and all Americans who resist their Communist takeover of the United States.

From its Socialist origins in the 1950s, the anti- Stalinist (Trotskyites) movement adopted the rhetoric of the anti-Communist in order to create a new paradigm that was more palatable to the American public.

It is already well-established that the neocons began with the Trotskyist Communists.

The United States of America has always been historically staunchly anti-Communist/Socialist, with such favorite catch phrases in the 1950s such as **"Better dead than red**," but what happens when the Trojan Horse of Communism appears from within the most conservative force in America itself, i.e., the Republican Party?

The Neocon founders included James Burnham, Max Shactman, Leo Strauss, Suzanne LaFollette, Willmoore Kendall, and Irving Kristol (father of Fox News pundit Bill Kristol).

All of them came from Communist (Trotskyist) backgrounds.

It is therefore incumbent upon each and every single patriotic American who cares about the future of their country (especially federal, state, and local law enforcement and prosecutor offices) to immediately begin to identify, isolate, marginalize, investigate, indict, arrest, prosecute, and incarcerate all neoconservatives as an internal and national security threat to the welfare of the United States of America.

CHAPTER 50

Dr. Paul Craig Roberts Is Former
Treasury Secretary Who Actually Cares

Another thing Donald Trump and Dr. Paul Craig Roberts have in common— they are both former "insiders" who turned against the Establishment.

H ere's an idea—how about appointing a US Treasury Secretary who actually *cares* for the ultimate welfare of the American people and the United States of America for a change, as opposed to using his position as a "revolving door" à la the cadre of treasonous "America-last" gaggle of premeditated criminals merely taking a leave of absence from their full-time jobs at Goldman Sachs and Covington & Burling LLP?

The American economy and its engineered 2008 crash wrought by such "financial luminaries" as Robert Rubin, Larry Summers, Gene Sperling, Hank Paulson, Tim Geithner, and others has left a lasting effect if not almost the total destruction of the American Economy.

Much has been written about how the above cabal literally, beginning with when they were working under the Bill Clinton presidency, forced and coerced Mr. Clinton to repeal the Glass-Steagall Act, which was the barrier separating risky investment bank behavior from "mom and pop" checking accounts and savings, thus essentially imbuing these massive financial institutions to proceed unfettered toward the shark-infested waters of bad deals, risky investments, speculative spending, and other crazy financial stunts, for "high-risk/high-yield" pyramid and Ponzi schemes more akin to a night at a seedy Las Vegas casino rather than what should supposedly have been judicious, well-planned, and risk- averse behavior on behalf of these banking behemoths.

Simultaneously, these same organized criminals used the Housing and Urban Development (HUD) headed up by then Chief Andrew Cuomo to put enormous pressure on such loan entities as Fannie Mae and Freddie Mac to lower and reduce the credit requirements to purchase a million-dollar home so that every burger flipper across America could buy a financial and un-payable "albatross" around their neck, and when the Federal Reserve eventually removed cash liquidity from the markets, all these new "homeowners" literally found themselves on a merry-go-round that suddenly stopped with their monthly mortgage payments coming due but no jobs or cash to pay them, thus resulting in tens of millions of massive housing defaults across the country.

Even more sickeningly, Goldman Sachs and others only a few years earlier created a "reverse credit swap derivative," betting on the ultimate failure within the housing market, again earning countless billions when this inevitable "housing bubble" burst.

Are these the same kind of people we want back in the United States Treasury engineering our "economic recovery"?

These bankers, unfettered by the protections guaranteed by Glass-Steagall, could feel confident that even if their bad investments went completely and totally south, they would eventually be bailed out by none other than the American taxpayer—and that's exactly what happened.

But what about a former assistant US Treasury Secretary, who previously was appointed by and served under one of the greatest US Presidents of all time, Ronald Reagan, and who was actually instrumental in pulling America out of the quagmire of idiotic and out of control government spending, a lazy un-stimulated economy, and the general malaise of the 1970s "disco economy" manned and presided over by Democrat President Jimmy Carter?

That individual is none other than the great Dr. Paul Craig Roberts, hero to the 300 million strong American people, personal mentor to hundreds of thousands, and demonstrated enemy of the oligarchy/plutocracy deep state elite, the latter of whom have been shown the proverbial "door" by the American people in their overwhelming support of President-Elect Donald J. Trump.

The American people were able to hoist Donald Trump to the presidency even in the face of the overwhelming "cheating mechanisms" of the deep state oligarch elite with their complete and total brainwashing control of the mainstream media, the awesome buying power of the international bankers, the co-opting of the vast majority of our legislative (senate and congress)/judiciary/executive branches, the "black bag/covert operations/color revolutions" of deep state *agent provocateurs*, such as George Soros, who previously used to only direct his regime change operations against foreign governments rather than fomenting "purple" revolutions here at home.

Dr. Paul Craig Roberts has been critical of the United States Department of the Treasury and the US financial regulatory authorities—particularly of the actions of the Federal Reserve System—from former Chairmen Alan

Greenspan and Ben Bernanke's terms to current Chairwoman Janet Yellen via quantitative easing policies and low interest rates, the latter of which he has argued (due to his view that official government data is biased) are actually negative interest rates.

One only has to peruse the countless and brilliantly incisive books and articles penned by Dr. Paul Craig Roberts over the past few decades, and especially within the past few years, freely available on the internet and in hard book format, to clearly and easily discern just what this man stands for, what his expertise is, how much he loves the United States of America, how much he values peace and the avoidance of "stupid foreign wars," his support, hope for, and measured loyalty to the incoming Donald Trump administration (for Trump, "loyalty is key"), his overall and general distrust for the US government and the awesome power it yields, his suspicion over the latest *du jour* "terrorist attacks" all over the world which he, as do the vast majority of Americans, believe are nothing but "false flags" designed to keep Americans and the rest of the global populace afraid and compliant, ever ready to sacrifice and unyieldingly relinquish even more of their God-given human rights, civil liberties, and constitutional protections for the sake of "state-sanctioned security" from the fabricated "boogeymen" of the Western/Saudi/Israeli/Turkish Intelligence Services known as ISIS or Al Qaeda.

His written works have also addressed and criticized outsourcing, economic deregulation, privatization of social services, Wall Street finance fraud and lax enforcement of environmental protection laws, as well as been a vocal opponent of taxing social-security payments, holding that this amounts to a "tax on a tax" or privatizing social-security believing this would create an opportunity for speculators to play with and lose the hard-earned savings of retirees.

There could be no better ally of the American people (and the Donald Trump administration) within the United States Treasury than Dr. Paul Craig Roberts, as he would be "our man within the US Treasury," and would take control and design the much-anticipated economic recovery so badly needed by the citizenry.

He has already done it before, successfully, under the Reagan administration, and he could easily and handily do it again under Trump.

Dr. Paul Craig Roberts was born on April 3, 1939, and is oftentimes described as an American economist, journalist, blogger, and former civil servant.

He reached the height of his government career when he became the United States Assistant Secretary of the Treasury for Economic Policy under President Reagan in 1981.

In office, he and his staff successfully combated the stagflation (price-inflation and stagnation) then plaguing the American economy.

Tighter monetary policy was used to restrain inflation, in addition lower marginal tax rates were used to increase the rewards to work and investment.

In recognition, he was awarded the US Treasury's Meritorious Service Award for "outstanding contributions to the formulation of United States economic policy."

Dr. Paul Craig Roberts has also been a huge supporter of common human decency, both in the United States and abroad.

As a supporter of the human rights of the population of the West Bank, he has criticized Israel's policies and harsh actions against the Palestinians as well as speaking out against what he calls the Israel Lobby's malign influence within US politics and academia.

Dr. Roberts is a graduate of the Georgia Institute of Technology (BS in industrial engineering) and holds a PhD from the University of Virginia.

He was a postgraduate at the University of California, Berkeley, and at Merton College, Oxford University.

From 1975 to 1978, Roberts served on congressional staff. As economic counsel to Congressman Jack Kemp, he drafted the Kemp-Roth Bill (which became the Economic Recovery Tax Act of 1981). He played a leading role in developing bipartisan support for a supply-side economic policy.

Due to his influential 1978 article on tax burden for *Harper's Magazine* while economic counsel to Senator Orrin Hatch, the *Wall Street Journal* editor Robert L. Bartley offered him an editorial slot.

He wrote for the *WSJ* until 1980.

He was a senior fellow in political economy at the Center for Strategic and International Studies, then part of Georgetown University.

From early 1981 to January 1982, Roberts served as assistant secretary of the treasury for economic policy, wherein President Ronald Reagan and Treasury Secretary Donald Regan credited him with a major role in the Economic Recovery Tax Act of 1981, and he was awarded the Treasury Department's Meritorious Service Award for "outstanding contributions to the formulation of United States economic policy."

After his time in government, he turned to journalism, holding positions of editor and columnist for the *Wall Street Journal*, columnist for *Business Week*, and the Scripps Howard News Service as well as contributing editor to *Harper's Magazine*.

In addition to numerous guest and visiting- professorships at US universities, he was professor of business administration and professor of economics at George Mason University and was the inaugural William E. Simon, chair in political economy at Georgetown University, serving for twelve years.

From 1993 to 1996, he was a distinguished fellow at the Cato Institute.

He also was a senior research fellow at the Hoover Institution.

This is another thing Donald Trump and Dr. Paul Craig Roberts have in common—they are both former "insiders" who turned against the establishment as an overwhelming gesture of heroic self-sacrifice to the American people rather than continuing to "play the game" in order to keep enriching their own pockets at the expense of the American people and the United States.

Dr. Roberts also has the great love and respect of foreign nations, governments, and dignitaries as did other previous and legendary US government / statesmen luminaries in centuries past, as Benjamin Franklin and Thomas Jefferson. In 1987 the French government recognized him as "the artisan of a renewal in economic science and policy after half a century of state interventionism," and inducted him into the Legion of Honor on March 20, 1987.

The French minister of economics and finance, Edouard Balladur, came to the US from France to present the medal to Roberts.

In 1992, Roberts received the Warren Brookes Award for Excellence in Journalism from the free-market American Legislative Exchange Council (ALEC).

In 1993 the Forbes Media Guide ranked him as one of the top seven journalists in the United States.

In 2015, the Mexican Press Club awarded Dr. Roberts its International Award for Excellence in Journalism in recognition of his lifelong commitment to truth and unbiased-reporting in exposing the inner workings of the global economic power-structure.

Dr. Paul Craig Roberts has written that "true conservatives" were the "first victims" of the neocons of the Bush administration.

He has criticized the Bush tax cuts, believing they "were nothing but a greedy grab" and were "not necessary policy adjustments but rewards to the mega- rich who underwrite political careers and provide grants to economic departments and think tanks," however, also stating that "they are not a significant cause of today's inequality."

Of the 9/11 Commission Report, Dr. Paul Craig Roberts wrote in 2006, "One would think that if the report could stand analysis, there would not be a taboo against calling attention to the inadequacy of its explanations."

He has asserted there is a large "energy deficit" in the official account of the collapse of the three WTC buildings, and this deficit remains unexplained.

This is yet another, out of thousands, of common ground similarities currently shared by President-Elect Donald Trump and Dr. Roberts—truly a government partnership/marriage made in heaven.

Roberts commented on the "scientific impossibility" of the official explanation for the events on 9/11, as did Donald Trump in a television interview when the Towers first went down in 2001.

On August 18, 2006, he wrote: "I will begin by stating what we know to be a solid incontrovertible scientific fact. We know that it is strictly impossible for any building, much less steel columned buildings, to 'pancake' at free fall speed. Therefore, it is a non- controversial fact that the official explanation of the collapse of the WTC buildings is false Since the damning incontrovertible fact has not been investigated, speculation and 'conspiracy theories' have filled the void."

He has written or co-written twelve books, contributed chapters to numerous books, and published many articles in scholarly journals.

Dr. Paul Craig Roberts, like President-Elect Donald Trump, has ultimate intestinal fortitude, as is evident by his countless papers, treatises, books, and articles, where he demonstrates an all-American fearlessness coupled with ingenuity, brilliance, common sense, and stalwartness, totally absent in our treasury departments over the past few decades.

President-Elect Donald Trump should give due consideration and thought to Dr. Paul Craig Roberts to be US Secretary of the Treasury, a living legend who is truly a testament to everything that is, and always has been, great about America.

CHAPTER 51

US Intelligence Community and
President-Elect Donald Trump Needs Philip Giraldi

If Donald Trump truly wants to "drain the swamp," and "make America great again," then perhaps he should start with ensuring that his daily intelligence briefings are honest, forthright, devoid of political bias, neutral, impartial, informative, and ultimately helpful to both him and the legislative branch in order to make the difficult foreign policy decisions during the Trump presidential administration.

There's something to be said for nominating a Central Intelligence Agency (CIA) director who actually knows and understands how to do their job—that is, honestly and truthfully collecting, disseminating, and analyzing intelligence.

For far too long, the position of CIA director has been like nearly every other executive-appointed or cabinet member position within the US government—just another popularity or political contest no different than choosing teammates in a grade-school kickball team or invitees to a Hamptons Party by the elitists of New York City.

This may be the exact same reason that the US government is failing on so many fronts—the wrong people are sitting in the wrong jobs and have either no idea what they are doing or are so heavily politicized and "owned" by certain special interests, lobbying groups, or foreign governments that they literally are unable or unwilling to do what is best for the American people and the United States of America.

One such case example is the eminent Philip Giraldi, who has a collective experience in the CIA spanning over eighteen years.

Israel to Get Biggest US Aid
Package in History: A Good Idea?

He is consistently a voice of sanity and reason, as is his colleague Ray McGovern, but has been consistently shut out, marginalized, driven out, and "disinvited" from all of the "intelligence parties" going on in Washington DC.

He is probably one of the most qualified, down-to- earth, matter-of-fact, no-nonsense career intelligence officers this country has ever had, but no one is throwing his name around as either an intelligence director or even as a "consultant" to the intelligence community in any of the sixteen intelligence agencies within the US government.

Instead, career politicians, neoconservative loyalists, "America-lasters," co-opted bureaucrats, ex-lobbyists, and bankster-owned stooges are consistently hoisted into these intelligence director and leadership positions, who routinely and without fail have either suppressed relevant intelligence so desperately needed by the congress and senate to pass legislation or navigate foreign affairs and conflict, or have outright misconstrued or lied about foreign intelligence in order to achieve "outcome determinative" goals of the banking and corporate oligarchy/plutocracy, bombing and killing and murdering millions of innocent people in the process, destroying viable and independent peaceful nation states around the world, assassinating duly elected foreign leaders who stand in the way of American oligarchy hegemony, and other sick and twisted outcomes.

Philip Giraldi was born in 1946 and is a former counterterrorism specialist and military intelligence officer of the CIA as well as a columnist and television commentator who is the executive director of the Council for the National Interest, a group that advocates for more even-handed policies by the US government in the Middle East.

He received a bachelor of arts with honors from the University of Chicago and a MA and a PhD from the University of London in European history.

Giraldi was employed by the CIA for eighteen years, working in Turkey, Italy, Germany, and Spain and is fluent in Turkish, Italian, German, and Spanish. Since 1992 Giraldi has consulted for several Fortune 500 corporate clients. He is the president of San Marco International, an international security management and risk assessment consulting firm and a partner in Cannistraro Associates, another security consultancy. Giraldi has written columns on terrorism, intelligence, and security issues for the American Conservative magazine, the *Huffington Post*, and Antiwar.com and op-ed pieces for the *Hearst Newspaper* chain.

He has been interviewed by *Good Morning America*, *60 Minutes*, MSNBC, Fox News Channel, National Public Radio, the Canadian Broadcasting Corporation, the British Broadcasting Corporation, al-Jazeera, al-Arabiya, *Iran Daily, Russia Today, Veterans Today, Press T*, and other media outlets. During the 2008 presidential primaries, Giraldi served as a foreign policy adviser to Ron Paul.

His writings always consistently cut through the mainstream media nonsense being propagated by the plutocratic deep state, a topic of which he has also written extensively about, based on his intelligence experience in Turkey, where the proverbial deep state was an integral and cultural way of life, consisting of, in Phil Giraldi's words, as "including all the obvious parties, both public and private, who benefit from the status quo: including key players in the police and intelligence agencies, the military, the treasury and justice departments, and the judiciary."

See "Deep State America" found at http://www.theamericanconservative .com/articles/deep- state-america/.

In 2004, Giraldi, with his partner Vincent Cannistraro, a retired CIA counterterrorism chief, wrote that Turkish sources had reported that Turkey was concerned by Israel's alleged encouragement of Kurdish ambitions to create an independent state and that Israeli intelligence operations in the area included anti-Syrian and anti- Iranian activity by Kurds. They predicted this might lead to a new alliance among Iran, Syria, and Turkey, which have Kurdish minorities.

In August 2005, Giraldi wrote that US Vice President Dick Cheney had instructed STRATCOM to prepare "a contingency plan to be employed in response to another 9/11-type terrorist attack on the United States including a large-scale air assault on Iran employing both conventional and tactical nuclear weapons not ... conditional on Iran actually being involved in the act of terrorism directed against the United States." The reason cited for the attack to use mini-nukes is that the targets are hardened or are deep underground and would not be destroyed by non-nuclear warheads.

The neoconservative impulse became visible in modern American foreign policy since Reagan but became dominant ideology and foreign policy practice during George W. Bush administration, which hijacked US Foreign policy and unleashed the disastrous Iraq War.

In 2005, Giraldi also wrote that the Italian Niger/yellowcake documents claiming an Iraqi interest in purchasing uranium from Niger were forgeries created by former CIA officers and Michael Ledeen. Giraldi also wrote that officials in the Office of Special Plans working for Undersecretary of Defense for Policy Douglas Feith had forged the Habbush letter allegedly written by Saddam Hussein's intelligence director regarding shipping the uranium.

In 2009, Giraldi wrote that unnamed intelligence sources had told him that a document published by *The Times*, which allegedly described an Iranian plan to experiment on a "neutron initiator" for an atomic weapon, was in fact a fabrication, which Giraldi speculated was created by the state of Israel. He claimed that Rupert Murdoch publications regularly published false intelligence from the Israeli and sometimes the British government. Further disclosures by *The Times* undermined the document's veracity.

The underlying theme and thread of all these revelations by Phil Giraldi underscores one glaring bright truth—that Mr. Giraldi has consistently, courageously, heroically, and patriotically always chosen to expose the truth and provide intelligence that serves the interests of the American people and the United States of America rather than the corporate/bankster plutocratic deep state elite.

This may be the essential reason Phil Giraldi has been consistently passed over for the credit and positions within the US Intelligence Community for nominations to essential national security positions for nearly every single presidential administration since he left the CIA.

Hopefully President-Elect Donald Trump will recognize this, and choose or ask Mr. Giraldi to serve in some capacity, as this man is a national treasure and living legend who could only strengthen and fortify US intelligence work, as well as begin to heal the open bloody wounds of decades of stupid foreign policy decisions and idiotic wars typified by the Neoconservative and previous establishment decisions and positions over the past few decades.

If Donald Trump truly wants to drain the swamp and make America great again, then perhaps he should start with ensuring that his daily intelligence briefings are honest, forthright, devoid of political bias, neutral, impartial, informative, and ultimately helpful to both him and the legislative branch in order to make the difficult foreign policy decisions during the Trump presidential administration.

Recently, Phil Giraldi has spent a great deal of his time in his capacity as a founding member of the Veteran Intelligence Professionals for Sanity (VIPS), which is a think tank made up of former intelligence officers dedicated to upholding the virtues of true intelligence work and analysis, offering countercurrent views often at odds with establishment plutocratic deep state outcome determinative intelligence and again is designed to serve the American people and the United States rather than the corporate/bankster oligarchs.

His work is all over the internet and in print, and he often appears in the *Unz Review* online journal, and his articles are always instrumental in helping to elucidate and crystallize the truth in a wilderness of dishonesty and falsities churned out by the mainstream media and their handlers within the US intelligence community.

In September 2015, Giraldi and twenty-seven other members of VIPS steering group wrote a letter to the president challenging a recently published book that claimed to rebut the report of the US Senate Intelligence Committee on the Central Intelligence Agency's use of torture.

In August, 2010 Giraldi wrote that unnamed "sources in the counterintelligence community" had told him that agents of Israel's Mossad intelligence agency were posing as American intelligence agents and visiting Arabs and Muslims in New York and New Jersey. This was allegedly done to help agents gain information about Iran, which they believed would not be forthcoming to known Israeli agents.

True to what must be habit, Phil Giraldi "does not tweet, and avoids all [except Facebook] social media."

CHAPTER 52

Deluge of American Crime Dramas
Acclimatizes Americans to Police State

Few, if any, Americans remember the pre- World War II days when freedom was rampant, and people actually believed, lived, fought, and died for their own independence, inalienable human rights, guarantees, and civil liberties. constitutional

One does not have to be a rocket science to deduce that it feels that 90 percent of the television shows being broadcast on the American mainstream media television/movie/cable networks consist of an avalanche of gritty crime dramas and, in the last decade or so, have become exceedingly technical in nature, lionizing police officers, detectives, special victims unit officers, prosecutors and others, charged with investigating, indicting, arresting, and incarcerating Americans from all walks of life.

But there is an agenda at work here—as part of the national security state / military-industrial complex of the United States, which first began to lay its tracks after World War II after the US began to accept *en masse* hordes of card-carrying NAZIs from Germany and other sympathetic nations, and immediately set to work conditioning and "cattle-herding" Americans from all walks of life into accepting the reality that they were now living in a technocratic police state, constantly under surveillance, and one step away from the "hoosgow" at any given moment, at any time, so they better stay in line.

On a daily basis, Americans are inundated on nearly all the major channels on their television sets, thanks to reruns, spinoffs, syndicated licenses, and other mechanisms, disturbing and threatening shows like *Law and Order* and its many spinoffs therein such as *Special Victims Unit and Criminal Intent, CSI, NCIS, The Blacklist, True Detective, Gotham, Criminal Minds*, and scores of others ever since the broadcast of the show *Dragnet* appearing from 1951 to 1959.

A truly astounding list of American police crime dramas can be found here at https://en.wikipedia.org/wiki/List_of_police_television_dr amas.

This is obviously being done by the deep state plutocrat elite to condition and acclimatize Americans to the perceived reality that they want them to not only accept, for ease of their control, but also to "enjoy their captivity," with highly entertaining, edge-of-your-seat plot structures, and highly attractive actors with sympathetic character traits so that in some sort of sick Stockholm syndrome methodology, we begin to fall in love with our captors/oppressors.

This mechanism is highly successful in large part because Americans as a rule remain willfully ignorant and blind to this brainwashing by the American mainstream media.

The message is clear—Americans are more akin to a "rat in a cage," susceptible at any time to stop and frisks unlawful surveillance, pretexted criminal arrests and harassment, hanging on by a thread, organized gang-stalking masquerading as "community-oriented policing," and to be able to be marginalized and cut out of society at the drop of a hat, if anyone within the national security state / military-industrial complex is so inclined.

These television shows glorify complete and total abuses of American civil and constitutional rights by "jack booted thugs," who always seem to be very attractive but tortured souls who are trying to do good, but in reality they are no different than any common criminal seeking to arbitrarily deprive you of your life, liberty, property, and pursuit of happiness.

And your anxiety while watching the television shows is expected to give rise to reluctant but willing acceptance rather than outrage at the blatant propaganda and enslavement being thrust in your face.

The message in these American crime dramas is essentially this: "You have no rights, and any rights that you currently enjoy are dispensed at the pleasure and discretion of the deep state oligarchical elite and can be removed from you within a moment's notice at any time that they want."

Lavrenty Beria, former chief of secret police in Jozef Stalin's Soviet police state used to openly brag: "Show me the man, and I will show you the crime."

Markus Wolf, originator and chief of East Germany's Stasi police state, also subscribed to this ideology but took it one step further when he developed the *Zersetzung* methodology of policing, incorporating organized gang-stalking and the recruitment of the targeted individual's family, friends, colleagues, fellow employees, neighbors, and any others similarly situated to jointly drive their intended target to madness, suicide, or incarceration.

Few, if any, Americans remember the pre-World War II days when freedom was rampant, and people actually believed, lived, fought, and died for their own independence, inalienable human rights, constitutional guarantees, and civil liberties.

The beacons of light and warning as to the changing and metastasizing transformation of America into the technocratic police state of today are few and far between, and some are getting older and more suppressed by the American national security / police state, such as legendary statesman former Texas Congressman Ron Paul and his contemporary, the heroic John Whitehead of the Rutherford Institute.

As the younger generation in America gets older and enters adulthood, their conditioning has been complete—they are no longer even able to break out of their mind-controlled way of thinking and even entertain the notion that they are somehow living in a "prison planet" devoid of any stable and God-given rights whatsoever.

Therefore, it is incumbent upon all Americans to see and view their oppressors in the naked and bright sunlight and truly acknowledge the condition that they are in and recognize that the major media and the 24/7 crime drama show television garbage that they purvey is truly part and parcel of their enslavement and disenfranchisement in order to become better controlled and ruled by their deep state plutocrat masters.

CHAPTER 53

John W. Whitehead Should
Be US Homeland Security Director

John W. Whitehead has been described as "this nation's Paul Revere of protecting civil liberties."

John W. Whitehead is a constitutional attorney and author and founder and president of the Rutherford Institute.

Mostly everyone in America has a sinking feeling that the US Department of Homeland Security (DHS) has gone way too far in trampling the civil liberties of average citizens, further augmenting and increasing the police state already stamped on the books with then President Bill Clinton and then Senator Joseph Biden's community-oriented policing (COPS) program, which was enacted as part of their draconian Violent Crime Control and Law Enforcement Act of 1994 (the Clinton Crime Bill or VCCLEA), which led to the mass incarceration of 1/3 of all blacks, 1/6 of all Latinos, and 1/10 of all whites since 1994, resulting in 70 million Americans with criminal records (one out of every three adults), greater than the population of France.

So there is a dire need for an individual who has made a living studying and critiquing the American police state in order to correct and recalibrate it, if not completely dismantle and replace it—sort of like President-Elect Donald Trump's appointment of Tom Price as head of the Department of Health and Human Services (DHHS), an avowed critic of the Affordable Care Act (Obamacare) in order to, at the very least, iron out and fix the myriad problems with the program.

Tom Price fine pick to head DHHS in new Donald Trump administration.

Or we can even point to Donald Trump's appointment of Jeff Miller, retired chairman of the House Veterans Affairs Committee, to run Veterans Affairs, who is also a fierce critic of that agency.

Therefore, it would make perfect sense to consider Mr. Whitehead (constitutional attorney and author John W. Whitehead is founder and president of The Rutherford Institute) whose seminal book *Battlefield America: The War on the American People* is an extraordinary treatise, in-depth study, and detailed analysis of just what went wrong with the hasty enactment of the DHS after the suspicious circumstances of September 11, 2001.

This book was a follow up to his award-winning book *A Government of Wolves: The Emerging American Police State*, which also set out the problems facing America due to the overreaching and increasing militant-style force that has become the American police state.

According to Amazon Books, John W. Whitehead "paints a terrifying portrait of a nation at war with itself and which is on the verge of undermining the basic freedoms guaranteed to the citizenry in the Constitution. Indeed, police have been transformed into extensions of the military, towns and cities have become battlefields, and the American people have been turned into enemy combatants, to be spied on, tracked, scanned, frisked, searched, subjected to all manner of intrusions, intimidated, invaded, raided, manhandled, censored, silenced, shot at, locked up, and denied due process.

"Yet this police state did not come about overnight. As Whitehead notes, this shift into totalitarianism cannot be traced back to a single individual or event. Rather, the evolution has been so subtle that most American citizens were hardly even aware of it taking place (like the 'boiling frog' analogy). Yet little by little, police authority expanded, one weapon after another was added to the police arsenal, and one exception after another was made to the standards that have historically restrained police authority. Add to this mix the merger of Internet mega corporations with government intelligence agencies, and you have the making of an electronic concentration camp that not only sees the citizenry as databits but will attempt to control every aspect of their lives. And if someone dares to step out of line, they will most likely find an armed SWAT team at their door."

John Whitehead describes the predicament facing America in the following manner:

"A government which will turn its tanks upon its people, for any reason, is a government with a taste of blood and a thirst for power and must either be smartly rebuked, or blindly obeyed in deadly fear" (John Salter).

We have entered into a particularly dismal chapter in the American narrative, one that shifts us from a swashbuckling tale of adventure into a bone-chilling horror story "We the people" have now come full circle, from being held captive by the British police state to being held captive by the

American police state. In between, we have charted a course from revolutionaries fighting for our independence and a free people establishing a new nation to pioneers and explorers, braving the wilderness and expanding into new territories Where we went wrong, however, was in ... allowing ourselves to become enthralled with and then held hostage by a military empire in bondage to a corporate state (the very definition of fascism). No longer would America hold the moral high ground as a champion of freedom and human rights. Instead, in the pursuit of profit, our overlords succumbed to greed, took pleasure in inflicting pain, exported torture, and imported the machinery of war, transforming the American landscape into a battlefield, complete with military personnel, tactics and weaponry to our dismay, we now find ourselves scrambling for a foothold as our once rock-solid constitutional foundation crumbles beneath us. And no longer can we rely on the president, Congress, the courts, or the police to protect us from wrongdoing Indeed, they have come to embody all that is wrong with America... "We the people" are being hijacked on the highway by government agents with little knowledge of or regard for the Constitution, who are hyped up on the power of their badge, outfitted for war, eager for combat, and taking a joy ride—on taxpayer time and money—in a military tank that has no business being on American soil... Rest assured, unless we slam on the brakes, this runaway tank will soon be charting a new course through terrain that bears no resemblance to land of our forefathers, where freedom meant more than just the freedom to exist and consume what the corporate powers dish out.

The Rutherford Institute is a nonprofit organization based in Charlottesville, Virginia, and dedicated to the defense of civil liberties and human rights.

The organization was founded in 1982 by John W. Whitehead, who continued to be its president as of 2015 and offers free legal services to those who have had their rights threatened or violated and has a network of affiliate attorneys across the United States and funds its efforts through donations.

In addition to its offer of legal services, the organization offers free educational materials for those interested in the US Constitution and Bill of Rights.

The Rutherford Institute also publishes a weekly commentary by Whitehead that is published in hundreds of newspapers and web publications, including the *Huffington Post* and LewRockwell.com.

The institute has been described as "a more conservative American Civil Liberties Union" (ACLU).

John Whitehead has been described by jazz historian and civil libertarian Nat Hentoff as "this nation's Paul Revere of protecting civil liberties."

The Rutherford Institute was named after Samuel Rutherford, a seventeenth-century theologian who wrote a book *Lex, Rex,* which challenged the concept of the divine right of kings.

When the Rutherford Institute was founded, conservative Protestants in the United States were reconsidering their role in American political and legal life, perceiving that the federal government was intent on encroaching on Americans' religious liberties.

Organizations such as the Rutherford Institute pursued matters of religious liberties in the courts, and the Rutherford Institute became the model for groups such as the National Legal Foundation, the Liberty Counsel, and the American Center for Law and Justice.

So, there is absolutely no question that President- Elect Donald Trump should either appoint John W. Whitehead as DHS director, or regularly consult with him on a rigorous basis in order to help steer the ship of state known as the United States of America back to calmer, smoother constitutional waters.

CHAPTER 54

What's Wrong with Pursuing Peace?

Diplomacy is always the best option, and warfare should be the last choice.

"Is it really necessary to say that one can recognize Trump's good points [see above] without becoming a partisan shill?" (Justin Raimondo).

To all the warmongers, foreign interventionists, rabid neocons, members of the military-industrial complex (MIC), armchair warriors, chickenhawks, and prepubescent boys still playing war games with their Xbox, the only question is, "What is wrong with pursuing global peace?"

Why is the United States of America being led around by the nose by the worst that this country has to offer in terms of naked aggression and hostility, clandestine operations designed to destabilize and destroy every other nation around us (friends and enemies alike), dumping trillions of dollars in hard-earned tax dollars from the US citizenry into useless stupid foreign wars and paramilitary operations, borrowing money into oblivion and enslaving the future of our children from the perpetual fiat currency printing Federal Reserve, churning out bunker buster bombs and TOW missiles by the hundreds of thousands, using billions of tons of precious steel which could be used to build bridges, hospitals, and schools in order to continue to wreak havoc around the globe?

If the last eight years of the President Obama administration has taught us one thing, it is that the United States of America has countless internecine problems, issues and imperfections that we need to take care of and iron out first, before we go around policing and lecturing the rest of the world on how they should live.

Barack Obama was like an exfoliate that brought out hundreds of years of anger, festering emotion, class warfare, and stifled expression that truly needed to be aired out once and for all and not further suppressed.

Obama Thanks Putin for Russia's Role in Iran Nuclear Deal

Additionally, for all of Obama's faults and missteps in the Middle East (mainly because of the erroneous and politically motivated and "foreign government paid for advice" of his thoroughly corrupted Secretary of State

Hillary Clinton and her "mini-me" Victoria "Cookies" Nuland), one of his greatest legacies was by either inadvertently or on purpose, avoiding and stopping World War III by enacting the Iran Nuclear Deal, by getting them to disarm without firing a single shot and by proxy allowing the rise of a multi-polar world wherein different countries, cultures, religions and races could now have a seat at the bargaining table of global affairs rather than simply the legacy of the colonial masters of yesterday, which by and large exploited the Third and Second Worlds in every capacity.

BRICS Nations, 2015

A perfect symbol of this was the rise of the BRICS (Brazil, Russia, India, China, South Africa) banking system, which poses an open challenge to the hegemony of the IMF / World Bank, ushering in healthy competition among global central banks to keep each other more honest and competitive in terms of loans and project finance to the world's people and countries.

Had the masters of chaos succeeded in getting President Obama to carpet-bomb Iran, this would most certainly have led to World War III by forcing Russia, China, Syria, Turkey, Saudi Arabia, Yemen, and other nations to jump into the fray to protect and defend their interests, quickly escalating matters coupled with multiple terrorist attacks all throughout the Middle East, Europe, and yes, even in America.

Diplomacy is always the best option, and warfare should be the last choice.

Neoconed Architects of Endless "Regime Change" Wars

But we as a nation have been too gung ho and obsessed with destroying other nations and their own sovereignty.

The United States should instead fix all its problems at home, such as joblessness, poverty, malnutrition, failing infrastructure, poor race relations, corrupt courts and government, broken families, poor educational standards, a $23-trillion-dollar debt, and other systematic problems and issues, perhaps use all of its reserves to heal America first and first use diplomacy and negotiation to solve any and all problems overseas.

The doctrine of foreign intervention "blowback" has yielded great disasters such as September 11.

The routine and constant violations of the "entangling alliances with other nations" doctrine as per Thomas Jefferson has destroyed our civil liberties and constitutional guarantees at home, while earning us myriad enemies abroad.

Live and let live.

Now that Donald Trump is president-elect, the USA can devote more time to building up America first rather than selling out the nation and its birthright to the highest bidder. Trump promises to increase jobs, straighten out Obamacare, rebuild infrastructure, pull out of stupid foreign wars, deal decisively with enemies, recalibrate the Middle East and relationships overseas, deal with the Federal Reserve and the $23-trillion-dollar debt, simplify extreme over-legislation and over-regulation, and other tasks necessary to make America great again.

CHAPTER 55

American People Must Hold Mainstream Media to Account

Why can't RICO charges (or civil lawsuits) be brought against the 6 heads of the major mainstream enterprise? media-organized criminal

One thing that the events of this latest political election have taught the American people is that the mainstream media has virtually no real credibility anymore and are essentially working for the deep state plutocratic elite, fully owned and co-opted by the central bankers of the City of London and other foreign nations/entities/individuals, with absolutely no loyalty to the people to provide them with real news that does not support their own agenda and self-enrichment.

Since 90 percent of American media is controlled by only 6 corporations, it is unfortunately now time for a new civil, legal, equitable, and non-violent American revolutionary war, this time dedicated to holding the CEOs of the 6 major mainstream media conglomerates to account with non-violent revolution.

This means that the people should rise up and begin to file lawsuits, left and right, against individual and corporate entities that make up the mainstream media for a whole series and litany of civil (as well as criminal) causes of action.

For example, we all now know that the US government, through the CIA's Operation Mockingbird, is an unconstitutional program developed to target and brainwash average Americans into supporting stupid foreign wars, getting tens of millions of people unnecessarily killed, spending US taxpayer dollars to the tune of $23 trillion in debt, and aiding and abetting major international and domestic criminal conspiracies and plots (such as the engineered financial crisis of 2008) by either refusing to report on them or outright lying to the American people by covering them up.

Here's the graphic:

Frugal Dad

From a criminal perspective, the mainstream American media, led by their CEOs, are at once guilty of treason, acting on behalf of (favored) foreign entities and governments (Foreign Agents Registration Act) and violating the Racketeering Organizations (RICO) Act. Influenced Corrupt

Treason

To avoid the abuses of the English law, treason was specifically defined in the US Constitution, the only crime so defined.

Article III, section 3 reads as follows, "Treason against the United States, shall consist only in levying War against them, or in adhering to their Enemies, giving them Aid and Comfort. No Person shall be convicted of Treason unless on the Testimony of two Witnesses to the same overt Act, or on Confession in open Court."

The United States Code at 18 USC § 2381 states, "Whoever, owing allegiance to the United States, levies war against them or adheres to their enemies, giving them aid and comfort within the United States or elsewhere, is guilty of treason and shall suffer death, or shall be imprisoned not less than five years and fined under this title but not less than $10,000; and shall be incapable of holding any office under the United States."

There is no question that the six major mainstream media conglomerates are owned and beholden to the international central banks which are by and large non-American actors and are instead sovereign foreign-based entities headquartered in the United Kingdom, specifically in the City of London and with other foreign nations/entities/individuals.

Foreign Agents Registration Act

The Foreign Agents Registration Act (FARA) is a United States law (22 USC § 611 et seq.), passed in 1938, requiring that agents representing the interests of foreign powers in a "political or quasi-political capacity" disclose their relationship with the foreign government and information about related activities and finances.

The purpose is to facilitate "evaluation by the government and the American people of the statements and activities of such persons."

The law is administered by the FARA registration unit of the Counterespionage Section (CES) in the National Security Division (NSD) of the United States Department of Justice.

For the same reasons as described above, the CEOS of the above-referenced 6 major media companies need to be criminally investigated, indicted, charged, arrested, prosecuted, and incarcerated as such.

They are just as dangerous and subversive as any of their foreign central bankers, the City of London, and other foreign nations/entities/individual masters.

The Act originally was administered by the Department of State until transferred to the Department of Justice in 1942.

From its passage in 1938 until 1966 when the Act was amended, enforcement focused on propagandists for foreign powers (in this case the City of London international central bankers and other foreign nations/entities/individuals), even if it was not "for or on behalf of those powers.

It was used in twenty-three criminal cases during World War II.

For cases not warranting prosecution, the Department of Justice sent letters advising prospective agents of the law.

In 1966 the Act was amended and narrowed to emphasize agents actually working with foreign powers who sought economic or political advantage by influencing governmental decision-making.

The amendments shifted the focus of the law from propaganda to political lobbying and narrowed the meaning of "foreign agent."

From that moment on, an organization (or person) could only be placed in the FARA database if the government proved that it (or he or she) was acting "at the order, request, or under the direction or control, of a foreign principal" and proved that it (or he or she) was engaged "in political activities for or in the interests of such foreign principal," by "representing the interests of such foreign principal before any agency or official of the government of the United States."

This increased the government's burden of proof. Since 1966, there have been no successful criminal prosecutions under the FARA Act.

However, a civil injunctive remedy also was added to allow the Department of Justice to warn individuals and entities of possible violations of the Act, ensuring more voluntary compliance but also making it clear when the law has been violated.

This has resulted in a number of successful civil cases and administrative resolutions since that time.

The Act requires periodic disclosure of all activities and finances by (1) people and organizations that are under control of a foreign government, of organizations, or of persons outside of the United States (foreign principal); (2) if they act "at the order, request, or under the direction or control" of this principal (i.e., as agents) or of persons who are "controlled or subsidized in major part" by this principal.

"I am sometimes asked if I have any regrets about publishing our book. As of today, my only regret is that it is not being published now. After the humiliations that Obama has endured at the hands of the Israel lobby and the Hagel circus, we would sell even more copies and we would not face nearly as much ill-informed criticism" (Stephen Walt, co-author of the book).

Organizations under such foreign control can include political agents, public relations counsel, publicity agents, information-service employees, political consultants, fundraisers, or those who represent the foreign power before any agency or official of the United States government.

The law **includes** news or press services owned by a foreign principal.

To that end, if any one of the 6 major media corporations has foreign owners or any relationships with the international foreign central bankers based out of the City of London and other foreign nations/entities/individuals, they are at once guilty of violating this Act.

Racketeering Influenced Corrupt Organizations (RICO) Act

The Racketeer Influenced and Corrupt Organizations Act, commonly referred to as the RICO Act or simply RICO, is a US federal law that provides for extended criminal penalties and a civil cause of action for acts performed as part of an ongoing criminal organization.

The RICO Act focuses specifically on racketeering, and it allows the leaders of a syndicate to be tried for the crimes which they ordered others to do or assisted them in doing, closing a perceived loophole that allowed a person who instructed someone else to, for example, murder, to be exempt from the trial because he did not actually commit the crime personally.

RICO was enacted by section 901(a) of the Organized Crime Control Act of 1970 (Public Law 91- 452, 84 Stat. 922, enacted October 15, 1970) and is codified at 18 USC ch. 96 as 18 USC §§ 1961-1968.

Racketeering businessman

G. Robert Blakey, an adviser to the United States Senate government Operations Committee, drafted the law under the close supervision of the committee's chairman, Senator John Little McClellan.

It was enacted as Title IX of the Organized Crime Control Act of 1970 and signed into law by Richard M. Nixon.

While its original use in the 1970s was to prosecute the mafia as well as others who were actively engaged in organized crime, its later application has been more widespread.

Beginning in 1972, thirty-three states adopted state RICO laws to be able to prosecute similar conduct.

Under RICO, a person who has committed "at least two acts of racketeering activity" drawn from a list of thirty-five crimes—twenty-seven federal crimes and eight state crimes—within a ten-year period can be charged with racketeering if such acts are related in one of four specified ways to an "enterprise."

Those found guilty of racketeering can be fined up to $250,000 and sentenced to twenty years in prison per racketeering count.

In addition, the racketeer must forfeit all ill-gotten gains and interest in any business gained through a pattern of "racketeering activity."

When the US Attorney decides to indict someone under RICO, he or she has the option of seeking a pretrial restraining order or injunction to temporarily seize a defendant's assets and prevent the transfer of potentially forfeitable property, as well as require the defendant to put up a performance bond.

This provision was placed in the law because the owners of mafia-related shell corporations often absconded with the assets.

An injunction and/or performance bond ensures that there is something to seize in the event of a guilty verdict.

Despite its harsh provisions, a RICO-related charge is considered easy to prove in court, as it focuses on patterns of behavior as opposed to criminal acts.

RICO also permits a private individual "damaged in his business or property" by a "racketeer" to file a civil suit.

The plaintiff must prove the existence of an "enterprise."

The defendant(s) are not the enterprise; in other words, the defendant(s) and the enterprise are not one and the same.

There must be one of four specified relationships between the defendant(s) and the enterprise: either the defendant(s) invested the proceeds of the pattern of racketeering activity into the enterprise (18 USC § 1962(a)); or the defendant(s) acquired or maintained an interest in, or control of, the enterprise through the pattern of racketeering activity (subsection (b)); or the defendant(s) conducted or participated in the affairs of the enterprise "through" the pattern of racketeering activity (subsection (c)); or the defendant(s) conspired to do one of the above (subsection (d)).

In essence, the enterprise is either the "prize," "instrument," "victim," or "perpetrator" of the racketeers.

A civil RICO action can be filed in either state or federal court.

Both the criminal and civil components allow the recovery of treble damages (damages in triple the amount of actual/compensatory damages).

Initially, prosecutors were skeptical of using RICO mainly because it was unproven.

However, during the 1980s and 1990s, federal prosecutors used the law to bring charges against several mafia figures.

The first major success was the Mafia Commission Trial, which resulted in several top leaders of New York City's Five Families getting what amounted to life sentences.

By the turn of the century, RICO cases resulted in virtually all of the top leaders of the New York mafia being sent to prison.

So why can't RICO charges (or civil lawsuits) be brought against the 6 heads of the major mainstream media-organized criminal enterprise?

Examples of required predicate criminal acts include bribery, extortion, fraud, obstruction of justice, racketeering, money laundering, or copyright infringement.

Although some of the most often used RICO predicate criminal acts are extortion and blackmail, one of the most successful applications of the RICO laws has been the ability to indict and or sanction individuals for their behavior and actions committed against witnesses and victims in alleged retaliation or retribution for cooperating with federal or state law enforcement or intelligence agencies.

It is well known that the mainstream media routinely engages in the above-described criminal acts, especially retaliation (defamation/slander/libel for example) when their targets don't tow the political line as issued by the City of London central bankers and other foreign nations/individuals /entities.

Just think of what happened to President-Elect Donald Trump by these six major mainstream media organizations simply because the central bankers of the City of London and other foreign nations/individuals/entities did not like him, or want him to win the election.

This is not even to mention the various and exclusively civil causes of action that the American people could collectively or individually bring against CEOs and various members of the mainstream media, such as defamation, libel, slander, tortious interference with contract, breach of fiduciary duty, breach of the duty of loyalty, unfair trade practices, false advertising, unlawful trespass, civil RICO, unjust enrichment, intentional infliction of emotional distress, negligent infliction of emotional distress, trademark infringement, copyright infringement, and myriad other purely civil claims, both federal and state.

The cases against the six major mainstream media corporation CEOs should involve the Federal Bureau of Investigation (FBI), the US Department of Justice (USDOJ), the US Department of State (USDOS), the Central Intelligence Agency (CIA), the Federal Trade Commission (FTC), the Federal Communications Commission (FCC), the Department of Homeland Security (DHS), the National Security Agency (NSA), and other agencies— but the only problem is that it appears that all of these "alphabet agencies" are, at the top, run by individuals who are also literally co-opted, bought off, and paid for by the same enemies of the American people the international central bankers of the City of London and other foreign nations/entities/ individuals.

Until and unless these linkages are more formally exposed and the relationships uncovered, the American people (and the rest of the world) will be hard-pressed to ever obtain any justice or release from the earthly and hellish bondage of the six CEO members of the mainstream media, mafia-organized criminal enterprise.

CHAPTER 56

Call to Develop Alternative Social Media
and Search Engine Platform Competitors (That Aren't Evil)

The successful election of President-Elect Donald Trump has proven this great and voracious demand from the people, all over the world.

I t appears that the major search engine and social media platforms have either succumbed to (or are in the process of succumbing) to the awesome monetary and political power of the deep state, plutocratic/oligarchic elite, in that they are either on their own or under the pressure of others engaging in a massive, wholesale, frontal attack on freedom of speech, censorship of views/opinions that they don't like, terminating accounts of those that the deep state deem to be antithetical to their interests, and overall, undermining democracy, freedom of speech and expression, competition, and undercutting legitimate debate and discourse.

This is why it is now vitally important that all socially conscious and anti-globalist/deep state, independent-thinking technical experts and finance/hedge fund owners start to work together in order to immediately start cross-pollinating, creating, funding, and marketing alternative social media and search engine platform websites to compete with the likes of Google, Facebook, and Twitter, amongst other thoroughly corrupted media platforms.

The essential theme of all successful business throughout history has always been the age-old mantra of "supply and demand."

Well, there is no greater demand in America and the rest of the world than open, free, and alternative search engine/social media website platforms that are not taking their marching orders and political censorship edicts from the deep state, as well as from other deep-pocket, obscenely wealthy, domestic and foreign nations/entities/individuals.

The successful election of President-Elect Donald Trump has proven this great and voracious demand from the people all over the world.

New search engine and social media platforms need to remember and ensure that their chief line of business should be the wholesale accountability to the people that they serve and the people alone, and not to the selfish, greedy, and violent needs of the oligarchs.

And at any time, if search engine and social media platforms start to sell out and kiss the proverbial "ring" of these oligarchs by throwing their own customers under the bus, then the people need to take notice and look elsewhere.

This is a formal call to develop alternative search engine and social media platforms.

CHAPTER 57

Israeli Penetration of US Media

The first step in fixing a problem is to acknowledge that it exists.

Much has been written over the past few weeks about how, allegedly, the Russian government has penetrated the American media in order to tell their side of the story and to counter the steady diet of anti-Russian propaganda by the thoroughly corrupted and co-opted US mainstream media by the neoconservatives, warmongers, and military-industrial complex in order to brainwash and motivate average Americans into hating Russia and to support clandestine and overt military and paramilitary operations against Russia and their interests overseas.

The American Mainstream Media (MSM) has been steadily beating the drum against Russia while vilifying Vladimir Putin in order to justify neoconservative incursions into that sovereign country, as well as undermine their relationships overseas and subjugate their entire country.

This type of media script is also pushing the United States dangerously close to World War III by constantly provoking and poking the Russian bear, aided and abetted by NATO who is constantly pushing its troops, military, tanks, missiles and other hardware right up to the border of Russia in an increasingly menacing and hostile manner.

"I am sometimes asked if I have any regrets about publishing our book. As of today, my only regret is that it is not being published now. After the humiliations that Obama has endured at the hands of the Israel lobby and the Hagel circus, we would sell even more copies, and we would not face nearly as much ill-informed criticism" (Stephen Walt, co-author of the book).

But next to nothing has been researched or written about the long-standing, ongoing, decades-long penetration of the US mainstream media by Israel and its vested spies within the US government.

In fact, many would argue that the neoconservative movement is simply a front group for Israel and has thoroughly and openly taken over and corrupted the US government in its legislative, executive, and judicial branches.

The US government, through its incredibly corrupted congress and senate, just swept through legislation outlawing "Russian propaganda" within the alternative media, but completely ignored Israeli, British, Qatari, Saudi Arabian, and other foreign national funding, support, and penetration of the MSM in America.

The double standards are glaring and obvious.

President-Elect Donald Trump was a major recipient of this Israeli-owned media abuse by their relentless, 24/7 attacks on him and his candidacy using their useful idiot-protected classes, also funded by them, consisting of hardcore militant feminist, homosexual, black, and Zionist groups to gather around and accuse him of being a misogynist, homophobe, racist, or anti-Semitic, all simply because Donald Trump is an "America-firster" and is against the oligarchy in America running the roost.

The Israeli-Zionist media character assassination of President-Elect Donald Trump was carried out in the exact same manner by the same exact people who have ruthlessly and aggressively targeted Russian President Vladimir Putin, and so clearly these forces are not only anti-Russian, but also anti-American.

To that end, as was explained in a previous article (http://www.veteran snewsnow.com/2016/12/03/the-american-people-must-hold-the-mainstream-media-to-account/), the US actors involved are all at once guilty of treason, violations of the Foreign Corrupt Practices Act, RICO, and the Foreign Agents Registration Act.

The US FBI and DHS are not doing anything about this is because they are obviously being told to "stand down," or their leaders have been thoroughly co-opted and corrupted by the Israeli government.

How the Israeli-Zionist Benjamin Netanyah received his "speech of a lifetime" standing ovations by his obedient Marionettes in the US Congress.

The first step in fixing a problem is to acknowledge that it exists. — Americans must put daily financial, logistical, telephone/email/fax pressure on each and every one of their elected representatives in the senate, congress, and local council, as well as the thoroughly corrupted and co-opted Federal Bureau of Investigation, to immediately and summarily "clean house" and terminate any and all links of Israeli influence in the United States mainstream media.

CHAPTER 58

Betrayal of People of India

People have rightfully called Narendra Modi and his act totally "demonic."

Any simpleton can make the obvious deduction that the job of government is **not** to take the people's gold, cash, material possessions, private wealth, tangible goods, and real property away from them to be deposited into the government's coffers so that they can be freely intermingled with the personal piggy bank accounts of the country's oligarchs and central bankers, two flip sides of the same coin as we are also seeing here in the United States more than ever over the past few decades.

So when Indian Prime Minister Narendra Modi decided a few weeks ago to issue executive orders ordering small cash denominations and gold holdings by India's massive middle class and poor to become a criminal offense and that they be turned over to the government, he has now effectively and openly declared war on India's huge and burgeoning middle class, one of the largest of any nation in the world, wherein the people fuel their economy through buying/spending, nurturing a rich and vibrant economy thereon.

Narendra Modi simply declared that anyone possessing five hundred- or one-thousand-rupee notes had to turn them in for new bills before December 31, 2016, and afterwards the money is worthless.

The problem is that Narendra Modi is only letting people replace a maximum of 4,500 rupees of notes for cash.

Anything more than that has to be deposited, thus forcing people to either pay taxes or render their private savings (some for countless generations) absolutely worthless.

Even more egregiously and as a fundamental deprivation of the inalienable human rights and civil liberties of the people, anyone retaining 250,000 rupees (approximately $3,500) will be criminally prosecuted.

Narendra Modi, by this criminal act, has only proven the ultimate conspiracy theory that he is in fact an agent of the international oligarchy/ plutocracy deep state, and is their "man in India" of the international central bankers, who want to be the only ones who actually enjoy tangible wealth rather than worthless fiat paper currency whose value can be instantly decimated or increased with a stroke of a pen or the tap of a computer keyboard on some central banker's laptop.

According to ZeroHedge, "After declaring large denomination notes illegal, India now targets gold ... It's not just gold bars or bullion. The government has raided houses, no questions asked, and confiscating jewelry" (http://www.zerohedge.com/news/2016-12-07/india-   confiscates-gold-even-jewelry-raids-hidden-money).

Unfortunately, the vast majority of India's poor are either too uneducated, disorganized, disunited, or too powerless to do anything about this massive and organized criminal conspiracy against them. If this were to occur in the United States, for example, there can be no doubt that the American people would not tolerate these acts by the unholy trinity of their oligarchs, corrupted leaders, and central bankers.

Although Franklin Delano Roosevelt (FDR) did engage in this type of wholesale theft from the American people with his gold seizure Executive Order 6102 signed on April 5, 1933, "forbidding the 'hoarding' of gold coin, gold bullion, and gold certificates within the continental United States," the effect of which was to criminalize the possession of monetary gold by any individual, partnership, association, or corporation.

But FDR was able to successfully hoodwink the American people, who at the time, were much more innocent and pliable, by his hiding behind "American patriotism" during a time of war (World War II) and also because he was trying to deceive the American people into thinking that this was the only remedy to combat the burgeoning Great Depression, which was completely and totally wrought on purpose by the newly formed Federal Reserve Bank enacted in 1913, but which the American people had not yet figured out at the time was neither "federal" nor a "reserve," but was in fact a completely and privately owned family business, emanating out of London under the Rothschild Banking Cartel, and FDR was their American agent in the White House.

As noted, Economist Jim Rickards has remarked, "The global elites are using negative interest rates and inflation to make your money disappear... The whole idea of the war on cash is to force savers into digital bank accounts so that their money can be taken from them in the form of negative interest rates."

So, to that end, armed with all of this history and hindsight, Narendra Modi has revealed himself to be the devil incarnate with this act. He is robbing the poor to give to the rich, which is the ultimate definition of evil.

This is an extremely dismal and disappointing development by a man who was touted as the "savior" and economic "liberalizer" of India, but has in fact revealed himself to be nothing but a tool of the oligarchs/plutocrats, placed into power in order to loot his own people and destroy his own country's middle class to drive them further into poverty, austerity, death, and destruction (just like Germany's Angela Merkel, USA's Barack Obama, UK's David Cameron, Italy's Matteo Renzi, and others recently being pushed out of office by the people in their awakening to their wholesale rape and pillaging by the oligarchy, now very much international in nature).

The traitor Narendra Modi overnight made approximately 85 percent of India's entire currency completely and totally worthless, causing the middle class and the poor to take to begging in the streets, gas stations, and stores to fill their car tanks, or to even buy food.

People have rightfully called Narendra Modi and his act totally "demonic."

Modi has defended his criminal behavior by stating that he wanted to root out corruption and get rid of hidden money within the Indian economy, but in reality this is exactly what constitutes private wealth vested within the middle class and the poor, who use it on a daily basis to live, survive, buy food and goods, and literally sustain their vibrant and private growth fueled economy, which is literally the lifeblood force of the Indian middle class and its economy, which Modi has now effectively killed on behalf of his plutocratic paymasters.

Six hundred million of India's poor and uneducated don't even have a bank account, and three hundred million people don't even have government identification, so this is also a type of "bird tagging" operation in order to eradicate personal freedom, as well as being a mass confiscation of "mom and pop money" being hidden under their mattress for a rainy day and away from the big bad wolves of government corruption, thieving oligarchs, and other organized criminal figures.

The hypocritical and deceptive Modi ran on a "minimum government, maximum governance" election platform, and this is how he has treated his people.

Some of the catastrophic results of Narendra Modi's ultimate betrayal are already in, and they involve the following:

1. Daily wage laborers haven't been paid due to the currency shortage.
2. People are only eating one meal a day.
3. Farmers and vendors can't sell their produce due to lack of cash to buy them with.
4. Produce has been ruined due to being spoiled.
5. Small businesses can't operate without cash and are therefore going bankrupt.
6. Massive deaths have been reported as a direct result of Narendra Modi's treachery.

Meanwhile Narendra Modi continues to enjoy wearing his $16,000 suits—a true "man of the people."

CHAPTER 59

Are the Neocons Dispatching Assassins?

The proverbial "jig" is finally up.

Having failed miserably in their global campaigns to unilaterally, in an unprovoked fashion, destroy, subjugate, and undermine the Ukraine and Russia, also using their proxy paramilitary force ISIS against Syria and other bordering Middle Eastern nations with their concurrent campaigns using proxy state Saudi Arabia against Yemen, and NATO against Libya coming under closer scrutiny and fire from heroic members of the US Congress and Senate- Led by patriotic and honest "America-Firsters" Rand Paul, Tulsi Gabbard, Chris Murphy, Ted Lieu and Trey Gowdy.

The neoconservatives appear to be frantically scaling the walls within the Pentagon, Intelligence Community, halls of the legislature, think-tanks, mainstream media outlets, and other US government/NGO/private enclaves, grasping at straws and throwing "Parthian shots" more akin to the temper tantrums of a child than a well-organized and amply financed intellectual force to be reckoned with.

Perhaps in their latest "Samson Option-type" acts and behavior, it appears that they may very well be behind the latest spate of targeted assassinations all over the world, but mainly focusing on high-level Russians in their own homes (Petr Polshikov), on the streets of Moscow (Boris Nemtsov), in art exhibits in Turkey (Andrey Karlov), and in hotels in Washington DC (Mikhail Lesin).

Whoever is carrying out these assassinations is either doing this out of blind frustrated rage, or trying to make it look like someone else's.

But the greatest lesson of "real-politik" and international conflicts should always begin and end with the Latin phrase "Cui Bono," i.e., "Who Benefits."

Now with the confirmed election of neocon hater President-Elect Donald Trump, it appears that the neoconservative movement's fate is sealed in each and every segment of the US government in which they have burrowed themselves like termites or maggots, whatever disgusting vermin insect appellation of choice.

So simply by the process of first grade-level deduction, it is easy to show that right now, the only victors after a hard- fought series of years-long battles on the battlefield, media, and in politics, are the Russians under President Vladimir Putin and the "America-firsters" under US President-Elect Donald Trump, and the vast majority of global humanity supporting them that are all unanimously welcoming a new chapter and epoch of peace and prosperity in the future of the global community.

Men of the Century-Putin and Trump

Underneath the protective and inspirational wings of Vladimir Putin and Donald Trump are nestled the vast majority of global humanity that care about their futures, their children, their jobs, their freedom, the avoidance of World War III, and their plot of earth that they like to call home.

This would probably be 99 percent of humanity.

So, who is not happy? Who represents the 1 percent of global humanity? Who is not happy with the outcome of the last few months/years of recent geopolitical developments? Who would literally kill to get even?

One does not have to be a brain surgeon to figure this out in only a few minutes.

This small, embittered, embattled, and spiteful minority of the global community are the only ones who would ruin a perfectly good global party of hope, prosperity, and optimism for the future, and they are all completely and totally controlled by the neoconservative movement in the United States, which has previously been described to be the intellectual, political, media, financial, and "armchair warrior-face" of the deep state, plutocratic/ oligarchic, global elite.

See previous articles as to the etiology and origin of these parasitic neoconservatives at http://www.veteransnewsnow.com/2016/11/26/the-hidden-communist-history-of-the-conservatives-neo-cons/.

So now that these neocons have also lost control of the mainstream media narrative, with their recent embarrassments chronicled and detailed in the war by and between the mainstream (MSM) and alternative media, with accusations and allegations of "fake news" being hurled and bandied about like pissed-off monkeys throwing their own feces (See http://www.veterans newsnow.com/2016/11/19/the-upcoming-war-on-the-alternative-media-by -the-deep-state-mainstream-media/), with the MSM emerging as the true loser as the vast majority of the world has awakened to the fact that they are just "arms" of the London central bankers and their foreign nation-state, family, or individual lackeys, the proverbial "jig" is finally up (http://www.veteransnewsnow.com/2016/12/03/the-american-people-must-hold-the-mainstream-media-to-account/).

Therefore, like any other spoiled brat armed to the teeth with jacked-up, private security and mercenaries, state-of-the-art military hardware and technology, layers and layers of secret societies dispensing orders from up on high like any other mafia/organized crime family, and under the "color of law and authority" of the US or other allied foreign government, these recent targeted assassinations by well-trained and connected "insiders" are no doubt being dispatched, like "Sith warriors," to the far corners of the globe in order to kill off their enemies in a retaliatory and bitter fashion.

It is too obvious a joke.

The quick, ad hoc assembling of high-level Russian intelligence operatives and government employees by Vladimir Putin to determine the exact perpetrators/planners/organizers of these latest assassinations is obviously being done for window dressing and also to vet any last-minute arguments against a finding against these neocon/deep state perps, but everyone (including Putin) must be pretty certain about who these culprits truly are.

And so, it goes. Now that the lid has been lifted off of Pandora's box with these recent targeted and unprovoked assassinations of innocent Russian diplomats, intelligence officers, ambassadors, and private citizens, expect the great "Jedi/Sith" targeted individual assassinations to continue on throughout the world, as this global conflict has now been reduced to veritable provocation "mob hits" by and between the neocons and the rest of the civilized world. The odds are glaringly against the neocons.

The neocons were never known for their long-term planning or ability to be accurate or successful in their strategies or predictions in the past fifty years, so why would they start now?

CHAPTER 60

President Barack Obama
Brings Balance Back to the Force

He has, in one single swoop, restored honor, dignity, and justice
to the long-suffering Palestinians.

I n a heroic gesture of complete and total decisive power, President
Barack Obama has restored balance to the Force and order to the
Universe.

He has, in one single swoop, restored honor, dignity, and justice to the
long-suffering Palestinians, while smiting down the evil perpetrated by the
ultra-extreme Zionist Israelis since 1967.

By engineering the United Nations Security Resolution 2334, reiterating
its demand that Israel immediately and completely cease all settlement
activities in the occupied Palestinian territory including East Jerusalem,
President Obama has rectified a long-existent evil.

The vote resulted to fourteen in favor of the resolution, with one
abstention (United States).

The Security Council reaffirmed that Israel's establishment of settlements
in Palestinian territory since the former's occupation of the former, including
East Jerusalem, in 1967 had no legal validity and constituted a flagrant
violation under international law and a major obstacle to the vision of two
states living side-by-side in peace and security within internationally
recognized borders, and a just, lasting, and comprehensive peace.

"The resolution is a significant step demonstrating the Council's much
needed leadership and the international community's collective efforts to
reconfirm that the vision of two states is still achievable," the UN chief's
spokesperson said in a statement.

"The Secretary-General takes this opportunity to encourage Israeli and
Palestinian leaders to work with the international community to create a
conducive environment for a return to meaningful negotiations," the
spokesperson added. "The United Nations stands ready to support all
concerned parties in achieving this goal."

The fifteen-member Council adopted the resolution by a vote of fourteen
in favor and one abstention. The United States abstained from the vote. The

resolution had been put forward by Malaysia, New Zealand, Senegal, and Venezuela.

In the resolution, the Council reiterated its demand that Israel "immediately and completely cease all settlement activities in the occupied Palestinian territory, including East Jerusalem, and that it fully respect all of its legal obligations in this regard."

The Council also underlined that it will not recognize any changes to the June 4, 1967, lines, including with regard to Jerusalem, other than those agreed by the parties through negotiations.

The resolution called for immediate steps to prevent all acts of violence against civilians, including acts of terror, as well as all acts of provocation and destruction, and promote accountability in that regard, as well as for both parties to act on the basis of international law, including international humanitarian law, and previous agreements and obligations, "to observe calm and restraint, and to refrain from provocative actions, incitement, and inflammatory rhetoric."

It further called for compliance with obligations under international law for the strengthening of ongoing efforts to combat terrorism, through existing security coordination, and to clearly condemn all acts of terrorism.

The Council also urged for intensification and acceleration of international and regional diplomatic efforts, and for support aimed at achieving, without delay, a comprehensive, just, and lasting peace in the Middle East on the basis of the relevant United Nations resolutions, the Madrid terms of reference, including the principle of land for peace, the Arab Peace Initiative and the Quartet Roadmap, and an end to the Israeli occupation that began in 1967.

Coupled with Barack Obama's brokering of the Iran nuclear deal, thereby preventing World War III, he has reinstated the international balance of power to keep nations honest, with respect for one another, with no one nation being able to trample over or steamroll anyone else.

CHAPTER 61

FBI Doesn't Care about Government Corruption

This is a secret society club, and you ain't in it.

T he reason the Federal Bureau of Investigation (FBI) doesn't care about governmental corruption (judicial, executive, and legislative) is because they are also in fact, completely and totally corrupt.

It appears that their main job is to protect the wealthy elite, deep state oligarchs/plutocrats while nailing to the wall free thinkers, political dissidents, patriots, soft targets, opponents of the oligarch elite, and other real or imagined targets.

The FBI has been caught engineering false terrorism arrests (http://www.veteranstoday.com/2013/02/19/fbi-terrorism-and-the-false-flag-war/), unlawfully surveilling and harassing innocent (https://www.aclu.org/other/more-about-fbi-spying), Americans developing and using "informants" who are actually arch-criminals themselves (http://www.usa today.com/story/news/nation/2013/08/04/fbi-informant-crimes-report/2613305/), and otherwise creating problems that don't exist in order to justify their annual federal budget.

Before 1975 when the Frank Church Senate Hearings outlawed this corruption, they did this under the aegis of the COINTELPRO program. After 1994 they have been doing this under the Bill Clinton/Joe Biden Community Oriented Policing (COPS) program.

See http://www.veteransnewsnow.com/2016/08/21/the- surreptitious-reincarnation-of-cointelpro-with-the-cops-gang- stalking-program/.

This should come as no surprise, since the FBI was founded by legendary cross dresser and alleged pedophile J Edgar Hoover (http://abcnews.go.com/Health/edgar-hoover-sex-men-homosexual/story?id=14948447), who was a high- level Freemason and Shriner (http://srjarchives.tripod.com/1997-05/deloach.htm) whose links can be connected to the grand pedophiles haunting London's national security apparatus GCHQ and other freaky masonic lodges scattered throughout the world (http://www.express.co.uk/news/uk/579523/Paedophile-Mason-lodge-GCHQ).

This is a secret society club, and you ain't in it.

Legendary FBI whistle-blower Ted Gunderson, who literally ran the FBI in several different jurisdictions throughout the United States, complained bitterly about how he was stifled and his investigations routinely "shit-canned" whenever he got close to the very real and underground satanic pedophile networks and other organized crime creeps that were being protected and covered up by the wealthy oligarchic/plutocratic powers that be (http://www.veteranstoday.com/2015/04/23/the-strange-case-of-ted-gunderson/), and many suspect that he was murdered surreptitiously for daring to go on the lecture circuit to announce his findings (https://white wraithe.wordpress.com/2012/01/28/ted-l-gunderson-ex-fbi-whistleblower-poisoned/).

Long-time NYPD Detective Jim Rothstein, assigned for more than forty years to a special investigative unit investigating, amongst other things, child prostitution/trafficking/pedophile networks, recently only last month did an interview wherein he echoed the same sentiments; that whenever he got too close to the source or origin of these satanic child molesters, he was routinely told to "back off" or "stand down," or face career destruction or even worse (https://www.youtube.com/watch?v=5cnT5amf6Ys).

This is apparently how the elite keep each other from talking, from divulging their secrets, or keep each other from testifying against one another.

When are we, the American people, going to demand that our lousy, dishonest Congress and Senate drag these criminals in front of them to conduct in-depth investigations on the FBI, members of the corrupt judiciary, and others "on the take" within the American government?

After all, the American people are the ultimate arbiters of justice. We should be faxing/emailing/texting/calling our representatives, incessantly demanding that they take investigative action immediately.

There are no doubt scores and countless numbers of patriotic, courageous, and heroic FBI Special Agents roaming the halls of all jurisdictions within this entity throughout the United States, but it appears that these "beat cops" are literally kept out of the loop and away from the levers of power by their higher ups, director, and special agents in charge within all of the various field offices because these "leaders" are also part and parcel of this same criminally corrupt, oligarchic/plutocratic power structure, going to the same parties, hanging out at the same clubs, making financial deals with one another, and otherwise covering up for the crimes and misdemeanors of their cronies in exchange for gifts, benefits, sweetheart deals, money, sex, drugs, and other types of bribes and coercions.

Since FBI whistleblowers have until recently had the worst protections for a government agency (https://www.rt.com/usa/369682-house-bill-protect-fbi-whistleblowers/), secrecy and retaliation are cultural problems within the FBI and many patriotic agents probably wonder what they were thinking by signing up for such a disgustingly corrupt and incompetent agency in the first place.

CHAPTER 62

Deep State Control of the American Courts and Judiciary

> Revolutionize the courts. It will not happen if the American people don't care or are apathetic about all of this.

C orrupt judges systematically provide advantages to those who have given them money and power, while they more often than not ignore the human rights, civil liberties, and constitutional rights of those who seek justice for acts of wrongdoing committed against them.

Not much attention has been paid to the insidious and hidden deep state plutocratic/oligarchic control of the US courts and its corresponding judiciary, whether state, federal, or local.

Perhaps it was inevitable, but the straying away from the US Constitution over the past 225 years or so has been so gradual and so muted that it has been almost impossible to recognize when the schisms occurred and when the greatest violations of the vision of the founding fathers actually happened.

Various events in American history, to be sure, have certainly "fast-tracked" the American court system and its judiciary away from the US Constitution, usually emanating out of fear-based legislation and ad hoc clandestine thief-in-the-night enactments, such as the events of the Oklahoma City bombing which ushered in the DOJ/FBI's resurgence of the COINTELPRO program outlawed in 1975 after the Frank Church hearings but reinstated by the 1995 Bill Clinton/Joe Biden Community Oriented Policing (COPS) gang- stalking/STASI program, or the obvious events of 9/11 which reinstated the CIA's mass assassination/propaganda/ MKULTRA program after its curtailing also by the Church senate hearings, or even relating to the creation of the Federal Reserve central banking system in 1913, which literally was surreptitiously passed on Christmas Eve in 1913 when 99 percent of the Congress and Senate were at home with their families for the holidays.

Many long-term surviving judges have reported that the Constitution intended that only elected lawmakers be permitted to create law, yet federal and state judges routinely and daily create their own law in the judicial system based on their own activism, personal opinions, corruption, bribery, and bias.

This court/judicial element is called "case law" and occurs daily through the rulings of federal and state judges.

When a judge hands down a ruling, and it survives appeal with the next tier of judges, it then becomes full-fledged, full- blown, case law or legal precedent.

But these constant and daily court rulings have now eclipsed the speed and pace of the legislative branch, and so therefore currently the American people are constantly subject to case rulings of individual judges who are much easier to corrupt and purchase than the entire congress/senate than the laws made by the legislature pursuant to the US Constitution.

The constant case law or legal precedent phenomenon consistently, continuously, and routinely alters and changes legislative and constitutional intent on a daily, if not hourly, basis.

Lawyers love this phenomenon because it constantly creates new business opportunities for them and their associated bar associations, highly profitable continuing legal education (CLE) programs, and other financial "hangers on" entities who feverishly mine these daily judicial court rulings for nuggets of gold to buy and sell to gain tactical advantages over others who may or may not know about them in order to make a fast buck.

Adding insult to injury is the fact that larger and powerful law firms who have banks, mega corporations, and wealthy individuals as "cash cow clients" routinely buy off and control federal, state, and local judges, and their corresponding court rulings reflect the agendas and visions of those wealthy powerful clients, at the complete and total expense of the common people and the masses.

The deep state, plutocratic/oligarchic elite control these financial purse-strings, and exercise this power on a daily basis so that our body of law and jurisprudence is, today and at once, totally unrecognizable from the visions of the founding fathers and our first American courts.

It is common knowledge within the legal profession that corrupt judges regularly refuse to identify potential conflicts of interest and refuse to step aside from cases where their personal bias, feelings, money trail, and connections might create a greater risk of them issuing an unfair ruling.

As a corollary to this truism, corrupted judges systematically provide advantages to those who have given them money and power, while they more often than not ignore the human rights, civil liberties, and constitutional rights of those who seek justice for acts of wrongdoing committed against them.

The only way to undo this vast quagmire of a mess is to meditate on these facts and "reset the clock" a bit to try and recapture the original intent of the founding fathers, the US Constitution, and the original legislatures, and quickly pare down and discount the various and cacophonous squawking of American judges over the past 225 years, but this is no mean feat. It will require an overall restocking of our nation's federal and state judiciary and a return to what made this country's legal system great in the first place the words and inherent meaning of the United States Constitution.

We, the People-United States Constitution

Once again, the only way the American people will ever see change is by incessantly calling/emailing/texting/faxing their local and federal congressional and senate leaders, as well as their local federal and state law enforcement agencies, to demand change at the local and federal level to investigate, arrest, prosecute, convict, and replace our nation's corrupt judges and court personnel, and thereupon revolutionize the courts.

It will not happen if the American people don't care or are apathetic to all of this.

CHAPTER 63

Liberate the Whistle-Blowers Now

The only test to determine if one qualifies for heroic whistle-blower status is whether or not more people were affected positively than negatively.

The founding fathers knew exactly the heroism and personal self-sacrifice of those who gave up their life, liberty and pursuit of happiness for the sake of freedom for all.

If one truly believes in American values, then one must also agree that whistle-blowers must be liberated, and freed immediately from earthly bondage, whether it be prison, home incarceration, vindictive prosecution/persecution by politically motivated government officials, disenfranchisement from voting or working, and all-around pariah status in the United States, and in the rest of the world.

Not every individual who leaks or pilfers confidential information to reveal it to third parties can be considered a whistle-blower, however.

A whistle-blower has been defined as a person who exposes any kind of information or activity that is deemed illegal, unethical, or not correct within an organization that is either private or public.

The information of alleged wrongdoing can be classified in many ways: violation of company policy/rules, law, regulation, or threat to public interest/national security, as well as fraud, and corruption.

Those who become whistle-blowers can choose to bring information or allegations to the surface either internally or externally.

Internally, a whistle-blower can bring his/her accusations to the attention of other people within the accused organization (unfortunately retaliation by that organization is often standard practice and de rigeur).

Externally, a whistle-blower can bring allegations to light by contacting a third party outside of an accused organization.

Whistle-blowers can reach out to the media, government, law enforcement, or those who are concerned but also face stiff reprisal and retaliation from those who are accused or alleged of wrongdoing.

The founding fathers knew exactly the heroism and personal self-sacrifice of those who gave up their life, liberty, and pursuit of happiness for the sake of freedom for all.

The progenitors of the founding fathers, i.e., those that influenced and inspired them to forge a new nation, **were also passionate whistle-blowers** who desperately tried to escape the yoke and slavery of colonial British England, which is exactly who still controls the purse strings today through the fiat power of the Bank of England and the other central banks located sporadically throughout the tiny City of London.

Thomas Paine in 1776 once said, "Those who expect to reap the blessings of freedom must, like men, undergo the fatigue of supporting it."

John Locke stated in 1689 that "where-ever law ends, tyranny begins, if the law be transgressed to another's harm; and whosoever in authority exceeds the power given him by the law, and makes use of the force he has under his command, to compass that upon the subject, which the law allows not, ceases in that to be a magistrate; and, acting without authority, may be opposed, as any other man, who by force invades the right of another. This is acknowledged in subordinate magistrates. He that hath authority to seize my person in the street, may be opposed as a thief and a robber, if he endeavors to break into my house to execute a writ, notwithstanding that I know he has such a warrant, and such a legal authority, as will empower him to arrest me abroad. And why this should not hold in the highest, as well as in the most inferior magistrate, I would gladly be informed."

So it can be no secret that today's crop of whistle-blowers are at once much more similar to the courageous founding fathers (and their progenitors) than the bought-off, paid-for bankster whores that populate our Congress, Senate, Judiciary, and Executive Branch, especially since the resurgence in 1995 of COINTELPRO by the DOJ/FBI/DHS after its outlawing in 1975 by the Frank Church Hearings with the Bill Clinton/Joe Biden Community-Oriented Policing (COPS) program brought on the by the suspiciously contrived Oklahoma City Bombings, or the reinstatement of the CIA mass assassination/MKULTRA/propaganda program onslaught after the equally suspect events of 9/11.

Today's whistle-blowers sacrificed themselves, their freedoms, and their "life, liberty, and pursuit of happiness" for the sake of their fellow American citizen, if not fellow man, should be immediately liberated from bondage, and then lionized in history, as such.

The only test to determine if one qualifies for heroic whistle-blower status is whether or not more people were affected positively than negatively.

If the calculus can be shown that their revelations operated to inform the American people about troubling programs, constitutional violations, and other mechanisms of corruption, then they should at once be liberated /freed/exonerated/lionized.

To be sure, not all leakers should be rescued from the earthly bondage of government retaliation, but a great many of the ones appearing in the modern news should be, because they have in fact ameliorated and improved the conditions and knowledge of their fellow citizenry, who have thereupon acted upon this knowledge to seek out change by throwing their elected (and non-elected) tyrants out of power to face public/private scrutiny and investigation.

Whistle-blower revelations have also illuminated brightly the money/ paper trails of the corrupted relationships within the government, allowing for a tracking of the origin/roots of their slavery, giving the American people the ability to collectively shut them down.

"Now we are all persons of interest" (NSA whistle-blower Thomas Drake).

Thomas Drake: Thomas Drake worked at the NSA in various analyst and management positions. He blew the whistle on the NSA's Trailblazer Project that he felt was a violation of the Fourth Amendment and other laws and regulations. He contacted The Baltimore Sun which published articles about waste, fraud, and abuse at the NSA, including stories about Trailblazer. In April 2010, Drake was indicted by a grand jury on various charges, including obstructing justice and making false statements. After the May 22, 2011, broadcast of a 60 Minutes episode on the Drake case, the government dropped all of the charges against Drake and agreed not to seek any jail time in return for Drake's agreement to plead guilty to a misdemeanor of misusing the agency's computer system. Drake was sentenced to one year of probation and community service.

John Kiriakou: In an interview with ABC News on December 10, CIA Officer Kiriakou disclosed that the agency waterboarded detainees and that this constituted torture.

In the months that followed, Kiriakou passed the identity of a covert CIA operative to a reporter.

He was convicted of violating the Intelligence Identities Protection Act and sentenced, on January 25, 2013, to 30 months imprisonment. Having served the first months of his service, he wrote an open letter describing the inhumane circumstances at the correctional facility.

Bradley "Chelsea" Manning: US Army intelligence analyst who released the largest set of classified documents ever, mostly published by WikiLeaks and their media partners. The material included videos of the July 12, 2007, Baghdad airstrike and the 2009 Granai airstrike in Afghanistan, 250,000 United States diplomatic cables, and 500,000 army reports that came to be known as the Iraq War logs and Afghan War logs. Manning was convicted of violating the Espionage Act and other offenses and was sentenced to thirty-five years in prison.

Jeffrey Sterling: Jeffrey Alexander Sterling is an American lawyer and former CIA employee who was arrested, charged, and convicted of violating the Espionage Act for revealing details about Operation Merlin to journalist James Risen. In April 2000, Sterling filed a complaint with the CIA's Equal Employment Office about management's alleged racial discrimination practices. The CIA subsequently revoked Sterling's authorization to receive or possess classified documents concerning the secret operation and placed him on administrative leave in March 2001. After the failure of two settlement attempts, his contract with the CIA was terminated on January 31, 2002.

Sterling's lawsuit accusing CIA officials of racial discrimination was dismissed by the judge after the government successfully argued the state secrets privilege by alleging the litigation would require disclosure of classified information. The 4th US Circuit Court of Appeals upheld the dismissal, ruling in 2005 that "there is no way for Sterling to prove employment discrimination without exposing at least some classified details of the covert employment that gives context to his claim." In May 2015, Sterling was sentenced to three and a half years in prison.

Edward Snowden: Booz Allen Hamilton contractor Snowden released classified material on top-secret NSA programs including the PRISM surveillance program to The Guardian and The Washington Post in June 2013.

Julian Paul Assange: Australian computer programmer, publisher and journalist. He is editor-in-chief of the organization WikiLeaks, which he founded in 2006. He has won numerous accolades for journalism, including the Sam Adams Award and Martha Gellhorn Prize for Journalism. Assange founded WikiLeaks in 2006 but came to global prominence in 2010 when WikiLeaks published a series of leaks, allegedly provided by Chelsea Manning. These leaks included the Collateral Murder video (April 2010), the Afghanistan war logs (July 2010), the Iraq war logs (October 2010), and CableGate (November 2010). Assange became even more globally recognized after WikiLeaks published more leaks-the DNC leaks and the Podesta emails during the United States 2016 presidential election. Following the 2010 leaks, the United States government launched a criminal investigation into WikiLeaks and asked allied nations for assistance. In November 2010, a request was made for Assange's extradition to Sweden, where he had been questioned months earlier over allegations of sexual assault and rape. Assange continued to deny the allegations after the case was re-opened and expressed concern that he would be extradited from Sweden to the United States due to his perceived role in publishing secret American documents. Assange surrendered himself to UK police on December 7, 2010, and was held for ten days in solitary confinement before being released on bail. Assange sought and was granted asylum by Ecuador in August 2012. Assange has since remained in the Embassy of Ecuador in London and is unable to leave without being arrested for breaching his bail conditions.

There are countless more heroic whistle-blowers throughout history, and if they can pass the test as described above, they should immediately be liberated/pardoned/exonerated either now while they are living, or posthumously if they are no longer with us.

CHAPTER 64

Follow the Money of the Deep State

In every vast criminal conspiracy, there has always been a leader or leaders, hiding in the shadows.

L ike any other criminal enterprise, there is always a leader, or series of leaders.

This is the essence of the RICO Laws, i.e., the Racketeering Influenced Corrupt Organization Act, wherein the US government (in a rare overture of actual beneficence to the American people) developed, enacted, and passed a series of federal statutes which allowed them to, in a much easier fashion, take down organized crime by attributing the criminal acts of their "lower-level henchmen" directly to the man upstairs, i.e., their leader, who, before the enactment of said statute, was usually able to evade liability or culpability of a sprawling criminal enterprise, which he/she, while in the shadows, was able to control and pull all of the strings.

To that end, every single patriot in America, and better yet if they are federal or state law enforcement, private investigators, lawyers, finance professionals, accountants, or anyone else trained/equipped to detect shadowy shell corporations, "hidden money trails," clandestine networks, and hidden corporate/organization structure, should immediately start and begin to attribute any and all criminal activity being felt by the masses in the United States and throughout the world, directly to one or several ultimate leaders.

It is no longer acceptable for the countless crimes being perpetrated against humanity to go unaccounted for and unpunished/uninvestigated.

The daily crimes that are constantly going uninvestigated and unaccounted for to their ultimate leader(s) consist of one or all of the following, both in the United States and the rest of the world: (1) false flag terrorism to get their populations to demand/accept more civil liberties violations/removal by their host governments; (2) acts of political and judicial corruption; (3) police and federal law enforcement misconduct or corruption; (4) mainstream media deceptions being passed off as "real news" in order to brainwash/influence a population; (5) war crimes or other paramilitary acts of unprovoked aggression against innocents throughout the world; (6) legal abuse and harassment using our nation's federal and state courts; (7) acts of STASI-like gang-stalking or community-oriented policing by the DHS, DOJ, and FBI working in conjunction with corrupted local police or private investigators/contractors against innocent people who run afoul of the National Security State or a member thereon; and (8) countless other crimes against humanity.

Thankfully, the RICO Laws that are used to take down these types of vast organized criminal entities/conspiracies do not require the federal or state government to investigate themselves, which rarely, if ever, works.

A RICO lawsuit can also be brought by any individual, or group of individuals, using forms freely available and provided by every Pro Se (self-representation) webpage on each and every US Federal District Court website in what is known as a private civil RICO lawsuit, i.e., whereby any one person or persons aggrieved or harmed by a criminal conspiracy, having a predicate criminal act(s), can sue any one, or all, of their perceived perpetrators, usually alongside 42 § 1983 (The Civil Rights Act).

One does not even need to have all of the proof required; just a colorable and cognizable claim or series of claims wherein the aggrieved party or parties believe that sufficient evidence exists to sue any or all of those defendants responsible for said predicate criminal act.

Hopefully the summons and complaint of the lawsuit will pass so that a federal judge will allow the case to continue on to the discovery stage, wherein the perpetrators of said criminal activity will be forced to turn over and yield any and all information and evidence to support that lawsuit, but this is also difficult because in the vast majority of cases, the federal judge/magistrate presiding is usually, completely, and totally "in bed" with the corrupt and shadowy criminal figure(s) who are victimizing you in the first place.

One of the greatest proponents of the aggrieved masses suing the "pants off" of the criminal element(s) masquerading within the deep state was none other than Eustace Mullins, one of the most underrated and undiscovered American heroes and patriots this country has ever known.

Eustace Mullins got a great kick and sense of enjoyment suing these criminal perpetrators on a regular basis, scoring win after win against corrupted members of the criminal deep state with his dogged persistence and laser-like focus on achieving justice against these nameless and faceless cowards hiding behind the color of law and authority or even standing outside of it.

It was reported that Eustace Mullins, himself a non-lawyer, scored back-to-back 30–50-million-dollar awards and judgments against his tormentors within the deep state, time after time again.

This also may have been attributed to the fact that he was also an amazing and great writer, linguist, and orator, having literally been the FIRST exposer of the criminal conspiracy involving the Federal Reserve, for example, amongst myriad other deep state revelations.

One of his seminal speeches can be found here at https://www.youtube.com/watch?v=deMAuq7zZV0 wherein he glorifies and discusses in detail, his unsung victories against some of the criminals who hide within the deep state and contains many glorious tidbits and pearls of wisdom, if you too, want to sue these cowardly people into oblivion for crimes against you, your family, or your friends.

CHAPTER 65

Markus Wolf: The New World
Order Anti-Christ Who Got Away with It

Markus Wolf's STASI was an Orwellian police-state using disturbing methods and murky operations.

There has never been so little written or so little information provided for one of the most diabolical, mentally sick, and twisted members of the human race as former East German STASI chief and founder, Markus Wolf, who literally embodied the word "evil" in everything that he did, or said, during the decades of terrorism against his own people and the rest of the world that was his life.

Even more disturbingly, this man (if one could even call him that) pretty much got away scot-free with his crimes against humanity and was even hired by the fledgling US Department of Homeland Security (DHS) in 2003 to recreate and add the final finishing touches to this anti-freedom governmental agency in the wake of September 11, 2001 (the American version of the Reichstag Fire).

The STASI that Markus Wolf created and led plunged Germany into state-sanctioned violence, tyranny, oppression, denial of civil rights/liberties of its citizenry, and otherwise spied on and surveillanced the entire East German population at the behest of their oligarchs/plutocrats, who insecurely clung to their own power in the face of ever- growing populist awareness and revolt by the purposefully deprived masses.

Indeed, this man, Markus Wolf, was, by self-admission, a sexual deviant and bully, similar to his mentor and protégé Lavrenty Beria, Secret Police Chief of former USSR Prime Minister Jozef Stalin, who often kidnapped, raped, and murdered girls as young as twelve years old, leaving them dead by the roadside, often incorporating both personality foibles in his grip of control over each and every aspect of his captive East German population, as well as on foreigners who dared to get involved with his daily trampling on the human rights of the people who he was ordered to corral and control on behalf of his oligarch/plutocrat paymasters within the big banks, corporations, royal families, and other well- heeled but insecure financial sponsors within East Germany.

Indeed, while Markus Wolf publicly espoused the "values" of austerity and living frugally in order to brainwash and fool the people he ruled over like a despot, privately he indulged in wild sexual orgies while eating and drinking the finest foods and wines using his illicit power and money to indulge in them.

His entire life and career within the East German STASI is a warning to the American people who could easily come under and fall prey to the ever increasing and encroaching power of the US Police State being assembled and formed under their very own eyes, unless the people take a stand and keep a watchful eye on the tyrannical men and women who are trying to recreate this spy agency within these fifty states.

Markus Johannes "Mischa" Wolf was born in Hechingen, Province of Hohenzollern (now Baden-Württemberg), to a Jewish father and a non-Jewish mother on January 19, 1923, and was founder and chief of the Main Directorate for Reconnaissance (Hauptverwaltung Aufklärung), the foreign intelligence division of East Germany's Ministry for State Security (MfS, commonly known as the "STASI").

He was the MfS's number two for thirty-four years, which spanned most of the Cold War.

It is said that Markus Wolf was totally ruthless and exploited any person's weaknesses with great precision and a total lack of compassion and that he often said that "no one who touched his intelligence service would be forgotten, and no debt would ever be cancelled."

Markus Wolf ran the East German security service for most of the Cold War and was accused of countless acts of kidnapping, coercion, and causing bodily harm amongst other myriad war crimes against humanity over the several decades that he was STASI chief.

His father was a member of the Communist Party of Germany and after Adolf Hitler gained power, Wolf escaped to Soviet Communist Moscow with his father via Switzerland and France because of their Communist connections, beliefs, and because Wolf's father was Jewish.

In 1953, at the age of thirty, Wolf was among the founding members of the East German foreign intelligence service within the Ministry for State Security.

As intelligence chief, he achieved great success in penetrating the government as well as business circles of West Germany with spies, predominantly using his targets' deviant sexual appetites, penchant for drugs, susceptibility to bribery, or just outright physical violence, blackmail, and extortion on his targets to do so.

For most of his career, Wolf was known as "the man without a face" due to his elusiveness, but also because the major banks/oligarchs/plutocrats actively protected his identity.

It was reported that Western agencies did not even know what the East German spy chief looked like until 1978, when he was photographed by Säpo, Sweden's National Security Service, during a visit to Sweden.

Markus Wolf's STASI was an Orwellian, police-state using disturbing methods and murky operations.

His STASI carried out widespread repression of its own people through a network of tens of thousands of informers and "gang-stalkers" using the "Zersetzung" program, meaning "targeted psychological degradation," and routinely harbored international terrorists, such as Carlos the Jackal, one of the world's most notorious terrorists, as well as the murderous Red Army Faction that terrorized West Germany, as well as the Palestine Liberation Organization (PLO).

Through Markus Wolf, the PLO was trained in hidden camps in East Germany in guns, explosives, and guerrilla tactics.

In September 1990, shortly before German reunification, Wolf fled the country and sought political asylum in Russia and Austria.

When he was denied entry, he returned to Germany where he was arrested by the recently reunited German police for crimes against humanity.

Markus Wolf claimed to have refused a lucrative financial offer, new identity, and home in California from the Central Intelligence Agency (CIA) to defect to the United States simply because the CIA apparently loves NAZIs and war criminals so much, as was evidenced by their taking in of fifteen thousand or more of them after World War II in Operation Paperclip.

In 1993, he was finally convicted of treason in Germany by the Oberlandesgericht Düsseldorf in a "sham/show trial" to satisfy the masses and other global human rights supporters, was and sentenced to six years imprisonment.

However, this conviction was later quashed by the German Supreme Court because Wolf was "acting from the territory of the then-independent GDR."

In 1997, he was convicted of unlawful detention, coercion, and bodily harm, and was given a "suspended sentence" of two years imprisonment, which was a complete and total slap on the wrist for his decades-long war crimes against his own people and the rest of the world.

Insanely, according to Adinda Akkermans in her seminal and informative article "Why Former Stasi Is Treated with Kid Gloves":

> Many former STASI members are still in public office in Germany today in fact, they're on the offensive when it comes to victims looking for recognition Former STASI Officers include former guards (of) Angela Merkel In 2009 it was ... revealed that approximately seventy thousand current employees of the German government used to work for the STASI the GDR secret service has been partly responsible for over 200,000 political prisoners, and about a thousand deaths of East Germans who tried to flee the GDR another explanation for the mild treatment of former STASI after the fall of the Wall is that it concerned 91 thousand Germans, and hundreds of thousands of "informal collaborators" who betrayed their friends, family and neighbors to the secret service (gang-stalking, i.e., Zersetzung) if all these people had lost their positions, it would have led to major turmoil and dissatisfaction within German society victims of the GDR regime ... have difficulty stomaching the fact that former STASI staff are still treated with kid gloves For example, names of STASI officers have been removed from public archives In fact, parts of these archives are no longer freely accessible because of lawsuits filed by former STASI members appealing to their privacy Many ... associates of the past secret service have managed to have references to their past removed from books and exhibitions.

Unfortunately, Markus Wolf died in his sleep at his Berlin home on November 9, 2006, rather than in a jail cell or by firing squad like he did to so many of his victims probably numbering in the hundreds of thousands, if not millions, of innocents during his lifetime and by his own hands.

CHAPTER 66

Donald Trump: The Great Liberator

We Americans are a brave, resilient and fearless lot, and Donald Trump reflects all that is great about America.

Very few, if any, presidents in recent history have had the personal reservoirs of strength, internal fortitude, character, vision, and endless energy that our new upcoming President Donald Trump has.

He has the singular goal of rescuing America from its tormentors who have held this nation and its people captive for at least the past fifty years since World War II, whose economic, social, and existential vice-grip has been growing more and more constrictive and oppressive with each and every cowardly successive administration that has come down the pike who preferred to slowly sell the American people out, then to take these social engineering enslavers head-on.

Even though his enemies and detractors have relentlessly sought to destroy and undermine his credibility, message, and momentum since the auspicious day that he announced his candidacy, Donald Trump is supported by the undying and eternal spirit that is America. Its patriots from all walks of life and skill sets have added the fuel to his fire, and through the power of the internet, real-time communication, and Donald Trump's direct Tweets to the American people, this bond has become even stronger.

There is nothing that can come between the American people and their chosen president, and the day that he ascends into the White House cannot come soon enough.

Donald Trump is the Great Liberator and will release Americans from all walks of life, economic and social groups, races, religions, and creeds, from their yokes of slavery in order to free all Americans once again, to fully realize each and every one of their innate potentials, and he is truly gifted with the missing Divine Providence that this country felt tangibly at its founding in 1776.

We Americans are a brave, resilient, and fearless lot, and Donald Trump reflects all that is great about America.

CHAPTER 67

In Defense of Israel from the Crazies

It seems Israel (and consequently the United States) is being driven off a cliff at the behest of people who don't care about the State of Israel in the first place.

nyone who has any shred of common decency realizes and recognizes that the State of Israel has every right to exist and prosper.

And also, that the Jews of the world have every right to have a homeland and a place on earth to call their own, with complete and total sovereignty, borders, right to defend itself, and the right to live in peace.

But what happens when leaders or other outside factors, with different and selfish agendas, co-opt and use the Israeli leadership to support and engage in behavior, actions, and methods which tend to overwhelmingly delegitimize, undermine, or defame the Israeli State and its people?

Even the Israeli Intelligence Services, the foreign agency Mossad and domestic Shin Bet agencies have come out in clear support and favor of the Iran Nuclear Deal Agreement, i.e., the Iran Nuclear Deal Framework (Joint Comprehensive Plan of Action [JCPOA]), which was a preliminary framework agreement reached in 2015 between the Islamic Republic of Iran and a group of world powers, i.e., the P5+1 (the permanent members of the United Nations Security Council—the United States, the United Kingdom, Russia, France, and China—plus Germany) and the European Union.

Even choice leadership of the Israeli military have vociferously supported this deal.

The Israeli intelligence services and security establishment, past and present, charged with the ultimate safeguarding and territorial integrity/security of the Jewish state above anything else, as well its leaders, have come out in full force and support of this agreement, stating that Iran has fully complied with its obligations under said contract, and to either void it or disrupt or repeal it would be foolhardy, stupid, and would ultimately undermine and harm Israel's security interests.

So why is it that Israeli Leader Benjamin Netanyahu, who is simply a political leader, is so vociferously against it?

Why does he continue to try to recruit US and European (and world) leadership to derail, destroy, amend, or repeal the Iran Nuclear Deal in spite of the deep Israeli indigenous intelligence and military strategic information that overwhelmingly supports it for the sake of the long-term security and survival of Israel?

Could it be because Netanyahu is not at all loyal to his own people of the state of Israel that he instead takes his marching and policy orders from outside Israel's borders, say for example, from wealthy and powerful oligarch/plutocratic institutions located in the city of London or in the deep state neocon/neoliberal/Hawkish halls of power within the United States of America?

That perhaps Benjamin Netanyahu does not owe fealty and allegiance to his own people but rather to overseas and foreign crazies who are hell-bent on stoking and provoking a major world war between militant Islam and extremist Zionism, bad for both sides?

US political leadership such as in the form of Mitt Romney keep pushing and encouraging the Israeli leadership to engage in open and horrible acts of violence, ethnic cleansing, police misconduct, human rights violations, war crimes, apartheid, random acts of violence against the beleaguered Palestinians, jailing/incarcerating children as young as seven within Israel's horrific jails and other evil and criminal acts in their isolation of the Palestinian people behind cages in Gaza, never to venture out again for even water, food, or medical care, let alone jobs or the right to migrate, which are enshrined as basic human rights in every culture in the world.

Could the answer be found in the Freemasonic Lodge that both Mitt Romney and Benjamin Netanyahu were recruited by in Boston when they were both kids working in the financial company, Bain Capital, back in the 1960s?

Could it be that these two leaders, for example, owe an allegiance to an invisible, clandestine, hidden power, and force, which forces them to abide by their edicts, in direct contravention to both common sense and the intelligence and military sections of the Israeli National Security State, if not the vast majority of humanity?

Albert Pike, a 33rd Degree Freemason, penned a famous book entitled *Morals and Dogma*, wherein he predicted (if not wrote the blueprints for) all three world wars, with the last installment being World War III and describing it as a war between militant Islam and militant Zionism.

This last war would result in a horrible and catastrophic "end of days," where the vast majority of the people of earth would be consumed by hellfire, death, and destruction.

Is this their final wish and goal?

To clear the earth of its "useless eaters," as Henry Kissinger once famously described in his National Security Memorandum 200, to establish a capitol and homeland for the Luciferian Freemasonic/Deep State elements within the world's political and wealth power structures and international deep state and to depopulate the planet to the tune of 500 million from its current and present 8 billion, according to the insidious George Guidestones found in Atlanta Georgia?

What else could support this insane reasoning in order to keep Israel engaged in overtly outlandish and criminal wanton acts of violence against the indigenous people of Palestine in the face of the overwhelming protests of the rest of the people of the world?

Could these insane leaders simply be using the good and innocent men and women of the Israeli Defense Forces and military police to ethnically cleanse and "settle" this land in preparation for their future New World Order government, with the people of Israel themselves to be finally and ultimately sacrificed in a cataclysmic war, destroying both Islam and Judaism in the process?

If one cares about the state of Israel and its long-term survival, one must always encourage the de-escalation of conflict, which delegitimizes the state of Israel through the embarrassing and random acts of violence and human rights violations being perpetrated on the orders of the crazy Israeli leadership, and its foreign and hitherto unknown, faceless and nameless foreign directors and their "hidden hands" on their open and described suicide mission.

It seems Israel (and consequently the United States) is being driven off a cliff at the behest of Luciferian people who don't care about the state of Israel in the first place.

Perhaps this was why President Obama, in one of his final acts of true love and concern for the state of Israel as US president, abstained from and essentially voted for United Nations Security Resolution 2334, which punished the Israeli leadership and its lunatic fringe by resetting its boundaries back to 1967, formally outlawing the illegal settlements and incursions being built in the face of worldwide and international condemnation, the continuation of which kept adding more and more enmity and hatred for the Jewish State and its innocent people, fomenting and increasing anti- Semitism all over the world.

Perhaps this act of "tough love" was necessary to blunt the insanity of Israel's crazies and bring back the country from the brink and state of abyss it was finding itself unable to extricate itself from.

CHAPTER 68

America Has a Moral Obligation
to Help Rebuild the Ravaged Middle East

Peace, commerce and honest friendship with all nations, entangling alliances with none.

Thomas Jefferson

Although the vast majority of Americans are grateful and happy to hear the news from President Donald Trump that he wishes to withdraw from the world, in terms of military conflicts, paramilitary affairs, and pointless regime changes that span the globe, in direct contravention to the abject insanity of the neoconservatives/neoliberals, which have plagued American foreign policy for the past fifteen years, it is vital to understand that even though these criminal acts were perpetrated by previous regimes/administrations of the United States, which gorged themselves on the proverbial meal in the proverbial restaurant, it is unfortunately incumbent upon the new administration to also pay the proverbial bill and to fix and rectify the mistakes of the past.

While it is fair and good to state as a matter of foreign policy that the USA will now try to adhere to Thomas Jefferson's mantra of "Peace, commerce and honest friendship with all nations, entangling alliances with none," it would be altogether grossly irresponsible and cruel to now leave the entire world in smoke and shambles, burning embers of once great civilizations that have often existed for thousands of years uninterrupted and unmolested.

So even though President Donald Trump and the vast majority of America (and the rest of the European world) wish to move forward into the future, it would be absolutely unforgivable if they did not also assist in actively rebuilding those damaged and destroyed societies, while not attempting to recolonize them again.

The United States through the World Bank and IMF, as well as Russia, Brazil, India, China and South Africa through the BRICS Bank, need to join hands and extend billions and billions of dollars in loans and project finance to those poor ravaged nations in order to help them rebuild their infrastructure, waterways, electric grids, internet, buildings, health facilities and hospitals, schools, and other major points of civilized life.

To turn our backs on the tens of millions of innocent men, women, and children, who had absolutely nothing to do with the "conflict of bankers/globalists," would be tantamount to condemning them to death and would be wholesale genocide.

Now that Europe, followed by America, has slammed the door shut on the tens of millions of poor refugees created by such monsters as NATO, George Soros, and other megalomaniacs, the latter of which had betted on simply incorporating these bedraggled refugees within Western societies, these poor masses have been relegated to drowning in the waters in between North Africa and Europe and dying or being raped at the hands of barbarians in the Middle East.

This reality is altogether unacceptable.

If the Western countries no longer want to take these newly created refugees within their own borders, then they must immediately recreate and rebuild the nations that they destroyed so that these people can go home.

The USA must immediately join hands with Europe and the emerging nations of the BRICS Bank paradigm in order to rebuild the horrific destruction wrought by the previous American administrations/regimes, war criminals, pirates, neocons, and their proxies Saudi Arabia, Turkey, NATO, ISIS, and other clandestine mercenaries.

We must also punish the war criminals involved in such horrendous atrocities spanning fifteen years, with convened "Nuremberg Trials" and other such international judicial congress in order to also deal with the devastating moral fallout of their behavior and actions, as these people cannot be allowed to get away with their fifteen-year raping and pillaging of humanity with impunity.

If the United States does not take the lead in this dispensation of much overdue justice, then the United Nations should do so with or without America at the table. This is just quite simply the morally correct thing to do.

Otherwise, the United States of America has no right to call itself a civilized nation.

CHAPTER 69

Time to Bring Lyndon LaRouche Out of Exile

Visionaries are always ahead of their time.

Novel thinkers and those with original ideas, coupled with gifts of clairvoyance, are always initially challenged and ostracized by the masses, who are then used by corrupt political leadership to justify horrific actions of exclusion, persecution, and damnation of their enemies.

For more than fifty years, Lyndon LaRouche has been writing, lecturing, teaching, and warning Americans and the rest of the people of the world about the exact same issues pertaining to economics, global governance, and the agenda of the oligarch /plutocrat / deep state lunatic fringe who Donald Trump and the majority of America (and the world) are now fighting against.

To be sure, at the time Lyndon LaRouche was railing against these enemies of humanity in the 1970s and 1980s, both before and during the Ronald Reagan administration, his enemies were so strong that they were able to character- assassinate and marginalize him from political power, and they were also able to set him up for what he alleges was a false and contrived criminal case, sentencing this wise, learned gentleman to prison for many years, where inside he was apparently attacked, and attempts were made to murder him.

But Lyndon LaRouche is not only one of the world's greatest thinkers/writers, but he is also one of its most resilient, and he survived this slow assassination plot hatched by his enemies and is now living in Germany.

His enemies and betrayers were allegedly people like George H. W. Bush and the rest of the New World Order globalist/skull-and-bones secret societies, which were beholden to the city of London within the United Kingdom and its crown rather than to the United States of America and its people.

To that end, Lyndon LaRouche's enemies have now been revealed over the past few years, especially to be the enemies of the American people.

One recalls at a media press conference in the late 1990s, wherein James Woolsey, formerly head of the CIA, who is an open and avowed NWO globalist, openly castigated, humiliated, and verbally assaulted a member of the press corps asking a question that was both intelligent and insightful as soon as Woolsey learned that this media representative was from the Executive Intelligence Review (EIR), funded, led and spearheaded by Lyndon LaRouche. James Woolsey has now been banished from the halls of power by the Donald Trump administration and the rest of America, for his political background/motivations have been revealed to the American public and the rest of the world, as have the rest of the rabid neocons, neoliberals, and other Trotsky-ite Communists and Stasi-like proponents of a technocratic global New World Order, where the masses are considered cattle, and their ruling oligarchs/plutocrats are designed to be their sheep-herders.

Oscar Wilde wrote that "you can always judge a man by the quality of his enemies." Well, if that is the case, then Lyndon LaLarouche may be the second coming of Christ.

Lyndon LaRouche has stated that the people who wanted him dead and gone were entities such as the Queen of the United Kingdom, the Council on Foreign Relations, the Justice Department, and the Mossad.

He further fingered the CIA and British intelligence, as well as Communists, extreme/militant Zionists, narcotics gangsters, the Rockefellers, powerful bankers, globalists, Henry Kissinger, Averell Harriman, international Socialists and Nazis, and international terrorists.

Whatever Lyndon LaRouche's history and evolution throughout his life, much of which has been controversial and difficult to understand, one must admit that this list of enemies is truly impressive, and have now been established to be enemies of the American people and the rest of the world.

The problem is that forty to fifty years ago, no one knew who these people were or why they were motivated against him as they had a complete and total stranglehold on the media and the power structure within the USA and the world, and so truly no one in the American masses knew about it.

Some of the issues and political agendas of Lyndon LaRouche that he has supported and espoused over the last forty to fifty years resulted in his powerful enemies removing him from political power, forcing him away from his American podium, exiling him from the United States of America and confining him to a prison for a dubious crime like Jean Valjean in *Les Misérables:*

1. He is against rabid environmental protectionism and instead opts for bolstering and growing the American and world economies through manufacturing, industry, and great jobs.

2. He has called out our corrupt political leadership who often engage in behavior/actions against the interests of the American people (and the world) because he has uncovered their allegiance to the city of London in the United Kingdom and British Crown rather than the interests of the American people.

3. He is a supporter of the international balance of power approach against stupid foreign wars of intervention as he discovered long ago that this was only in the interest of the international oligarch/plutocrat elite while undermining and disenfranchising the American people (and the rest of the world).

4. He is a supporter of better relations with all nations and countries of the world, trading honestly with all, entangling alliances with none, as was typified and instructed by Thomas Jefferson.

5. He is a supporter of the BRICS banking paradigm, which seeks to challenge the bankster hegemony being foisted and perpetrated against the Third and Second World and its people, while simultaneously devaluing American currency and oppressing the citizens of the USA.

6. He is 100 percent in favor of bringing high-paying quality jobs in manufacturing, industry, and other hard employment with higher salaries and better longevity and working conditions back to the United States after the awful carnage that was inflicted on the American people by the pro-NAFTA corporate/government fascist crowd, which sent tens of millions of American jobs and its corporations overseas (President Donald Trump has made this a cornerstone of his entire presidential administration, if not all of the above issues as well).

7. He is for abolishing (or at least auditing) the Federal Reserve, which he views as the ultimate harbinger and source of evil, for which countless intellectual luminaries of the modern age have profoundly supported and espoused, but Lyndon LaRouche was talking about this fifty years ago.

8. He is against wholesale and systematic corruption within all three branches of the US government, having traced its economic and financial fount to the city of London and its UK proponents.

9. He is against a biased and corrupted media, speaking out against its rapid consolidation so that it could better brainwash and

mind-control the American people and the rest of the world into accepting the long-term enslavement visions of the global oligarchs and plutocratic feudal masters who lurk in the shadows.

10. He is completely against the doctrines of neoconservatism in our foreign policy against useless stupid foreign wars and routinely calls out people like US State Department Chief Victoria Nuland for destroying and sabotaging other sovereign foreign nations in their bloodlust and thirst for global hegemony at the expense of the world's people and only beneficial to its oligarch masters.

11. A return to the Bretton Woods system, including a gold-based national and world monetary system, fixed exchange rates, and ending the IMF.

12. Replacement of the central bank system, including the US Federal Reserve System, with a national bank.

13. A war on drug trafficking and prosecution of banks involved in money laundering.

14. Building of nuclear power plants.

15. Opposition to excessive environmentalism, deregulation, outcome-based education, and abortion.

16. Immediate reinstatement of the Glass-Steagall Act, which separated private mom-and-pop checking/savings accounts from the risky casino- like investment habits/tactics of the major banks, the repeal of which in 1998 by then President Bill Clinton under pressure from Goldman Sachs/Treasury Secretaries/Economic Advisors Robert Rubin, Larry Summers, Gene Sperling and others within the central banker cabal led directly to the financial cataclysm of 2008 wherein the American people were forced to bail out these reckless banks with their taxpayer dollars.

These are only a few of Lyndon LaRouche's original and greatest original contributions to humanity for the past fifty years.

In December 1980, LaRouche and his followers started what came to be known as the October Surprise allegation, namely that in October 1980 Ronald Reagan's campaign staff conspired with the Iranian government during the Iran hostage crisis to delay the release of fifty-two American hostages held in Iran, with the aim of helping Reagan win the 1980 presidential election against Jimmy Carter. The Iranians had agreed to this, according to the theory, in exchange for future weapons sales from the Reagan administration. The first publication of the story was in LaRouche's

Executive Intelligence Review on December 2, 1980, followed by his New Solidarity on September 2, 1983, alleging that Henry Kissinger, one of LaRouche's regular targets, had met Iran's Ayatollah Beheshti in Paris, according to Iranian sources in Paris. The theory was later echoed by former Iranian President Abulhassan Banisadr and former naval intelligence officer and National Security Council member Gary Sick. This of course all led to the famous Iran Contra Affair, which resulted in several prosecutions and congressional inquiry into the "hidden hands" of backroom black market clandestine operations at the expense of the American people.

In 2002 LaRouche's Executive Intelligence Review argued that the September 11, 2001, attacks had been an "inside job" and "attempted coup d'état," and that Iran was the first country to question it. The article received wide coverage in Iran and was cited by senior Iranian government officials, including Akbar Hashemi Rafsanjani and Hassan Rowhani. Mahmoud Alinejad writes that, in a subsequent telephone interview with the Voice of the Islamic Republic of Iran, LaRouche said the attacks had been organized by rogue elements inside the United States, aiming to use the incident to promote a war against Islam, and that Israel was a dictatorial regime prepared to commit Nazi-style crimes against the Palestinians.

There are countless thousands of anecdotes and pieces of essential and important trivia regarding this great man's life, and it would be impossible to list them all here.

According to George Johnson, LaRouche sees history as a battle between Platonists (e.g., Beethoven, Mozart, Shakespeare, Leonardo da Vinci, and Leibniz) who believe in absolute truth, and Aristotelians (e.g., Hobbes, Locke, Berkeley, and Hume), who rely on empirical data.

According to Lyndon LaRouche, industry, technology, and classical music should be used to enlighten the world, whereas psychotherapy, drugs, rock music, jazz, environmentalism, and quantum theory simply bring about a new dark age in which the world will be ruled by the oligarchs.

LaRouche and his ideas have been called anti-Semitic since at least the mid-1970s by dozens of individuals and organizations in countries across Europe and North America. LaRouche and his followers have responded to these allegations by claiming that LaRouche has countless Jewish supporters in his inner circle and has vociferously denied these allegations.

In 1977 LaRouche married his current wife, Helga Zepp- LaRouche, who is German and twenty-seven years younger than him. Her 1984 book *The Hitler Book* argues that "we need a movement that can finally free Germany from the control of the Versailles and Yalta treaties, thanks to which we have staggered from one catastrophe to another for an entire century." Helga founded the Schiller Institute, which has been accused of anti-Semitism by the Berliner Zeitung and Political Research Associates, a nonprofit research group that studies right wing, white supremacist, and militia groups.

LaRouche maintains that he is anti-Zionist, not anti- Semitic. When the Anti-Defamation League accused LaRouche of anti-Semitism in 1979, he filed a $26-million libel suit.

Lyndon LaRouche said in 2006 that "religious and racial hatred, such as anti-Semitism, or hatred against Islam, or hatred of Christians, is, on record of known history, the evilest expression of criminality to be seen on the planet today."

Now that Donald Trump is president of the United States, perhaps Lyndon LaRouche will be allowed to emerge from forced exile, as his enemies have now been outed and routed, and he should take his rightful place among one of America's greatest heroes, thinkers, philosophers, writers, lovers of humanity and the United States of America.

CHAPTER 70

Drain the Neocon/Neoliberal Deep State Micro-Swamp

The enormous potential for sabotage, politically motivated investigations/prosecutions/indictments/civil lawsuits, and other types of proverbial "throwing a monkey wrench" into the well-oiled pro-America First machine that President Donald Trump is now trying to feverishly reconstruct and rebuild is at huge, great risk from potential enemies within.

Now that President Donald Trump is, in a lightning fast, almost blitzkrieg manner, using his first weeks to pass monumentally powerful executive orders in order to demolish and devastate the existing United States deep state neoconservative/neoliberal establishment, he must also simultaneously watch his back and be cognizant of the tens of millions of government micro-infiltrators, still taking their marching orders from the proverbial "head of the snake."

In other words, the devil is in the details in that the minions, troops, order-followers, agents, and hatchet men (and women) of the US deep state neoconservative/neoliberal establishment still lurk in the shadows, populating nearly every aspect and level of the US government, from the top on down, to the most low-level staffer in the administrative offices of every locale, in every state, city, town, and municipality in America.

And just because their jobs may be small, or their jurisdiction, their potential to do great harm still exists.

When Vladimir Putin took power back from the oligarchs/plutocrats in Russia in the late 1990s early 2000s, he was also faced with a daunting task, but Donald Trump's job is going to be much harder.

Because in Russia, they did not have as much of a free press who could criticize him so freely, and also Russia had a much more top-down, executory, and iron-fist brand of legislative/executive power, wherein the president could issue edicts and orders, smashing the obstacles to his power and would-be usurpers/saboteurs within his own government one by one or group by group, thus helping to ensure the ultimate success of his agenda of pure love and loyalty to his Russian people.

But in America, we have these great gifts with the free press, freedom of speech, and whistle-blower protection, which, if taken at face value, are extremely great and wonderful things, but if taken in the context that our macro (and micro) government employees have been thoroughly stocked and decked with deep state neocon/neoliberal loyalists for the better part of the last eight years under the Obama administration, and actually even twenty-eight to thirty years if you include the successive neocon/neoliberal regimes under Presidents Obama, George W. Bush, Clinton, and George H. W. Bush Sr., the American people might be in big trouble.

This is because these deep state neocon/neoliberal establishment government infiltrators/agents by and large have been conditioned to **HATE** Donald Trump, everything that he stands for, and by proxy, everything that the vast majority of Americans have also woken up to stand for- which is a peaceful nonviolent revolution against the globalist New World Order deep state oligarchs/plutocrats manifesting themselves with their neocon/neoliberal agents manning every governmental (and mainstream media) job from the lowest level post office worker to the local police department/district attorney/prosecutors office, federal and state judiciary, attorneys general in all fifty states, governors, congressmen, senators—hell, even the DMV in each and every state.

The enormous potential for sabotage, politically motivated investigations, prosecutions, indictments, civil lawsuits, and other types of proverbial throwing a monkey wrench into the well-oiled pro-America- First machine that President Donald Trump is now trying to feverishly reconstruct and rebuild is at huge, great risk from the potential enemies within.

President Donald Trump needs to take immediate preventative and precautionary measures to ensure that none of his executive actions, Cabinet members, government appointees, agenda, or even citizen loyalists do not get "picked off" one by one by the deep state neocon/neoliberal remnant infiltrators currently inhabiting his own government, like so many sleeper cells within any terrorist infrastructure.

Each and every investigation, prosecution, indictment, civil lawsuit, or targeted legal harassment against President Donald Trump must now be fully vetted and viewed with a jaundiced eye by the American people, because George Soros's self-described "purple revolution" declared after the defeat of his handpicked successor, Hillary and Bill Clinton, is far from over yet.

And people like George Soros, who recently went on record stating that he was lobbying and paying for new prosecutors and district attorneys all across the United States to "go after" individual conservatives or other pro-

America-Firsters, or anyone else on his and his colleagues' "shit list," should fill every patriotic American's heart with abject cold and icy fear, terror, and then anger.

The Second American Revolution isn't over just yet. In fact, it is only just beginning, and the globalist deep state neocon/neoliberal establishment empire is 100 percent totally and completely confident that it will eventually quash this "impudent insurrection," and mightily and handily crush this "upstart rebellion" in the form of Donald Trump and his hundreds of millions of American (and global) followers.

We as Americans must be eternally vigilant, especially now, if we wish to remain as a free people-and this must be accomplished by staying loyal to our president, being exceedingly wary and suspicious over any investigation, prosecution, indictment, civil lawsuit instigated by any of the deep state oligarch/plutocrat neocon/neoliberal establishment infiltrator remnants of the previous thirty years of their regime control, or any other targeted harassment/sabotage against both him, his Cabinet, his newly forming government, and above all, his loyalists within the American general population on both the federal macro level, all the way down to the local micro level, just like the Russian people did under their much-beloved and heroic President Vladimir Putin of Russia, who, as promised, eventually and ultimately delivered his people from the evil of the oligarchs/plutocrats in the form of the Communists, plaguing his nation from 1917 to 1999.

CHAPTER 71

Perhaps President Donald Trump Needs to Chill Out a Bit

> These refugee/immigration executive orders appear to be knee-jerk, fear-based, and xenophobic acts of reflexive anger and emotional "lashing out," rather than well-thought-out policy and heavily researched executive action.

While the vast majority of President Donald Trump's lightning-fast and blitzkrieg-like executive orders over the past week and a half appear to have been positively aimed primarily at improving the US economy, augmenting the creation of US well-paying and stable jobs, building and reinstituting industry and manufacturing within the United States, and by and large removing excessive governmental largesse and overregulation that stifles job growth and economic freedom. The recent executive orders pertaining to blanket refugee bans and immigration shutdowns from countries based primarily on religion, race, or ethnicity appear to go way too far and punish the victims of the global oligarchs/plutocrats and their stupid foreign wars and conflicts, the latter of which presidential candidate Donald Trump appeared to want to take on.

The last few executive orders pertaining to refugees and immigration appear to not have been very well thought through, and the etiology/genesis of the refugee crisis and immigration issues were either completely ignored, or Trump and his administration don't understand it very well.

These refugee/immigration executive orders appear to be knee-jerk, fear-based, and xenophobic acts of reflexive anger and emotional "lashing out," rather than well-thought- out policy and heavily researched executive action.

In fact, as immediate responses to these misguided executive actions, Iran (a potential ally actually fighting against ISIS along with Russia) has angrily also clamped down and shut down visa issuance to Americans, as have several other nations important to the US economy, international relations, and human rights, while North Korea has responded by bizarrely firing up its nuclear reactor today in preparation for something not so nice.

This is actually worsening our relationship with countries that the United States could do great things with economically, strategically, militarily, and internationally.

Only Saudi Arabia, one of the greatest violators of international human rights, and allegedly the main proxy ring leader of the 9/11 attacks, can still travel freely in and out of the United States-because it is not even on that seven-country ban list. How in the hell does that make any sense?

Not only that, but Trump's enemies and detractors within the United States like Democrat Senate Majority Leader Chuck Schumer and his ilk are also milking this one as much as they can, in order to completely and totally undermine Donald Trump's presidency and the truly great things that he wants to accomplish over the next four years, falling into their trap, adding fuel to their fire, alienating his loyalists and supporters, and weakening his own bully pulpit.

Meanwhile, Israel's Benjamin Netanyahu is smiling and rubbing his hands because for the first time in a few years, someone else is being accused of being the greatest human/civil rights violator in the universe.

Politics is not business, and this is the type of arena where swift, decisive, uninformed, "both feet in," ill-advised executive action is not always the best decision, because of the vast domestic and international political/economic fallout.

We are not dealing with "widgets" here, but with people.

This is also where it appears that the similarities between Donald Trump and Vladimir Putin end-the latter being a calm, cool, collected, deliberate, and icy-cold decision-maker after having first been provided full intelligence briefings, understanding the political/economic fallout/risks, and then making a quick lightning-like move as if he was playing a game of chess.

Sun Tzu once said, "All battles are won before they are fought."

There is no question that these last above-described executive orders need to be tempered down, amended, and possibly modified as soon as possible in order to prevent further damage to the United States and its interests.

Donald Trump and his administration need to go back to their intelligence community and reeducate themselves on the origin and genesis of terrorism and the individuals involved. More often than not, they are agents of the wealthy globalists, oligarchs, and plutocrats (like Saudi Arabia, who are laughing their collective asses off because they are not being banned), not the poor men, women, children and war- ravaged refugees of the countries that America, European NATO, Saudi Arabia, Turkey and Israel have preemptively and without provocation bombed the shit out of in the first place.

This is a classic case of treating the symptoms and not the disease.

CHAPTER 72

The Importance of Maintaining the Balance of Power

The United States should become more and more the implementer of the diplomatic balance of power of the whole globe, without resorting to war and conflict.

N o one, or country, no matter how novel or inventive they are, has any right, or can be trusted, with absolute power over everyone else.

It is absolutely essential for political leaders all across the world to ensure that the balance of power exists in all spheres of power and the body politic, both domestically as well as internationally, because there is no way that any one individual or government can ensure the equal protection of the people in all their myriad conflicts and challenges from the very large to the very small.

Therefore, it is important that care should be taken that each and every individual voice has enough of a power structure to keep in check their polar opposites.

Violence is of course never a good option, whether through warfare or terrorism, but political balance of power always normally results in a standoff of nonviolence.

It is only when one side of a conflict is so powerful, so wealthy, and so militarily superior, that violence and injustice become an inevitability.

According to Kegley and Wittkopf in *World Politics—Trends and Transformation*, the balance of power theory in international relations suggests that national security is enhanced when military capability is distributed so that no one state is strong enough to dominate all others.

If one state becomes much stronger than others, the theory predicts that it will take advantage of its strength and attack weaker neighbors, thereby providing an incentive for those threatened to unite in a defensive coalition.

Some realists maintain that this would be more stable as aggression would appear unattractive and would be averted if there was equilibrium of power between the rival coalitions.

The principle involved in preserving the balance of power as a conscious goal of both domestic and foreign policy, as David Hume pointed out in his *Essay on the Balance of Power*, is as old as history, and was used by Greeks such as Thucydides both as political theories and practical statesmanship.

During the Renaissance, with regard to Italian city-states in the fifteenth century, Francesco Sforza, duke of Milan, and Lorenzo de' Medici, ruler of Florence, were the first rulers actively to pursue such a policy within *the Italic League*.

Many would argue that their political and financial descendants are still in power, so there is little chance of them giving up on this strategy of global governance at this moment of time.

It was not until the beginning of the seventeenth century when international law became structured under Hugo Grotius and others that the theory of the "balance of power" was formulated as a fundamental principle of modern diplomacy.

It was held to be the interest, the right, and the duty of every power to interfere, even by force of arms, when any of the conditions of this settlement were infringed upon or assailed by any other member of the community.

The principle formed the basis of the coalitions against Louis XIV and Napoleon, and the reason for most of the wars of Europe experienced between the Peace of Westphalia (1648) and the Congress of Vienna (1814), and World War I.

The fact remains that if a nation-state's culture, economy, way of life, national character, and inherent value systems are attractive, then other nation-states will either strive to seek out an alliance, diplomacy, friendship, or comity with it by organic methods rather than by actively seeking out conflict and that no violence or force is necessary to subjugate, convert, or conquer others, which the now thoroughly exposed neocons often try to do.

It is argued that the ultimate goal of diplomacy is to stay or direct the elemental forces of nationalism let loose by revolution, for which the ostensible object is the preservation of peace.

No one state should ever be strong enough to devour the rest, and the greatest responsibility of the Great Powers is to maintain the small states, which cannot adequately protect themselves.

However, former US Secretary of Defense and arch- neocon Dick Cheney stated, "It is not in our interest or those of the other democracies to return to earlier periods in which multiple military powers balanced one against another in what passed for security structures while regional or even global peace hung in the balance."

This type of world view outlook has wrought the devastating destruction and near bankrupting of the USA for the better part of the past fifteen years.

Sir Esme Howard wrote that England adopted the balance of power as "a cornerstone of English policy, unconsciously during the sixteenth, subconsciously during the seventeenth, and consciously during the eighteenth, nineteenth and twentieth centuries, because for England it represented the only plan of preserving her own independence, political and economic."

In 1941, Winston Churchill was criticized by his rival Adolf Hitler for his adherence to the balance of power, stating "Churchill is a man with an out-of-date political idea—that of the balance of power. It no longer belongs to the sphere of realities."

Many would argue that more than fifteen thousand of Adolf Hitler's adherents, loyalists, and followers migrated to the United States after World War II in Operation Paperclip, which ultimately led to the creation of the American National Security State, otherwise known as the military-industrial complex, mainly responsible for America's stupid foreign wars of intervention, especially over the past fifteen years.

Critics point out that traditional balance of power theory fails to explain state behavior in the post-Cold War era.

These critics state that since the end of the Cold War, the United States has been expanding its economic and political power and more recently has begun to engage in increasingly unilateralist military policy, wherein despite these growing material capabilities, major powers such as China, France, Germany, India, and Russia have not responded with significant increases in their defense spending.

These critics add that these countries have not formed military coalitions to counteract US power as traditional balance of power theory would predict.

For example, Council on Foreign Relations (CFR) member and CNN host Fareed Zakaria asked, "Why is no one ganging up against the United States?"

John Ikenberry and John M. Owen asked the same question.

Two American neocon leaders, Robert Kagan and William Kristol, completely agreed when they said that "today's international system is built not around a balance of power but around American hegemony."

However, what these critics fail to notice is that these other major great powers are merely waiting for the USA to exhaust itself militarily, financially, and existentially so that knocking it over would be an easy task. This is why the USA needs to pull out or cease from rampant military adventurism and instead focus on forging alliances and working relationships with the other great powers and to avoid any and all military conflict, completely and finally.

This is the only way it can hope to maintain its power.

Perhaps a fusion should now be the guiding principle—that the United States should become more and more the implementer of the diplomatic balance of power of the whole globe without resorting to war and conflict.

CHAPTER 73

Deep State Rebelling against
Donald Trump's Cleaning Up of the Judiciary

President Donald Trump is cleaning up the corrupted and activist judiciary, and they are not too happy about it.

O ne of President Donald Trump's campaign promises was to clean up the judiciary, i.e., one of the three main branch pools of fetid water known as the governmental "swamp" that he intends to "drain."

But no other branch of the US government will ever more feverishly resist going quietly into the night as this nation's judiciary.

This is because this third branch of government is entirely made up of people who are literally experts in the law, trials, evidence, discovery, and jurisprudence.

This means that these people have literal "black belts" in dispensing tyranny, all under the color of law and authority.

One of the greatest tragedies and hallmarks of modern American jurisprudence is that any judge, at any time, can rationalize or justify, under the color of law and authority, any and all tyrannical, unconstitutional, malicious, judicially activist, unjust, unfair, unethical, politically biased, racist, sexist, unethical, and even illegal court decisions with enough "legal mumbo jumbo," and this is one of the greatest weaknesses of the common law system (judicial based/interpreted legal decisions) rather than a Civil Code type of law (black and white, right and wrong judicial decisions), such as can be found in Europe.

This immense power vested in judges is the **GREATEST** reason that they need to be closely and deeply vetted for any and all ties to foreign powers, financial institutions and banks, fringe-groups, political groups, extremist protected class groups, activist groups, and other potential pollutants to a clean and pure judiciary that respects the US Constitution. In fact, judges should be vetted and scrutinized more than the standards used to determine whether or not a foreign visitor is a terrorist or not, as promulgated by the US Department of Homeland Security, because a bad judge can do far more harm to the United States and its citizenry than any terrorist ever could.

Where once the common law was a very useful and in fact helpful type of body of law choice in America, leading to universally acceptable progressive decisions such as giving women and minorities the right to vote, civil rights laws and amendments, questioning and then eradicating out-of-date concepts and value systems that did not comport with modern life. Today it has literally been hijacked by the most extreme, activist, anti-American, unconstitutional, civil liberties hating gaggle of deep state oligarch/plutocrat- controlled screeching neoconservative/neoliberal Communist hysterics that have, over the past few decades, reduced our body of law and US Constitution to a shambles.

The deep state oligarchs/plutocrats have learned that by funding and supporting the various and different "protected classes" and "tapping into their passions" that they could then control them and direct them as "useful idiots" to attack and turn them on their enemies, i.e., anyone who stands in the way of their total and complete, unbridled, and unopposed power.

In other words, the most wealthy and powerful have learned to use these protected classes, the most repressed and beaten-down of American society to destroy or undermine anyone that interferes with their tyranny.

Donald Trump has come out in the open, lambasting this nation's thoroughly corrupted judiciary, railing against those corrupted and beholden judges (both federal and state), who have now decided to take up their legal arms against him to both destroy and undermine his vision and presidency, and these judges are retaliating and lashing out with the vim and vinegar of hellfire and scorn.

They repeatedly support the issuance of press statements or using their fellow likeminded and similarly controlled scoundrels in the legislature (US senate and congress) about how they, like the Federal Reserve, are "above politics" and should not be questioned in their unbridled authority or that their comfy and cushy judicial positions (sometimes lifetime appointments) should not and cannot ever be questioned or usurped in the most unconstitutional displays of jealously holding on to their gilded power thrones.

Their sheer shamelessness and unabashed thirst for power and refusal or "offended sensibilities" to be questioned by the American people that they serve or the president of the United States, who was elected by the people, is truly disgusting to watch, and often speakers like American Bar Association President Linda Klein come out and publicly attack and castigate the president of the United States, just because he has recently dared to exercise his First Amendment Rights to criticize what he perceives to be rampant judicial corruption in the federal and state judiciary, first as a regular US citizen, then as a presidential candidate, and now as this country's full-fledged elected US president.

The bad news for these jealous vampire-like corrupted and activist judges is that now President Donald Trump can actually **do something** about this serious judicial corruption problem in the United States, while before, as a regular citizen, he also had to just sit there, shut up, and take their abuse.

President Donald Trump has proven his love for the US Constitution when he hoisted and submitted Judge Neil Gorsuch to the US Supreme Court in a heroic and herculean effort to save the American Republic and to rescue it from the evil satanic cabal that has subverted and undermined its courts all throughout America, from the civil to the criminal, to the family, from the federal bench all the way down to the state and local.

The character of the US Supreme Court is ultimately what will shape and filter what goes on at the federal, state, local level, but this will take time, possibly many years.

However, it is worth the wait, and the smart and intelligent judges will know that the writing is on the wall—either they love and respect the US Constitution and abstain from activism and monetary/political corruption, or they will be handily and quickly swept out of power (at best) or jailed (at worst) by the very document and people that they loath, abuse, and hate.

ABOUT THE AUTHOR

Rahul Manchanda rose to the top of Wall Street lawyer fame during the 2000s, often showcased and making appearances on FoxNews, CNN, CourtTV, MSNBC, and other news networks dealing with the most earthshattering and groundbreaking international law cases of the post-9/11 world. A philosophical and ideological founder of the Anonymous movement, with one of his own Associate Attorneys going on to start/lead the Occupy Wall Street/99% Movement at Zuccotti Park in Lower Manhattan, he published vast amounts of political/deep state exposing articles anonymously until he was targeted by federal/state/local government mixed in conjunction with organized crime/foreign/domestic espionage and Edward Snowden revealed that there was no anonymity on the internet, whereupon Mr. Manchanda started writing and publishing his essays using his real name and identity. The articles contained in this book are some of those articles written under his real name. He also taught Immigration Law at some of the finest universities in New York City as well as gave countless lectures on Civil Rights and National Security in America as well as lectures pertaining to International Law, Immigration, and Civil Rights Law. He has traveled extensively throughout the world and has been on the inside of key foreign and domestic policy decisions and changes over the past fifteen years, and coupled with his vast experience in federal and state litigation as well as dealing with foreign consulates and international legal forums, he has developed a bird's eye view of the world when it comes to multi-variate areas of expertise. He condenses some of his observations and analysis in this book as well as exposes some of the selfish "divide-and-conquer" motivations behind some of the most controversial laws, regulations, foreign and domestic policy decisions, and culprits behind the Deep State/New World Order.